The
University Teacher
as Artist

*Toward an Aesthetics of Teaching
with Emphasis on the Humanities*

JOSEPH AXELROD

The University
Teacher
as Artist

Jossey-Bass Publishers
San Francisco · Washington · London · 1973

THE UNIVERSITY TEACHER AS ARTIST
Toward an Aesthetics of Teaching with Emphasis on the Humanities
by Joseph Axelrod

Copyright © 1973 by: Jossey-Bass, Inc., Publishers
615 Montgomery Street
San Francisco, California 94111

and

Jossey-Bass Limited
3 Henrietta Street
London WC2E 8LU

Library of Congress Catalogue Card Number LC 73-3773

International Standard Book Number ISBN 0-87589-183-7

Manufactured in the United States of America

JACKET DESIGN BY WILLI BAUM

FIRST EDITION
Code 7325

The Jossey-Bass
Series in Higher Education

A Publication of
THE CENTER FOR RESEARCH AND DEVELOPMENT IN HIGHER EDUCATION
The University of California, Berkeley

LYMAN A. GLENNY, DIRECTOR

Foreword

For most teachers, the longest, loneliest minute of life occurs in facing the first class for the very first time, when the students quiet down and look up expectantly. For some, the lonely isolation continues through an entire career. This is especially true on college and university campuses since so little effort is given to prepare the graduate student to move to the other side of the desk.

In this book, Joseph Axelrod gives us a detailed study of the dynamics of the college and university class, where we can see concretely the various effects on student learning of what the teacher does or does not do. The book is rich in anecdotes and examples that bring to life the models and prototypes, and it even includes transcriptions of actual class sessions to illustrate various teaching styles. Old-timers will recognize much here, learned by experience; but I suspect they will learn much more. I commend the book also to the new, young college teacher, even one who is still a graduate student.

Axelrod's concept of the teacher-artist is of importance to everyone interested in the future of higher education. If it is true, as Axelrod believes, that educational technology will free college and university teachers to pursue the evocative kind of teaching described in this book, then the possibilities are exciting and challenging, particularly for teachers in the humanities.

Kenneth W. Mildenberger
Deputy Executive Secretary
Modern Language Association of America

Preface

The University Teacher as Artist grew out of a research project that I directed at the Center for Research and Development in Higher Education at the University of California, Berkeley. The objectives of that project were, first, to prepare a theoretical model of the curricular-instructional process—the degree system, as it is called in this book—and, second, to work out a typology of college and university teachers. The methods used to attain these objectives included interviews with more than sixty faculty members at six campuses in the San Francisco Bay Area, along with observation of the teaching practices of these professors. My three research assistants and I attended several hundred class sessions, many of which were recorded and later transcribed for intensive study.

One of the professors included in the study was a faculty member to whom we have given the name Stephen Abbot. We were impressed by Professor Abbot from our first encounter with him, for it was apparent that he was seriously interested in becoming an artist at teaching. By one of those happy coincidences which sometimes occur in research, he had also used in his self-evaluation one of the techniques we had developed for use in our project: he had been recording his own class sessions, so that he could study his teaching techniques objectively. He made these recordings available to us, and he allowed us to make additional tapes in subsequent class sessions. Professor Abbot became, in fact, one of the major subjects in our research, and he continued to work with us even after the Berkeley project ended. The chapters of Part Two attest to his dedication—he became our Stephen Hero.

For almost two years after the research which has contributed to the substance of *The University Teacher as Artist* ended, I personally continued to interview faculty members and visit classes at three of the six campuses included in the study. By the time the writing of the book began, more than a hundred faculty members had been interviewed, and we had also tested and refined the theoretical models presented in Parts One and Three.

The development of the Berkeley project, along with the methodology applied at each stage, is described in detail in the final technical report of the project, *Model Building in the Undergraduate College* (Washington, D.C.: U.S. Department of Health, Education, and Welfare, 1969). Readers who are familiar with that report will probably notice that while the principles constituting the theoretical framework are basically the same as those presented here, an entirely new terminology has now been introduced. The terms originally used to describe the six dimensions of the degree system, as well as the terms applied to the four prototypes of evocative teaching, seemed to us, as we progressed, too cumbersome to appeal to general readers. The terms used in *The University Teacher as Artist,* therefore, are words in general use in the academic vocabulary. Although they avoid many of the difficulties of the more technical language, they require the addition of a Glossary for the use of those readers who choose not to read the chapters in sequence. Words with special meanings are fully defined where they are first introduced, but the Glossary enables all readers to check precise meanings wherever the special terms appear. Serious readers may, in fact, find it profitable to take a look at the Glossary before they begin reading the book.

A few words should be said about the transcriptions of class sessions and recorded interviews. Anyone who has ever attempted to transcribe actual dialogue knows what almost insuperable problems are encountered. Our standard writing system is not capable of representing all levels of meaning in the spoken language, and the punctuation commonly in use in English provides only a primitive means of presenting such suprasegmental phonemes as stress, intonation, and tempo. Even the representation of speech sounds is almost entirely stylized, and only in rare instances—for example, standard contractions like *isn't* or *he'd*—is there any alternative to the formal spelling of an utterance. Of course, it is possible to transcribe certain expressions such as "Hi!" or "Hiya!" without transforming them into the more formal "How are you?"—but that is only because acceptable spellings for these less formal levels of the greeting are already in existence. Choices such as these are rare, however.

We have approached the problem of transcription with only one guiding principle: to capture as accurately as possible the tone of the spoken statement in words and syntax that are already in common written usage and are therefore readable on the printed page. Let us give one example of how this principle has worked in practice. The example, taken directly from the tape, would appear thus. ALLEN: "That's not . . . uh . . . the— I mean, how can . . . how can you . . . how can you say

three? Three . . . three— I mean, how can you— It just isn't— Uh . . .
I just can't . . . uh . . . see how . . . uh—" We have rendered this
passage as follows. ALLEN: "That's not the— [Hesitates.] I mean, how
can you say "three"? I just can't see how—" In spite of all our efforts,
however, only a fraction of the meanings in the real-life dialogues can
be captured in this way. As we state elsewhere in the book, the transcripts
of the class sessions reproduce the original statements about as well as an
ordinary black-and-white newspaper photograph reproduces a Bonnard
painting.

An additional problem is involved in the transcripts of the interviews. In early drafts of our manuscript, we had retained the sexual
identification of the professors interviewed, and readers of those manuscript drafts, we noticed, tended to attach significance to this sexual identification. One of our women readers, in fact, read into our selection of
transcripts a bias against women academics which, she assured us, may
not have been intended but existed nonetheless. She called our attention
to an illustration which appears in Chapter One, where a professor of
French is reprimanded by the department chairman. In the original version, this professor of French was a woman, and when she was reprimanded for not teaching a lower-division French course at an appropriately elementary level, she replied: "When you hire a Julia Child, you
don't expect her to cook hamburgers!" Such a simple illustration, we discovered, could carry sexist overtones. We solved the problem by turning
our female professors into males—and thus encountered another problem.
There is a difference between male and female speech (though it is less
noticeable among highly educated persons), and so we had to edit the
interview passages again to remove any suggestion of sexual identification.
Readers will notice that all the professors quoted from interviews are now
presented as men, and we hope that nothing remains that can possibly be
interpreted as sexist in intention.

For much of what appears in *The University Teacher as Artist,* I
am deeply indebted to the Center for Research and Development in
Higher Education at the University of California, Berkeley. The two years
I spent as a project director at the Center were among the most important
years in my entire professional life. A spirit of inquiry pervades the Center,
and a cooperative environment has been created there—two qualities, I
am sure, that are rare even in the academic world. These qualities recall
the ethos that characterized the University of Chicago College when I
served on its faculty in the late 1940s. My association with the Center has
continued since my project there ended, and some of the material in this
book, particularly parts of Chapter Twelve, has been influenced by this
continuing association.

If I were to attempt to name the Center staff members who deserve my thanks, I would need to list the entire staff. In Program Two, where my project was located, I want to mention Warren Martin, the coordinator, and project directors Algo Henderson, T. R. McConnell, Terry Lunsford, Ann Heiss, Gilbert Paltridge, Ernest Palola, Troy Duster, and Harold Hodgkinson. These Center researchers had an enormous influence on my own research and, consequently, on this book. I also want to give special thanks to the official Center readers of my study: Leland Medsker and Warren Martin, who read an early draft, and T. R. McConnell and Robert Wilson, who read the final draft.

Friends outside the Center have also contributed extensively to my research. A complete list would cover several pages, beginning with Frank Abbott and ending with Harold Zyskind. So let me limit myself here to those colleagues who have read the manuscript: Mervin Freedman, who gave valuable advice during the Berkeley research and who read the entire manuscript critically at several stages of its life; David Riesman, who commented extensively on an earlier version of the typology of teaching styles presented in Part One; and JB Hefferlin, who read the final draft with great care and made a number of valuable suggestions, including one which led to the present order of the four parts of the book. I would like also to thank Gene Tanke, of Jossey-Bass, Inc., for his suggestions, and in particular for the simplification of Table 1.

I should like, in addition, to name six colleagues in the School of Humanities at San Francisco State University, who have been influential in my thinking about aesthetics—Edward Kaufmann, Kai-Yu Hsu, Herbert Kauffman, Ralph Pomeroy, Daniel Gerould, and the late Sidney Zink, who had been my office mate at the University of Chicago for five years and good friend for almost twenty years. I want also to express thanks to two extraordinary teacher-artists: C. E. Parmenter, who symbolizes the teachers with whom I studied at the University of Chicago, and Chaim Rothblatt, who symbolizes the professors under whose influence I came at the College of Jewish Studies in Chicago. And my thanks also to my wife, Addie, whose insights into art and aesthetics have been invaluable to me.

Finally, my heartiest thanks go to John Warner, who worked with me on the last two drafts of the manuscript, paragraph by paragraph, editing and rewriting, as we strove to make the book lucid and directly meaningful. It was he who helped fasten the wings securely to Daedalus' shoulders.

San Francisco   JOSEPH AXELROD
June 1973

Contents

The
University Teacher
as Artist

※※※※※※※※※※※※※※※※※※※※※※

*Toward an Aesthetics of Teaching
with Emphasis on the Humanities*

Prologue

Daedalus in the Classroom, 1975

The central subject of this book is college and university teaching. The hero of the book is the professor of humanities who attempts to escape the labyrinth of academic life, who seeks the freedom he needs in order to be an effective university teacher. The thesis of the book is that there is only one way: he must become an artist in the classroom. He must turn his mind toward unknown arts.

Every professor of humanities is reliving the Daedalus myth. It was Daedalus who designed and built the Labyrinth for King Minos of Crete and showed Ariadne how the imprisoned Theseus might escape from it. But for this he was himself imprisoned in it, along with his son, Icarus. His plight is described by Ovid:

> With prisoner's pain, and exile's too, he broods,
> And, fired with yearning for his native woods,
> He cries, "Though Minos held all else beside,
> Yet doth the air for all men free abide"—
> And turns his mind toward unknown arts. . . [1]

[1] Ovid, *Metamorphoses,* VIII, 184–188. Adapted by Adeline Axelrod from Arthur Golding's translation of 1567.

1

This passage fascinated James Joyce, who used its last line—Et ignotas animum dimittit in artes—as the epigraph for *A Portrait of the Artist As a Young Man.*

There are thousands of humanities professors in American colleges and universities today who feel imprisoned in the academic labyrinth and long to escape. We shall try, in this book, to describe the labyrinth and to show that the best means of escape is similar to the method employed by Daedalus—a turning "toward unknown arts." Parts One and Two suggest what some of the unknown arts might be; Parts Three and Four examine the labyrinth in detail and demonstrate that all alternate routes—other than a turning to art—are almost completely closed off for professors in the humanities.

In Part One, we distinguish between two major categories of university teaching (Chapter One) and we draw and study four portraits of what we call evocative teaching prototypes (Chapters Two and Three). From them, we learn, as Daedalus told his son, that we can escape the labyrinth, not by searching for the earthly way out, but by taking to wings.

Part Two shows our Daedalus, Professor Stephen Abbot, at three stages in his career as a university teacher. Chapters Four, Five, and Six show that the creative process is long and slow, that it is hard labor and requires hard study. They also show that each pair of wings must suit the person they are constructed for, and that he must be able to use them wisely. Each university teacher must create the wings that are precisely right for him and for his students; he must choose his own style and fit it to his own person and his own conditions.

Part Three explores the labyrinthine structures of the academic world and its setting, structures abounding in intricate passageways and blind alleys. The labyrinth is particularly complex inside the system in which the university teacher is most intimately involved: the degree system. We first locate the degree system among the other systems of the university (Chapter Seven), then describe the giant supersystems of which the university is itself a component (Chapter Eight), and finally analyze the degree system itself (Chapter Nine). It consists of six interrelated dimensions; each of these is unusually complex, and this complexity is multiplied many times over as each dimension interacts with all the others.

The nature of the labyrinth is further explored in Part Four, which focuses particularly on alternate routes of escape. Like Theseus, we follow a thread which, during the 1960s, many professors hoped might lead to liberation—educational reform through changes in the grading system and in other aspects of the curriculum. But we discover (Chapter Ten) that the more the grading system changes, the more it stays the same. Nor do innovative programs offer a means of escape for more than a few faculty members (Chapter Eleven). And as we examine foreseeable trends in the next decade (Chapter Twelve), unlike Theseus, we do not find an escape. As we explore the future, we find ourselves constantly retracing our steps to the same place: Plus ça change, plus c'est la même chose.

The university teacher will not escape the labyrinth by following its passageways. Like Daedalus, he must turn to art. Only as a teacher-artist can the professor make his flight to freedom.

Socrates: [To the much older teacher-philosopher, Protagoras; with respect]. *I have a wretched memory, Protagoras, and when anyone makes a long speech, I never remember what he has said. So I beg you to cut your speeches shorter if you want me to learn your meaning.*

Protagoras: *How am I to shorten them? Shall I leave them just hanging in air?*

Socrates: *Certainly not.*

Protagoras: *But you want them short.*

Socrates: *Yes.*

Protagoras: *What appears to me to be short, or what appears to you to be short?*

Socrates: *Protagoras, I do not wish to force this conversation, but when you are willing to converse with me in such a way that I can follow you, then I will converse with you. Now you—as is said of you by others and as you say of yourself—are able to have discussions in shorter forms of speech as well as in the form of lectures, for you are a master of wisdom. But I cannot manage the lectures. You, on the other hand, who are capable of either, ought to choose the shorter form, as I beg you, so that we might then pursue the inquiry. [Protagoras shows impatience.] But I see you are unwilling, and as I have an engagement that prevents my staying to hear you, I shall depart.*

Plato, *Protagoras*

PART I

The Art of University Teaching

In the first three chapters of the book, we attempt to identify classroom practices that are typical of teacher-artists. We begin by distinguishing teacher-artists from their colleagues, teacher-craftsmen. In Chapter One, two kinds of teaching styles are defined: the *didactic* modes, employed by teacher-craftsmen, and the *evocative* modes, employed by teacher-artists. All university teachers strive to achieve excellence in teaching by using one or the other of these two general teaching modes.

The evocative teaching modes fall into four categories. These categories are identified by *teaching prototypes* which are followed by all university teachers whose teaching styles can be described as evocative. Chapter Two presents portraits of four faculty members in various humanistic disciplines who exemplify these prototypes, and Chapter Three discusses the distinguishing features of the four evocative teaching modes. The prototype illustrated by Professor Prince emphasizes principles, facts, and other aspects of the subject matter of his discipline. The prototype illustrated by Professor Innis emphasizes the individual viewpoint of the instructor. The remaining two prototypes are student-centered: the one illustrated by Professor Minter focuses on the development of students' minds, and the one illustrated by Professor Persey focuses on the development of students as whole persons. Within each of the four modes, the teaching task can be performed excellently or poorly, and within each it is possible for the professor to lift his practice to the level of art.

Chapter 1

Didactic and Evocative
Teaching Modes

Among professors in the humanistic disciplines, there can be found three common conceptions of the teacher as artist and of the kind of artwork he brings into existence. The first of these rests upon the ancient metaphor of the teacher as midwife, as the person who helps students give birth to ideas. The second more grandly casts the teacher in the role of Jehovah, who breathes a soul into the clod (a college freshman) that is placed before him. In a third conception, teaching becomes a kind of horticultural art: the teacher is depicted as a sower of seeds that fall sometimes on fertile soil, sometimes on soil that is barren. As this metaphor is generally understood, it is not the sower's responsibility to try to improve the soil—to determine, for example, which nutrients might render it more fertile—but simply to sow.

But these conceptions, we are convinced, cannot contribute anything useful to serious attempts at evolving an aesthetics of teaching. It would seem more promising to begin empirically by examining the work of a great artist at teaching, in order to see what it is that he creates. Socrates has traditionally been regarded as the greatest teacher-figure of Western civilization, and it is unfortunate that his artwork is not available to us now for study; but like all teaching, it was evanescent. Happily for us, however, we have access to indirect evidence from several first-hand witnesses, and what they have written enables us to make three observations about the body of Socrates's work.

First, it is not enough to say that the products created by the teacher-artist are evanescent; one must add that in Socrates's conception of the teacher's art, such products must be so necessarily. Second, the art that Socrates created was improvisational. Neither he nor his intimates, neither his friends nor the strangers with whom he carried on an inquiry, could predict, when a conversation began, where it would lead. Participants could not know what they would discover during the course of the inquiry, or how and when discoveries would actually be made. And third, it is clear that the work of art was not created by Socrates alone, although he was surely the master and the leader in the group. It was created jointly by him and by every member of the group who entered into a relationship with him during the discussion. It is precisely that relationship which was crucial. More than any other factor, it determined the kind and the quality of the artwork that emerged.

This third observation about Socratic art illustrates an important principle about the teaching art in general: all members of the teaching-learning group—and not its leader alone—must become artists if a work of art is to come into existence. This is not to say that there is no difference between the contributions of the leader and the group members: unlike the leader, the members of the group generally do not *know* they are creating art. They believe they are only talking—inquiring, defining, exploring, discovering, accepting and rejecting, being turned on or off, sometimes laughing and playing with words; but what they are doing is not simply talking, any more than a poem on a printed page is simply a sequence of words. And much of the pleasure and excitement they experience during the sessions comes from their participation in the creation of art.

If the teacher has not been able to engage his students in the creative process, then he has failed as teacher-artist. Nor can he induce creativity in the learning group by calling attention to it, by exhortation, as art; the absence of self-conscious "creativity" is essential to the success of the teacher-artist's creation of art.

As the humanities teacher works at building his own systematic aesthetics of teaching, he must take care to distinguish between the improvisational arts and the standard literary, visual, and musical arts whose products have some sort of permanence. Further, the inquiry requires differentiation between those improvisational arts, such as teaching, which have not become institutionalized and those that have, such as commedia dell' arte or jazz or "living theater." In building his aesthetic theory, the humanities teacher must not distort the teaching art by drawing false analogies between teaching and these other arts. While they have essential features in common, the features which differentiate them must be clearly determined. It might also be profitable to consider the popular arts (or "entertainments," as some professors prefer to call them), about which provocative questions can be raised. For example, does a soap opera bear the same relationship to the art of Sophocles as a television talk show does to the art of Socrates?

In the end, we shall find that every teacher-artist, like the artist in any sphere, attacks his task in the only way he can: he develops his own style, and he expresses himself in his own personal ways. Each person's talent, being unique, pushes him or her in a particular direction. What is more, the teacher-artist (again like any artist) is influenced in his own particular way by the hundred external factors that surround his art: the precise nature of his subject matter, the sophistication and motivation of his students, the conditions imposed by his own department, the campus ethos within which he carries out his task as teacher, and—beyond that— the influences of all of the systems and supersystems that we describe in Parts Three and Four.

Every teacher who takes his work seriously, from the best teacher to the worst, holds in his mind a vision of the teaching style that he believes is most effective. Not every teacher is able to describe his vision upon request, but it remains nonetheless ever-present in his mind. It is the teaching style that he actually exemplifies in his classes during those moments when external reality and inner vision meet. It is an image of the teacher-at-his-best. It is a portrait that he believes he resembles most closely on those particular occasions when he feels happiest about his classes, when he is convinced he has achieved his greatest success in the art of teaching.

These mental portraits—*prototypes,* we shall call them—vary greatly from one teacher to another. By means of interviews we held with almost a hundred professors and by subsequent analysis, we examined the mental images that university teachers hold, and we discovered some significant differences among them. As a result of our interviews and class visits, we have classified teacher prototypes in two major categories. The first includes those teaching modes in which inquiry on the part of the student is not required or encouraged for the successful completion of the learning tasks set by the professor. We call these teaching styles the *didactic modes.* The other category includes those teaching modes in which inquiry on the part of the student *is* required if he is to complete successfully the tasks set by the teacher. We call these teaching styles the *evoca-*

tive modes. Those teachers who achieve excellence in the didactic modes we shall call craftsmen; those teachers who achieve excellence in the evocative modes we shall call artists.

Didactic Modes

The teaching styles we classify under the didactic modes are designed to achieve objectives that are generally clear and relatively easy to formulate. These objectives include the mastery of a definite body of information or the acquisition of specific motor-kinetic skills or specific mathematical or verbal skills (in English as well as in other languages). The didactic modes thus stress either cognitive knowledge acquired primarily by memorization, or mastery of skills acquired primarily by repetition and practice.

Among the teachers whose classes we visited and whose teaching styles clearly fell among the didactic modes were many whose classes—given the objectives of the teachers—were unusually effective. One of these, whom we shall call Professor Daniel Garcia, was recommended to us as one of the best foreign-language audio-lingual instructors in the United States. Professor Garcia's field is Spanish. He often gives professional demonstrations of his drill techniques at modern language meetings; and observers, whether they know Spanish or not, find his talent extraordinary. In the drill work of the audio-lingual method, tempo must be varied, but it must also be regulated to the split-second if the drill is to be completely successful. Professor Garcia's timing is as subtle and varied as that of a great actor. The audio-lingual approach is based on principles derived from Skinnerian psychology and structural linguistic theory, and the teaching methodology that has resulted from this combination has been developed by Professor Garcia to the finest point. Our admiration for Professor Garcia as a first-class craftsman was increased when he told us that his methodology was "in a somewhat confused stage" because within recent years, a new school of linguistics—the school of transformational or generative grammer—has called into question whether the principles of Skinnerian psychology are really appropriate for language learning.

Teachers of modern languages often work under paranoia-inducing conditions, and their colleagues around the campus—including those in neighboring departments in other humanistic studies—scarcely understand the problems that beset the language instructor who wants to achieve excellence as a teacher. A large part of the language teacher's frustration arises from the peculiar shape of his discipline, for in order to practice it, he is expected to be four or more different kinds of specialists. He is expected to be a teacher-craftsman helping students acquire language skills, but he is also expected to teach linguistics courses, courses in foreign civilization, and literature courses (where he must function at different times as literary historian, aesthetician, critic, poet-translator, and text explicator). All of the facets of his discipline—except the teaching of language skills—merit by anyone's standards the highest status in the world of traditional scholarship. But it is the lot of the foreign language teacher that he is often imagined by his colleagues to be a mere polyglot who is uninterested in ideas, inquiry, and intellectual exploration.

The teaching of language skills has its own distinctive excellence, and the craftsman who achieves this excellence must command our respect. But due to the very nature of these skills, any teaching style by which they are taught must be classified among the modes we have called didactic. All of the other kinds of knowledge traditionally transmitted by the foreign language teacher, however—literature in all its facets, linguistics, civilization—constitute fields in which excellence can be achieved only if a professor is a teacher-artist. While the didactic modes were much in evidence as we visited various classrooms in the foreign language field, we also saw many classes in literature and civilization, and a few in linguistics, in which foreign language teachers followed evocative teaching prototypes.

The didactic modes are followed by teachers in a number of disciplines, particularly in classes where the skill to be acquired does not depend on reasoning and where the teacher's objective is to develop in the student an automatic or semiautomatic response. When the teacher's aim is to induce in the student an ability to respond immediately, without reflection, he would be teaching *against* his aim to encourage the student to reason out his responses for each exercise. Thus in sessions led by a teacher whose prototypic model falls in one of the didactic modes, the ratiocinative processes are kept at a minimum. The acquisition of the skill (or the mastery of a body of information, if that is the objective of the course) is attained by repetition and practice, rather than by problem solving. In a skills course, the emphasis is placed on "learning to do," rather than on "learning about." In a course where a body of information is to be learned, the emphasis is placed on the direct presentation and memorization of facts and generalizations, rather than on the process of learning through discovery or inquiry. But whether the objective in a class following a didactic prototype is the acquisition of a skill or the mastery of information, the teacher is regarded by all parties as the ultimate authority and the student is not at any time presented with genuine alternatives. Once he has decided to participate—and he faces penalties if he decides not to participate—he discovers that there is only one way to respond to each cue that is given in a class discusssion or in a written test. For each cue, there is only one response that the teacher regards as best.

Our observation of classes falling in the didactic modes included a variety of skills courses in humanistic disciplines—for example, courses in elementary piano, elementary Russian, introduction to logic, beginning photography, and freshman English. We also observed some skills classes outside the humanities, such as courses in statistics, algebra, and typewriting. And we visited a number of courses dealing with substantive materials in the natural and social sciences—as well as in the humanities—where we observed students who did little more than recite, almost as a catechism, answers to questions about facts and generalizations presented in the textbook. In these classes, no time was devoted to inquiry or, in any significant sense, to weighing alternatives.

Evocative Modes

The basic difference between the didactic modes and the evocative modes is the method used in the learning process: the major means employed in the evocative modes are inquiry and discovery. Among the evocative modes, we discovered several major prototypes. If we analyze the teaching-learning process and divide it into its component elements, it is evident that three are basic: teacher, learner, and the subject matter or skill being taught. The major prototypes of evocative teachers can be differentiated according to different views that professors hold about their relationships to the other two elements involved in the process—the learners and the subject matter. The relationships between these three elements—what we might call their "fit"—are extensively varied. Typically, one of the elements moves to the center of the teaching-learning process, and the other two elements are expected to accommodate themselves to its demands and requirements. In the university classroom, it is the teaching style of the professor that determines which two of the elements are expected to make the greatest amount of accommodation and which one remains relatively stable.

One of the major teaching prototypes focuses on subject matter, and it is therefore the other two elements—teachers and learners—that must undergo adjustment. Neither teachers nor learners are permitted to reshape the subject matter, except in quite minor ways. The subject matter is simply not expected to accommodate itself to them, no matter what their requirements or special conditions might be. Teachers who are subject-matter-oriented usually view with alarm any suggestion that the subject matter of a course ought to be changed. They protest that any altering of subject matter would be tampering with academic standards. They believe that changing the subject matter in any basic way in order to accommodate the special needs of students would be detrimental to society, to the university, and in the long run to the students themselves.

But those professors who take as their teaching model one of the other major prototypes in the evocative mode insist that such a view is based largely on an academic myth. What, they ask, is "subject matter" anyway? They hold that the conventional boundaries and content of each field of knowledge are determined by historical accident and are preserved (although often revised and updated) by the learned societies—those guilds which the professionals in each subject field have created to protect and nurture themselves. The prototypes followed by these professors, then, focus on other elements of the teaching-learning process.

The second major teaching prototype focuses on the second element—the professor himself. The instructor-centered teacher believes that the other two elements—students and subject matter—should accommodate themselves to him. He is, after all, the possessor of knowledge and a model for learners. He could hardly submit to alteration for the sake of the other two elements because that would be to surrender his ego to unknown and possibly hostile forces. When a nationally famous American professor of French was reprimanded by his department chairman for not teaching his sophomore French class at an appropriately elementary level, he replied: "When a restaurateur hires an Escoffier, he does not ask him to make hamburgers!" The instructor-centered teacher, when he is not reduced to such a defensive stance, however, builds his argument on a different basis: if the university teacher is to be pushed into a shape that is not his own, then the humanity and the individuality of the professor are lost and we might as well invest in more efficient types of programmed learning. Students and subject matter remain important for the instructor-centered teacher, but *they* must be adjusted to fit what *he* is.

The third teaching prototype places its emphasis on the student. Student-centered professors argue that the teaching-learning process will not be effective if conditions require the student element to be vastly reshaped before the process can get started. Their view is that if the student is expected to accommodate himself to the other two elements in the educational transaction, if he is pushed into a shape other than his own, the whole educational process is endangered. The student's requirements—the steps needed for his development—are what is important. In this view, the whole undergraduate enterprise—classes and courses and professors—exists to meet the student's needs as a growing human being.

These three prototypes are based, then, on the three elements of the teaching-learning process. Those teachers who focus on subject matter follow the Principles-and-facts Prototype. Their teaching is organized around their desire to help students master principles, concepts, analytic tools, theories, applications, and relevant facts. It is characterized by two main features: an emphasis on cognitive knowledge, and the systematic coverage of a given segment of that knowledge in each of their courses.

Those teachers who focus on themselves and their own ideas follow the Instructor-centered Prototype. These teachers organize class sessions around their desire to help the student learn to approach problems in the field as they themselves approach them. Like their colleagues who follow the Principles-and-facts Prototype, they concentrate on transmitting segments of cognitive knowledge, but unlike those colleagues they use the force of their own personalities and their own unique points of view to give shape to that knowledge.

It became apparent during our investigation and analysis of student-centered teachers that there are two student-centered prototypes. One type of professor emphasizes the personal development of the student but limits the scope of his endeavor to the development of the student's mind. These professors follow the Student-as-mind Prototype. The class sessions of such a teacher are typically organized around his desire to help his students acquire a set of skills and abilities that are intellectual in nature. Students are taught to adopt reason and language as their major tools and to use problem-solving as the major means of investigating subject matter. The second type of student-centered professor emphasizes the personal development of the whole student—his entire personality and not just his mind. These professors follow the Student-as-person Prototype. Such a teacher organizes his class sessions around his desire to help students develop as individuals, along all the dimensions—particularly the nonintellectual dimensions—where growth appears necessary or desirable. The student's peer group (his classmates in a given course, for example) is used as a means for accomplishing such development.

The Prototypes and Teacher Evaluation

In our interviews with humanities professors, we learned that while the prototype a particular teacher follows is fairly constant during a single period of his life, it can vary greatly from one period to another in his own professional development. In fact, if a teacher is "exhibiting growth" (as some faculty evaluation forms put it), then this vision of the ideal teacher, in all probability, *will* vary from one stage of his professional life to the next.

Whenever a department chairman or a promotions committee evaluates a professor's teaching performance, such developmental possibilities are not always taken into consideration. Judgment about a professor's teaching ability cannot be made solely in terms of the image he holds of the ideal university teacher and how closely he succeeds in realizing that ideal; it must also include the direction in which the professor is moving, in his development as teacher-artist, and the rate at which he moves. The judgment required of the evaluator in such circumstances is very much like the judgment required of an automobile driver who is trying to avoid collision with another vehicle—he must know the precise location of the other vehicle on the road, but he must also know the direction in which it is traveling and its rate of movement.

Judgments which take these factors into account may be devilishly difficult to make, but such factors must be considered if department chairmen and others are to arrive at wise decisions. Let us consider for a moment a judgment of this kind involving a tenure decision. It is obvious that today's tenure decision will probably have more important consequences for a department ten or fifteen years from now than in the years immediately ahead. But more often than not, a candidate for tenure is looked upon as though he were a static entity. The decision-maker asks: "How capable is he?"—a question that focuses on his present ability and does not specifically ask about likely directions of change. Some more significant questions would be: "Where is he now on the scales we think important for his job as a teacher? In regard to those scales, how does his present position compare with where he was a year ago? How is he likely to develop as the years pass?" Judgment about the candidate, in short, should be based on his direction and rate of movement, rather than on the precise point he has reached at a given moment.

Changes in a teacher's mental image, then, must play a central role in any description we give of him. But aside from how this image is altered and developed—how it affects his own future and the future of his department—what we must look at first is the image itself. No analysis of the concrete behavior of a teacher in action can take place without reference to this mental image, the teacher prototype. When we observe a teacher in action, it is impossible to understand why he is doing what he is doing what he does, or how well he is doing it, unless we have some idea of the prototype that serves as his model. This principle is fundamental, and no description or evaluation of any professor's teaching should disregard it.

It is true, of course, that some teacher prototypes are well known, for several of them belong to a common academic tradition. A sensitive observer, sitting in a classroon of a teacher following one of these models, will probably be able to identify it. If, however, the teacher takes as his model one of the less common of the "evocative" prototypes (which will be described presently), the observer may need the help of some special identifying clues. Our experience in visiting classrooms has shown that, for reasons which will be clear in a moment, a teacher's intentions can easily be inaccurately perceived. This is not surprising when we consider that for many teachers the prototype model may not always be clear in their own minds. When the image is incomplete or confused, an observer in the classroom would find it impossible to discern any pattern that accounts for the way in which the professor behaves. A confused teaching prototype often accounts for ineffective teaching.

But a confused prototype is not the most common cause of ineffective teaching. More frequently, the prototype is clear in the teacher's mind, but he lacks proper control of his teacher's tools. His work as a technician and craftsman is so poor that he is unable to approach the level of his artistic vision.

As we discovered during our investigations, an observer can be thoroughly mystified by a teacher who is unable to approach his own image of the teacher-at-his-best. The professor's external behavior in the classroom gives the observer completely unreliable clues to his intention, and these poor clues can lead to unsound analysis and even mistaken judgment about teaching quality. The same kind of thing can happen with any work of art, whether we are dealing with an improvisational art like teaching or with one of the "hard" arts like painting. If a painter paints a dog which an art critic can only imagine to be a rabbit, the critic is not performing well when he complains that the rabbit is unrecognizable. Since he has misunderstood the painter's intention, he is not in a position to give an accurate description of the work or a sound artistic judgment. Until he obtains the clues that enable him to understand the artist's intention, all he can do is refrain from making any statements at all. So it is that the observer-critic in a classroom cannot understand what the professor is doing unless he has a fairly accurate picture of the teacher prototype the professor has in his mind. Without a knowledge of this prototypic model, the observer cannot presume to understand why the professor does what he does or to judge how well the professor is succeeding in terms of his own vision.

Chapter 2

Portraits of Evocative Teachers

To illustrate the four prototypes in the evocative mode which were introduced in the preceding chapter, we now present portraits of four teachers who exemplify these models. The most common of the models, the Principles-and-facts Prototype, is represented by Professor Prince, an art historian considered by his students and colleagues to be one of the best teachers on his campus. The second most common model is the Instructor-centered Prototype, represented by Professor Innis, a professor of French literature. The student-centered models—the Student-as-mind Prototype and the Student-as-person Prototype—are represented, respectively, by Professor Minter and Professor Persey. (Not all of the faculty members who served as the original models for these portraits were men; but we decided to portray all of them here as males.) The portraits of these four professors are intended to show the attitudes toward themselves and students, toward teaching and learning, upon which their classroom practices are based.

Professor Prince: "I Teach What I Know"

Professor Prince is in his late fifties and has spent most of his professional life at the small private college where he now teaches. His reputation in the field of art history extends far beyond the limits of his own campus, however, and he is proud of his reputation as a scholar and teacher. At first he appears somewhat aloof in manner, and his voice strikes the listener as rather harsh. He is formal and precise, and his pronouncements often seem severe. Yet he soon impresses his visitor as extremely knowledgeable and completely fair, and a genuine warmth emerges as one becomes better acquainted with him. His clothes, which are neat but slightly out-of-style, and his relaxed self-assurance, ingrown from habit, suggest that he is a man who has earned the right to express his views with authority.

Professor Prince speaks easily about his work as a teacher. He finds neither his tasks nor his discipline ambiguous. His primary task, he feels, is to cover the materials of his discipline in a systematic way in order to help his students master those materials. He is quite clear about what subject matter ought to be covered in the various courses offered by his department, how the subject matter should be divided into courses, and how specific topics should be arranged. He and his colleagues in the field of art history throughout the country, he explained during one of our interviews, have a standard way of ordering their subject matter. Consequently, courses carrying the same label at different campuses cover the same general topics. He said, for example, that courses labeled "Classic and Early Christian Art" or "The French Impressionists" would cover about the same subject matter regardless of where they were offered.

Just as Professor Prince has a clear view of his own role in the classroom, he also has a clear sense of the student's role. When he was asked "How do you conceive of the teaching-learning process?" he replied: "How do you mean—the teaching-learning *process?* They are two quite different processes." Professor Prince does not agree, obviously, with those educators who believe that teaching and learning are really two aspects of the same process. Nor does he accept the view that teaching and learning are a "joint inquiry" made by student and teacher. On this point, as we observed in Professor Prince's classroom, his practice was consistent with his philosophy. When joint inquiry does take place in his class encounters with students, we observed, it is not so much an inquiry carried on by teacher and students working together as it is a pedagogic device through which the student arrives at Professor Prince's solution to a prestructured problem.

During our interviews with Professor Prince, he elaborated further on this matter. It is his job, he said, to help the student master material that has already been discovered by workers in the field. It would be ridiculous, he told us, to think that an undergraduate student could actually discover something significant that qualified scholars had not yet learned. Thus, in his courses for undergraduates, students are led to the answers—or if necessary given those answers directly—which are already known and agreed upon by scholars such as Professor Prince himself. When we asked him whether it might not be possible for a professor, during a class discussion with undergraduates, to learn something he had not known before, the possibility seemed totally foreign to his view of his role as a teacher.

Professor Prince emphasizes the mastery of subject matter. His conception of subject matter demonstrates that he thinks of knowledge as a *product* (even when a methodological question is under discussion) rather than as a *process*. The matter, although complex, can be simply stated: Knowledge has generally been defined either as an *activity* of the human mind or as a set of *products* that result from such activity. Professor Prince's point of view on this question sharply distinguishes him from the other teachers whose portraits we shall look at. As we shall see, among the four prototypes in the evocative mode, only the Principles-and-facts Prototype conceives of the educative process in such a way as to subscribe to the concept of knowledge *qua* product.

Two basic notions about students organize Professor Prince's view of himself as a teacher and his activity in the classroom. The first is his image of the ideal student. This image is identical for everyone enrolled in his courses. The ideal student, in Professor Prince's mind, is someone who (a) has perfectly mastered the subject matter—the facts and principles—that have been presented in the course and assigned for out-of-class study, and (b) can restate those facts and principles in ways Professor Prince considers relevant and appropriate.

The second notion basic to Professor Prince's concept of teaching has to do with student growth. In his view, the change that takes place in students as a result of his influence is identical in nature—though not, of course, in degree—for *all* students; and, in general, it is an orderly change. To put the matter simply, it is a movement from ignorance to knowledge. Professor Prince offered this example: When a student takes his Primitive Art course—a course dealing with the arts of Africa, Polynesia, and Pre-Columbian America—it is his expectation that the student will enter the course knowing next to nothing about the arts of those cultures and that the student will slowly, under his tutelage, move from ignorance to a modest degree of knowledge in the area. The precise degree differs for each student and is largely determined by his willingness to work hard in the course.

This clear and rather simple philosophy gives Professor Prince the basis for his grading policy. He is quite without conflict about the grading system. Standards of mastery are set for each unit of learning, and the student, as he completes each stage, is judged and graded by comparison with those standards. Such a process—if it is not to depend on the pure whimsy of a teacher—must assume, of course, widespread agreement in the discipline as to the order and sequence of the various facets of the subject matter, as well as uniform standards of achievement. Professor Prince believes that such widespread agreement does, in fact, exist among art history departments throughout the country.

It is interesting to note, incidentally, what Professor Prince's officemate said to us in private on this subject. The officemate, also an art historian, asserted that there perhaps had been, at one time, widespread agreement among art historians about which periods, movements, and figures were to be covered in an undergraduate program, but that now many art history departments have broken away from the old pattern. According to the officemate, "several new patterns are now emerging, with resultant confusion" in undergraduate curriculum planning.

In interview, Professor Prince expressed a preference for "an emotion-free atmosphere" in his classroom. As a result of our visits to his classes, we knew that he generally manages to achieve it. His classroom, like his person, is characterized by an aura of scholarly objectivity and noninvolvement, and he maintains a cool and rational approach to problems. His relationship to students, both in class and out, is also cool and distant, although not positively unfriendly. His students are aware, as were we, that he wants to keep a private space where students must not penetrate. He carries this private space with him wherever he goes. The materials he deals with are intrinsically interesting (at least we found them so), and Professor Prince has the good sense not to get in their way. In this regard, he appears to be typical of teachers who follow the Principles-and-facts Prototype: they attempt to minimize personal opinions and predilections and to emphasize the body of knowledge that all scholars in the field accept.

We pursued this subject further in one of our interviews with Professor Prince:

INTERVIEWER: Since the department is fairly large, I assume that certain courses are taught by more than one faculty member.
PROFESSOR PRINCE: Yes, of course.
I: Does it make any difference to your students—I'm speaking now only of undergraduates—whether they take a given course from you or from one of your colleagues?
P: Yes, I should think—
I: [Interrupting.] Sorry, but I didn't ask the question properly. I meant: In your view, *should* it make any difference to one of your undergraduate students whether he has you or one of your colleagues for the course in, say, "Renaissance and Baroque Art?"
P: It apparently does make some difference to students. They appear to see some differences between us. But that wasn't your question—

you asked whether it *should* make a difference. Actually, it shouldn't. Most of my colleagues and I would cover the same material in about the same way in the same course. But I don't want to overstate the matter. Of course there would be many variations—maybe hundreds —from one to the other. But none of these differences should be significant. Occasionally, though, students might be influenced in their motivation or in other ways by these differences.

I: If you could conceive of a state of perfection—in this connection—the differences between you and your colleagues as you teach any given course, then, would be so insignificant as to make *no* difference to any student?

P: That's a peculiar way of putting it—but, yes, I agree.

In another of our interviews, we approached the subject of how Professor Prince views the teaching-learning process:

I: How do you conceive of the teaching-learning process?

P: How do you mean—the teaching-learning *process?* They are two quite different processes.

I: You do not agree with those educators who regard them as two aspects of a single process?

P: I suppose that is possible, but I don't see the advantage. Teaching and learning are closely related, of course, but they are distinctly different. I see the two processes as distinctly separate—though, of course, related.

I: Many of the professors we have been interviewing here on this campus tell us they also see learning and teaching as distinct and separate processes. It usually turns out that they see the student and the professor in what we might call their characteristic "roles"—the student is the learner and the professor is the teacher. Do you agree with this? I mean, do you see this clear differentiation of roles between teacher and student during the times when the professor and his students are working together?

P: Yes, I suppose so. In its most basic sense, the campus is the place where student and professor come together—the student to learn and the professor to teach. Does that answer the question?

I: What do you consider to be the learner's role or task?

P: It is the student's task, first of all, to master certain facts and principles and tools in my field. There is a special vocabulary, for instance, and there are a certain number of concepts. And it happens also in my field that there is a small number of physical tools to be mastered. And finally there is a total analytic framework to which all of this leads, which must also be mastered.

I: In your field, how long does it take to master all of that? Or am I asking a foolish question?

P: Not exactly foolish. But of course I can't give you a single, direct answer because there are various levels of mastery. After the introductory courses have been completed, as students continue their studies in the field—I'm thinking now of those who choose to major in it—their knowledge of the special vocabulary and the concepts and the tools and the general analytic framework all becomes more refined. More detailed. More complex.

I: Perhaps a better way of asking my question: How long must your students study facts, principles, tools, and total analytic framework before any of the "problems" relevant to your field can be systematically explored by students?

P: It's necessary to master the fundamentals quite well and accurately before any problems as such can be explored. Of course, we invent some rather artificial and relatively simple "problems" to use illustratively, even in our most elementary courses. But that is, I take it, not what you meant.

I: I meant real life problems, as it were. The problems newspapers and magazines talk about.

P: The real problems in the field. Probably not until the senior seminar. But even then, the student is hardly equipped to grapple with the intricacies of problems that actually exist. We formulate a few academic problems for pedagogic and analytic purposes—but as I said, we do that even in elementary courses. I don't think you can say that these so-called problems in any way resemble the overwhelming problems that exist outside the classroom. Many of those aren't solvable by anybody—not even the experts.

I: I don't mean to push the point, but do you ever use class time to present some of those unsolvable problems? Do you discuss them with students?

P: Indeed we do. It adds to the excitement of the class, maybe even gives a feeling of relevance. But that's really only incidental to our study of the basic and fundamental material in the field that we need to cover in an undergraduate program.

I: There has been a great deal written about changes in students that take place in college—that is, ways in which they are different when they finish college from what they were when they entered. How would you describe the major change you see taking place in your students?

P: The major change is that they get a systematic knowledge of my field that they did not have before.

I: Is that the main basis, then, for the course grade that you give each student?

P: Yes. I expect a certain knowledge to be mastered. How much of it is mastered can be measured. Not with precision, of course, but we have several good yardsticks in our field. And we have standards according to which we assign each student his grade for the course.

I: Do you and your colleagues plan together what should be covered in each one of the courses offered in your department? Is it done cooperatively?

P: Yes.

I: Is there very much of a problem in planning the courses?

P: I don't think so. No. In our field, there is a fairly standard way of ordering the subject matter. Some of it is arbitrary, I suppose— quite arbitrary. But a good deal is based on the logical and natural divisions within the material itself.

I: It's not a very controversial topic, then.

P: I'm speaking with reference to the undergraduate program. On the graduate level, there are different problems in the organization of the courses. There's some controversy between my more theoretical and my more pragmatic colleagues. But on the undergraduate level there is a standard way of arranging the courses which is traditional.

I: In some other departments there are some faculty members who sometimes talk about organizing a brand new course and then learning it along with the students. Is there any way in which you do this in any of your undergraduate courses?

P: Occasionally. For example, when we adopt a new textbook and are using it for the first time.

I: But is there actually any new substantive material you are learning with your students when you do this? Do you have, for instance, any new insights into the nature of your subject that you didn't have before? As a result of discussions with your students?

P: I would have to answer no to that. It doesn't seem to me possible for a qualified college professor really to learn anything within his own field from an undergraduate. I should think that would be true in all fields. After all, we have already mastered the materials we are teaching—hence, we couldn't actually be learning *with* our students. We pretend to sometimes, of course, for pedagogical reasons.

I: I was referring to genuine insights which might come to you during the course of a class discussion.

P: That isn't likely to happen in a course with undergraduates. My colleagues and I continue to advance in the field, and we do often stand at the growing edge, working together with a very advanced student, of course, but it's at a stage far beyond what undergraduate students do. It just isn't the same thing. Undergraduates are learning the basic materials in the field—we're way beyond that.

I: What is your feeling about the development of students as people— you know, the growth of the whole person?

P: That is very important, of course. And to the elementary or secondary teacher, it is exceedingly important. Though in the secondary schools now, a great deal more attention is being paid to the academic side of an individual's education. On the college level, we have always been concerned primarily with academic development. The other aspects of a person's growth are important, too, and our college provides ample opportunity for them. But that is not part of *my* job. I am interested in the intellectual side—in professional development.

I: It is often said that the factors which motivate students are mainly irrational and nonintellectual. What is your attitude about that? Are you influenced by such considerations in your teaching?

P: Not very much. I like to work in an atmosphere that is as emotion-free as possible.

I: Forgive me for putting the question this way, but your remark suggests it. Wouldn't you like to be admired by your students?

P: That's more or less irrelevant to me.

I: [Smiling.] Then I assume you don't ask for *love*.

P: [Seriously.] I do not. I think such emotions are only an interference in the classroom.

I: You are saying that they don't—as some people claim—help students learn?

P: I can't speak for my colleagues, and I'm sure there are a number of people on this campus who disagree with me. But speaking for myself, I say definitely that my task can best be done in an emotion-free atmosphere. And I expect my students to do their part in keeping the atmosphere unpolluted.

Professor Innis: "I Teach What I Am"

After the Principles-and-facts Prototype represented by Professor Prince, the most common teaching model among faculty members in the humanistic disciplines is the Instructor-centered Prototype. Among the professors we interviewed, the best representative of those who follow this prototype was Professor Innis, a specialist in the field of French literature.

Professor Innis is one of the best known and most talked about faculty members on his campus. He is, in fact, a famous man, having written several widely read novels (including a bestseller which was sub-

sequently filmed), reviews and commentary published in national magazines, and half a dozen volumes of critical essays in literature. Now past
sixty, he remains a glamorous figure, both for his students and for the
public. He is sometimes absent from his classes at the small, elite girls
school where he has taught for almost twenty years, because he also enjoys a reputation as a speaker for women's clubs and literary societies. He
is a very attractive man, much in demand for both social and scholarly
functions. He makes an impressive appearance—lean, stylishly dressed,
with a thatch of white hair and a full white moustache—and he is the
center of attention wherever he goes. Still at the height of a distinguished
career, he is a fascinating storyteller and a lively personality.

Such a distinguished man plays a very special role in the classroom. Professor Innis, it is soon apparent to a visitor, dominates his classes
and quite obviously plays the role of model literary critic for his students.
By his own behavior and personality, he demonstrates to his students what
he believes are the best ways of understanding and handling the concepts
of literature. In his interviews with us, Professor Innis emphasized his
competence not only as a specialist in the field of literature but also as a
liberally educated man. We asked him how he transmits his specialized
knowledge to students, and his response speaks directly to his educational
philosophy:

PROFESSOR INNIS: Giving my students special knowledge is only one part
of my job. There is a more important part. I do not regard myself
simply as a specialist in my field—I am also an educated man. If
I did not regard myself as an educated man, I would not be teaching in a college.
INTERVIEWER: You feel, then, that it's possible to be both a competent
specialist and an educated man generally?
INNIS: It's not only possible—for a college teacher, it's imperative. As a
teacher of undergraduate students, I must be something more than
a specialist. I must be a specialist who looks at the world around
him and sees the relationship between my specialty and all of the
problems facing mankind. To be able to do that is to be educated.

Since Professor Innis believes that his major task is to provide students with a model of an educated man, he uses his class time to demonstrate what an educated man does with the materials of French literature.
For Professor Innis, then, it is not the subject matter that is at the center
of class activity, but what the instructor does with that subject matter.
For him, it is not mastery of subject matter that is set as a goal for students.
Students are expected, instead, to demonstrate—in papers and examinations—that they can imitate his particular way of conceiving problems,

defining them, formulating them, reasoning about them, and handling data pertaining to them. Professor Innis, like Professor Prince, is interested in the transmission of cognitive knowledge, but it is not primarily knowledge as *product*. It is knowledge as *process*. For Professor Innis's students, he represents that conception of knowledge: not a set of static products, but an ever-changing, ever-alive activity.

Judging from what we observed in Professor Innis's classroom, his students are given some opportunity, during almost every class session, to apply the knowledge-as-process principle for themselves. His class meetings are generally divided into two parts: lectures, which he calls "demonstrations," and question-and-answer periods, which he calls "discussions." A large number of his students—especially the more intellectually aggressive ones, we observed—use the after-lecture question-and-answer period to challenge his point of view. They point out what they consider to be inconsistencies in the lecture, and they raise questions about the points of view of other critics. Occasionally a student presents an alternative view. Professor Innis obviously enjoys these challenges, encourages them, and (since he is an excellent showman) almost always emerges victorious. No one, however, objects to his taking advantage of his position at the podium, and students expect that he will invariably have the last word.

It was clear to us that Professor Innis is interested in the teaching process, that he has a coherent conception of his role as a teacher, and that he definitely plays a central role in the class. He is *always* at the center. He prepares for his role with great diligence, and he obviously enjoys being "on stage." He carries a rather dramatic aura of authority and independence which attracts students, and he takes the education of undergraduates seriously.

During the question-and-answer discussions and in after-class conversations, he responds warmly to students, especially to those who show warmth for him. His excellent rapport with many of his students, however, does not mean that their ideas, per se, have importance for him: he uses ideas expressed by students to highlight his own conceptions. All of his conversations with students, we noticed—either in class or after class —begin with him and his ideas and, sooner or later, return to him and his ideas. He remains at the center, outside the classroom as well as inside it.

Although we did not ask Professor Innis specific questions about his grading procedures, his policy became apparent during the course of our interviews. Like Professor Prince, he is generally satisfied with the standard grading system. He uses a single basic criterion for evaluating students: in examinations, they are asked to demonstrate the exactitude with which they are able to imitate his approaches, perspectives, conceptions, and formulations—or, alternatively, those of other important critics in the field whom Professor Innis admires. It should not be assumed, however, that Professor Innis is like anyone else in the field. As his students recognize, he is a unique "character" who feels passionately about his ideas, which he expresses with verve, originality, great seriousness, and infectious humor.

The difference between Professor Prince and Professor Innis—the difference between the teacher who follows the Principles-and-facts Prototype and the teacher who follows the Instructor-centered Prototype—is exactly the difference that exists, according to Daniel Bell, between a "scholar" and an "intellectual." A scholar, Bell says, "has a bounded field of knowledge, a tradition, and seeks to find his place in it, adding to the accumulated, tested knowledge of the past as a mosaic." The intellectual, on the other hand, "begins with *his* experience, *his* individual perceptions of the world, *his* privileges and deprivations, and judges the world by these sensibilities."[1]

This distinction between the scholar and the intellectual is essential to an understanding of the two teaching styles exemplified by Professor Prince and Professor Innis. Two class sessions presided over by two professors who follow the Principles-and-facts Prototype, dealing with the same or very similar subject matter, look very much the same. The professors keep out of the way of their materials; they cover the same main points; and they carry on their classroom operations in similar fashion. We saw this duplication many times during our class visits: one session with a Principles-and-facts professor was very much like another session with another Principles-and-facts professor in the same field. But the opposite was true in our observations of Instructor-centered Prototype professors. Each professor had a unique perspective, and an experience with one was rarely similar to an experience with another.

We commented on this difference in one of our interviews with Professor Innis. "That is how it should be," he said. "There ought to be a diversity of teacher models in a single department." The members of Professor Innis's department represent several different schools of literary criticism, we discovered, and Professor Innis was himself instrumental in bringing some of these representatives of opposing views to his campus. The department also contains some professors who have no approach at all to literary criticism, belonging to that generation when the literary scholar was trained to engage in value-free historical research. Professor Innis's department, then, has the diversity which he recommends. Since no single faculty member can serve as model for all styles and all modes of learning and inquiry in the field of literature, Professor Innis feels

[1] Daniel Bell, *The End of Ideology* (New York: Free Press, 1960), p. 372.

that one of the important factors on which excellence in a particular program depends is the very diversity of faculty models to which the student is exposed. "If one instructor," he said, "demands and illustrates a particular perspective in criticism—say, that of the Chicago School— another may take the position, as I myself do, that art is one of the modes of exploring the nature of things. In my view, art is the mode by which we perceive truth in the most intense way."

In Professor Innis's educational philosophy, it is not only desirable but actually necessary for members of the various departments of humanistic studies to model different approaches and different perspectives. Faculty colleagues should not reinforce each other's biases, he points out. The welter of diversity would not, in the end, confuse the student but would help him realize that no single perspective or mode of inquiry is accepted in the field as the only possible one. For Professor Innis, the best model is the best teacher, and an excellent educational program will assure that the student is exposed to a variety of models. This view is illustrated by his answers to some of our questions:

INT: In your view, how can students best learn to become educated?
INNIS: The answer is simple, but the process is complex. They can become educated by imitating people who are already educated. I mean by imitating models of educated men who are respected by the world of higher education and by society in general.
INT: In other words, by imitating you—among others.
INNIS: To speak plainly, yes. If I could not be imitated, I would have no right to be here.
INT: But surely you don't mean imitated in *every* way. That would make a professor's job impossible, or certainly unbearable. In what ways, precisely?
INNIS: Basically, my job is to demonstrate to students what an educated man does with the materials in the field of French literature. It is not the actual works of French literature that are important—ultimately. It's what I do with them.
INT: Do you do very much that is different from what your colleagues do?
INNIS: I don't understand the question.
INT: Is what you do in your classes unique? Or do most of your colleagues—in the same field—do pretty much the same thing? Your colleagues not only on this campus, but everywhere.
INNIS: Of course those that I admire usually do very much as I do. Or I do as they do. But each one of us is unique. It isn't conceivable that we would all, as you put it, do pretty much the same thing.

In one of our interviews we tried to get Professor Innis to talk about student participation in his classes:

INT: Do you teach mainly by lecturing?

INNIS: Yes. But you must understand that the lectures are not what you might call straight presentations. They aren't the kind of thing you might get from a textbook. Actually, I think of them as demonstrations.

INT: Do students participate in these demonstrations in any way?

INNIS: I always allow time for discussion following my lectures. As you've observed, my classes are not huge. We do things informally here. There's a substantial period set aside at the end of each class period, mainly to clarify points in the lecture that may not come through. Students participate freely at that time.

INT: What evidence do you give the student to assure her that you are interested in her, that you aren't neglecting her?

INNIS: The evidence is clear, I think. I give as perfect a performance as possible, and I think the students feel that. For my part, a perfect performance is imperative—otherwise, I would run a grave risk. I must be as perfect a model as it is possible for me to be, because I can't predict which one of the myriad things I say or do will take root. Students will imitate what they want to imitate, and what they can. And since I can't predict which precise feature of my performance will find its way into a given student's mind or heart, I must strive for perfection throughout.

Professor Minter: "I Train Minds"

As we have seen, Professor Innis, as representative of those teachers who follow the Instructor-centered Prototype, has expressed his belief that there ought to be considerable diversity in point of view and in teaching style within each department of humanistic studies. It is desirable, he said, to expose the student to different approaches to the subject matter traditionally covered in a given discipline. There are many professors of humanistic studies, however, who wonder whether such diversity is pedagogically sound. Some university teachers believe that every student ought to receive intensive training in one intellectual framework. Any respectable framework will do, they say—the important thing is to motivate the student to work at it in sufficient depth and with sufficient intensity to enable him to master it and use it with ease.

This is the view of most university professors who follow the Student-as-mind Prototype in their teaching. We have chosen as our example of this prototype Professor Minter, a professor of humanities at a large private university. Professor Minter strongly identifies with this university, having taken one of his graduate degrees there and having developed strong admiration for certain older professors in his department. He is a large man in his early forties, broad-shouldered and balding, who on first meeting apears excessively aggressive. He expresses his views with complete openness—indeed, he is eager to have them heard—but he also displays vitality and wit, along with an exceptionally broad knowledge of his field. He seems to be interested in everything—art, literature, music, philosophy, science, languages—and will avidly discuss any subject with anyone he believes to be mentally alert. He has great respect for analytic ability, and he prizes it and encourages it in his students. He possesses a great zest for life and demonstrates it by speaking glowingly of the accomplishments of his students and colleagues. Although his manner is sometimes brusque, one is constantly aware of his brilliance and his good-hearted intentions. The word to describe Professor Minter is *intense,* but he is also extremely meticulous.

Professor Minter believes in training of a particularly rigorous intellectual sort. He does not ordinarily, however, have the opportunity to test his belief in this kind of education because, with the exception of a handful of campus followers, students do not remain under his tutelage long enough for him to be able to carry his program of training through to a satisfactory conclusion. His teaching philosophy emerged in the course of our interviews with him:

INTERVIEWER: In previous conversations you have emphasized the distinction between knowledge as product and knowledge as process, and—
PROFESSOR MINTER: [Interrupting.] You have touched on one of my most important principles. There are, of course, courses in my department that derive from the conception of knowledge as product. Traditionally, courses in the humanities have taken as their base what has been established as the body of knowledge within the field, along with whatever methods and principles and content go along with it. The emphasis in courses of that kind is placed on subject matter per se—or on themes and problems that cut across several subject matters within the humanities. Sometimes on lists of great books, for instance. That is what I mean by courses that derive from the conception of knowledge as product—as something given, a thing with its own corporate limits.
I: What is *your* approach?
M: Obviously, I am on the other side. I believe that we do better to treat knowledge as process.
I: And what does that imply for you, exactly?
M: It means that we must shift the focus of concern to the nature of rational activity itself. We must cultivate rational activity as activity. Knowledge isn't just the *product* of such activity.
I: As you organize your courses, how does this view of knowledge affect

what you do? Do you cover the same materials that students are required to master—or at any rate be exposed to—when they study with professors who take the knowledge-as-product approach?

M: In the courses I give, the materials, the methods, the principles, the contents, the concepts, the structures—whatever is involved in the traditional courses—are, you might say, *traversed*. But during the traversal, the emphasis is on the *how* and the *why* of knowledge, not on the *what*.

I: What does this approach—your approach—do for the student? What does the student get in your course that he doesn't get in a traditional course with a subject-matter approach?

M: I emphasize rational activity. The kind of course I try to give provides the student with the basis for cultivating within himself the fundamental activities by which man fulfills himself as man—that is, realizes the function peculiar to his nature—and hence moves toward that excellence of which only man is capable.

I: For your approach to be effective, though, wouldn't it have to be adopted by your whole department?

M: That's the trouble with it, of course. But not just my own department. To be really effective, it ought to be adopted by the whole university.

I: How about people in the fine arts and those areas of study that deal with works that aren't verbal in nature? How would your view fit them?

M: I can't answer for them. In my classes, I spend a good deal of time with my students exploring nonverbal modes of communication. But the dominant mode of communication in my classes is definitely verbal. Our approach is analytic, rational, logical. I would not find it appropriate to teach the humanities any other way.

What characterizes teachers who follow the Student-as-mind Prototype is their strong concern for the intellectual development of students. Away from Professor Minter, we explored the matter of verbal and nonverbal modes of communication with teachers in art and music departments who follow the Student-as-mind Prototype. Many of these teachers in the fine arts speak of the "intellectual *and* intuitive development" of students, but their ideas generally agree with those expressed by Professor Minter. There appears to be fundamental agreement in educational philosophy among all teachers following the Student-as-mind Prototype, whether they teach in fields that are traditionally verbal and book-centered—fields where ideas and concepts play a central role—or whether they teach in fields that are considered creative—fields that are not traditionally verbal and book-centered. In both situations, the teacher's emphasis in class—if he is following the Student-as-mind Prototype—is on analysis, on the use of reason and language as major tools in teaching, and on the problem-solving process as the major device by means of which he tests and grades his students.

Professor Persey: "I Work with Students As People"

Our representative of the university teacher who follows the Student-as-person Prototype is Professor Barton Persey, a professor of English literature at a large, urban state university. In physical appearance, Professor Persey is scarcely distinguishable from some of his students: he is slender and youthful-looking, and he dresses in extremely casual styles. In one of his classes which we visited, he was wearing chopped-off blue jeans, white sneakers, and a tie-dyed shirt. His hair is long, and he occasionally dons wire-rimmed glasses. In manner, he is totally spontaneous, thoroughly relaxed. He has large hands, and when he speaks they visually shape his ideas for his listeners. He is "hip," and most of his students adore him for it. They told us eagerly that "there is nothing uptight about Bart." That his easy manner is not a pose was revealed in our private conversations with him. He appeared as casual with us, and with his colleagues, as with his students. He is obviously a man who is completely at ease with the person he knows himself to be. As his students say, "He knows where he's at."

Professor Persey, like Professor Minter, is a student-centered instructor, but he believes that Professor Minter's emphasis on intellectual development and on rational activity is based on a false principle. He believes that intellectual development cannot be split from other aspects of the human personality. "Worse," he told us, "if an instructor succeeded in effecting such a split, his success could only be taken as an actual failure." Since the object of an education, in Professor Persey's view, is to build wholeness and prevent fragmentation, an educational program that succeeds in encouraging fragmentation in the student must be regarded as having failed.

In spite of this difference, however, Professor Persey and Professor Minter share a fundamental assumption. They both believe that a teaching philosophy must be grounded in a theory of human development, a theory of how human beings achieve their fullest powers of humanity. Each defines *humanness* in his own way. Professor Minter, as we have seen, defines it in terms of rational development; he believes that a university can and ought to keep the two developmental cycles in the student separate—progress in academic matters on the one hand, and progress in matters of student life on the other. Professor Persey defines *humanness* in terms of the whole person; he believes that the two cycles should not be kept separate, that each cycle should work to support the other. He believes, further, that it is the responsibility of every faculty member to help in that process.

A portion of one of our interviews with Professor Persey illustrates this point of view, which characterizes teachers who follow the Student-as-person Prototype:

INTERVIEWER: Are you saying that we can distinguish two life lines for the typical student—that is, two developmental cycles which are separate?

PROFESSOR PERSEY: No, I'm not. But for purposes of discussion, it's possible to distinguish two separate cycles. One of them consists of the student's academic assignments and crises—meeting deadlines for papers, exploring new intellectual worlds, making decisions about his field of concentration, his career. The other consists of the parts of his life that aren't academic—friends, sex, his decision whether to stay on at Malcolm X Hall or move into a commune in the city, his struggle to divest himself of his parents, and things of that sort.

I: And the two things can be separated, you're saying, but shouldn't be? They should become one?

P: Not exactly. If we could reach the condition as faculty members that we all ought to be striving for, then these two cycles would be related. Related in a creative way. When a major decision has to be made in one cycle, everything in the other cycle should be ready to help. I'm speaking ideally, of course. And if there's a crisis in the other cycle, then everything and everybody in the first ought to work hand-in-hand. But that hardly ever happens, needless to say—at least on this campus.

Although Professor Persey and Professor Minter are similar to each other in certain significant ways—and more similar to each other than to either Professor Innis or Professor Prince—their similarity is mainly related to their attitude that the student lies at the center of the teaching-learning process. In other significant ways, Professor Persey's beliefs and practices are distinctly different from Professor Minter's. One of these ways has to do with the use of the student group. Both professors use the student group in their teaching; both take advantage of pressures felt in the group, and of opinions expressed in it, to motivate its members. But Professor Persey goes considerably farther than Professor Minter. Professor Minter, even while using the group, never becomes a member of it, but Professor Persey does. Professor Persey therefore willingly subjects himself to group pressures. He tries, although he is the teacher, to assert no more authority than any other member of the group who moves in and out of leadership roles.

Even though Professor Persey has no formal training in psychology, he appears conversant with recent personality theory. During our interviews, he explained his conception of what a student does when he learns something. This conception can be summarized as follows: A student does not learn unless the task he is required to perform demands resources and strategies that are somehow new, that had not been used before, in exactly the same way, in the achievement of other tasks. When a student encounters situations he can manage with his existing resources, he will of course not invent new ones. From the point of view of educational effectiveness, such an exercise is actually harmful, for it yields nothing; and in addition, the student is bored. The behavior is mere repetitiousness, following a path already known and used. But where the assignment is such that the student cannot manage with his existing resources, he must find or invent new responses. They may not always work, but when they do, then they are integrated into the sum total of the student's behavior. He has now *learned* something. This is the kind of learning that Professor Persey tries to induce in his students. He explained his educational philosophy in somewhat greater detail during our interviews with him:

I: Let's talk for a moment about the kinds of assignments you give your students. How do they differ from those given in more traditional courses?

P: College teachers typically present students with tasks that they can easily manage with their existing repertoire of responses—those that they learned during their previous years of schooling. I don't see that as very effective teaching.

I: Can you offer some examples? What sorts of tasks can be so easily managed with existing responses?

P: College students are very adept at memorizing all kinds of details and generalizations. They've learned in previous school experiences how to memorize facts presented by others and generalizations drawn and formulated by others. And most of their college courses require them to memorize still more facts and principles. So there are no new elements in the responses those students are called upon to make in meeting the demands of the teacher. They can simply maintain—or maybe strengthen somewhat—the behavioral structures they came into college with. The way of organizing experience they already possess fits the demands that are made on them. There's no need for them to seek a more complex way to organize experience.

I: Do you believe that is true of *most* college courses? Even today?

P: Yes. In most classes, the student is actually discouraged from seeking *new* ways to organize experience. He learns the first week of the quarter that it's risky to try the new thing—that is, if he's out to get an A. And if he discovers that his existing behavioral structure is adequate for all the demands made on it by the assignments the professor gives him, naturally he'll resist whatever other pressures might encourage him to expand that structure.

I: And could you offer some examples of that?

P: Most of the courses on this campus—and everywhere—don't urge the student to expand, to develop new resources, to discover himself and the world. They operate the opposite way. They help him resist the forces that push in the direction of real learning. They give him a false impression of the world. They may teach him that less complex and relatively undeveloped responses bring the highest rewards. They bring him an A in the classroom, and he assumes they will buy his future as a professional.

We noticed during our visits to Professor Persey's classes that he makes an attempt to persuade students to discuss with their friends and relatives (if the students live at home) the novels and plays which are being read for his courses. He appeared to be unusually insistent on this matter—although he suggested that students not push *too* hard—and so we asked about it during one of our interviews:

I: You seem terribly serious about students getting their parents or wives or brothers and sisters to read the novels which the students themselves are reading. May I ask why this is so important to you?

P: There are several reasons. One reason is that this is a way for a student to get into communication with his mother or father or brother or sister. I mean communication on a new basis—on a person-to-person basis. What does a student talk about with his parents? What does a son talk about with his mother, for instance? Usually it's about some family matter, and so the son's relationship to his mother remains a relationship of a child and a parent. But if the son talks to his mother about Sally Bowles's love affairs, it ought to be possible for him to speak to her as an adult. That's one reason. I want literature to serve students in their growth as *people,* to confirm them in their status as adults. Then, too, I want literature to be a natural part of their lives—not something they do just for school, not something that they will want to stop doing as soon as they stop going to school.

I: That's very good.

P: But there's another reason that may be even more important. When a student takes the initiative and starts a discussion at home about a novel he's reading for my class, something subtle happens to him. He makes a commitment. Assuming, of course, that he sparks some interest in his mother or father or wife or girl friend—then he is making a commitment that goes way beyond his commitment to me. He commits himself to the book at hand, and he commits himself to literature.

I: But you don't, of course, *insist* that your students do this? You don't make it sound like a requirement for passing the course, I presume.

P: Oh, of course not. If my suggestion works, fine! But if the conditions at home, or wherever, are against it, then there's no point in creating a frustrating situation.

Another feature of Professor Persey's teaching style appears to us to be of unusual importance. During class discussions, when students give reports about their reading and other activities—when they share their experiences with their classmates, so to speak—Professor Persey does not at once indicate his personal reactions or offer criticism. He jots down some notes during the discussion and makes collections of these notes over a period of two or three weeks. Then, organizing his impressions around two or three major themes, he uses one whole class period for a well-structured, although informal, lecture to the class. In the lecture, he illustrates each of his points with quotations or paraphrases from the earlier student reports. He told us that he finds this method an ideal solution for a problem he had not been able to solve in his earlier years of teaching: how to react to student contributions during discussion without delivering "lecturettes" that always seemed to transform him into an instructor-as-authority figure, which could only interfere with his concept of his role as a teacher. In Chapter Six we shall see this technique illustrated in a transcript of a class taught by Professor Stephen Abbot, who is a colleague and friend of Professor Persey's and who has been much influenced since 1970 by Persey's educational philosophy and teaching techniques.

Because Professor Persey saves his comments and criticisms for the special lecture sessions, he is able to remain relatively quiet during the discussion sessions. He plays the roles of resource person and traffic manager, but he purposely avoids saying anything that is more than necessary. After we had visited one of his classes where he said practically nothing, we asked one of the students, Peter Moorhead, how he felt about Professor Persey's general silence. The student's response indicates the effectiveness of Persey's method:

INTERVIEWER: I noticed during the class that Bart didn't do very much talking. Does he often just sit at the table taking notes without saying anything for a long time?

PETER: He usually says *something*.

I: I don't mean just calling on students or saying "That's fine" or something. I'm talking about the way he lets the students do practically all of the talking.

P: We wants *us* to talk, and he lets us talk.

I: Suppose he didn't come to class at all. Suppose he just wasn't there some day. Would it make any difference to you?

P: It certainly would.

I: But what's the difference between not being there at all and being there but not saying anything—the way he did today? Isn't it pretty much the same thing?

P: It's not the same at all. He doesn't have to *say* anything. Just having him there is important to us.

Meanings of "Student-Centered"

While investigating teaching styles, we often used the term *student-centered* in talking to professors. For a number of professors whom we interviewed, the term held only one meaning: they used it to refer to classes in which students overtly participated in discussions. In our research, however, we discovered that there is no strict correlation of student-centered teaching styles with discussion classes or of subject-centered teaching styles with lecture courses. We found many discussion classes (like those of Professor Prince) to be subject-centered, and we observed a number of lecture sessions (like those of Professor Persey) that were unambiguously student-centered. Here are two examples taken from our notes of class visits.

We visited an English language course given in the evening and designed for practicing secondary school English teachers. The subject matter: various ways of analyzing the syntax of English. The course seemed to be devoted mainly to the fundamentals of transformational grammar. The professor gave a formal lecture on the day we visited. He presented to the class, in considerable detail, an actual problem that had been brought to him by one of the students in the class. It appeared that the student, a teacher in a ghetto school, had encountered a number of difficulties in his attempts to teach "standard" English and that he was suffering great anxiety over what he believed to be his teaching failure.

After a brief description of the situation—the type of school where the student was teaching, and so forth—which the student himself presented, the professor delivered his formal lecture. He analyzed the problem by delving first into its socio-linguistic aspects and then by suggesting how it could be approached through the methods of transformational grammar. He then offered several possible solutions (which, he explained, he and the student had previously discussed in private conference), and he analyzed these solutions in terms of their possible consequences. As part of this analysis, he pointed out the difficulties inherent in each one.

A second class we visited also illustrates nicely the student-centered lecture. The class was a senior seminar devoted to selected problems in literary historiography. On the day we visited, the professor posed a problem in literary chronology that concerned the dating of a newly discovered poem by a poet of the Romantic period. First, the professor presented a variety of relevant data, and then he outlined a number of hypotheses all of which could account for the data. During this presentation, the professor rather cleverly (and quite seriously) pretended he was this or that member of the class, actually "quoting" what they *would say* (even though they actually said nothing), and assuming that each student he named *had* presented one of the hypotheses.

The professor then continued the lecture by checking each hypothesis against the data. Whenever it became apparent that new data were needed, the professor played a different role: he became a resource person who supplied the new data. As the exploration proceeded, several of the hypotheses had to be abandoned, for they did not "fit" the new data. But several of them appeared tentatively acceptable, and the class ended with an open question about further steps that needed to be taken in order to determine which of the tentatively acceptable hypotheses was most appropriate.

Both of these classes remained lectures but (as in Professor Persey's lecture sessions) the relationship between the material, the students, and the professor was of such a nature as to render the lectures student-centered. They were student-centered in a way in which most university lecture sessions are not—and in a way that many discussion classes (Professor Prince's, for example) are not. The term *student-centered* thus retains a certain ambiguity in academic conversation and, indeed, in the literature of higher education itself. If we analyze the term carefully, we find that it currently carries three distinct layers of meaning. We can clarify these meanings by taking a close look at the terms which are frequently set in opposition to the term *student-centered*.

Almost half a century ago, the progressive education movement gave us the important opposition between subject matter and student, asserting that the class should focus on the student. From this opposition comes the movement's shibboleth, "We teach students, not courses." In brief, the movement's philosophy opposes the view that a course of study is to be regarded primarily as a body of information to be learned, a set of disciplines to be mastered, or a group of textbooks to be analyzed. An academic course, as the progressive education movement saw it, should be conceived primarily as a series of related experiences the students undergo, and it has as its goal changes in students' attitudes and behavior. The first and deepest layer of meaning of the term *student-centered,* then, derives from its opposition to the term *subject-matter-centered,* which appeared during the heyday of the progressive education movement.

A decade or two later, however, a second layer of meaning was added. It arose from the application to teaching of the principles of nondirective therapy. In this variety of psychotherapy, the key word is *client-centered*—the basic term, for example, in Carl Rogers' work—and it is opposed to the term *counselor-centered.* Like the teacher, the counselor tries to help his client "learn" in the most profound sense—that is, undergo change in behavioral habits. The objective of this type of counseling is not simply the temporary alleviation of anxieties, but genuine growth during which the client comes to develop new insights into himself and the world around him. Rogers and the school which followed him believed that this objective could be reached only "nondirectly," and their concept of client-centered therapy was built on that philosophy. The aspects of nondirective therapy that were of interest to educators in the 1940s and 1950s were not the specific techniques recommended by Carl Rogers or his disciples, but the attitudes that the counselor held about himself and about his client—attitudes by means of which the counselor was able to help his client grow.

When educators wrote about the translation into the classroom context of the principles of nondirective counseling,[2] they referred primarily to the adoption of a philosophy about human relations and about the learning process. Their concern was not the mechanical application of techniques. The client-centered concept, translated into the classroom context, was called student-centered in imitation of its source, and its opposite was named instructor-centered. These terms and their meanings can thus be best understood if we look back at their origins in the counseling field. The counselor-centered therapist asks the questions he thinks are relevant, does the probing, makes the diagnosis, submits his interpretations to the client, and suggests his solution to the problem. In the same way, the instructor-centered teacher (Professor Innis, for example) poses the problems to his students, presents the relevant data, submits his interpretations, and provides the solutions.

The second layer of meaning of the term *student-centered* is thus differently focused from the first layer of meaning. The first layer has as its opposite *subject-matter-centered.* The second layer has as its opposite *instructor-centered.* The two layers of meaning contain a number of com-

---

[2] See, for example, an article written during that period by the present writer: "Group Dynamics, Nondirective Therapy, and College Teaching," *Journal of Higher Education,* XXVI, 4 (April 1955), pp. 200–208.

mon elements, but there are great differences in their specific emphases and in their total configurations.

A third layer of meaning was added to the term *student-centered* during the 1950s and 1960s by researchers and practitioners influenced by the theory of group dynamics. In this theory, it is neither the group member nor the group leader as an individual upon whom attention is primarily focused. It is the group itself which, in its own right and with its power as a distinct living organism, plays the central role in the teaching-learning process. According to this theory, both member and leader, in an ideally constituted group, become subservient to this larger organism. Both become integral parts of it: the leader relinquishes his exclusive leadership, and the members go beyond their exclusive followership. Every member of the group becomes leader and follower alternately and together, as the interests of the group dictate.

In the teaching context, the group dynamics elements of leader-member-group become teacher-student-class. While exploring ways of injecting this concept into the teaching-learning process, researchers have become aware of a wide variety of leader roles that it is possible for both instructors and students to assume. Investigation in this area has shown, among other things, the markedly different functions which the instructor serves, both before and after he is genuinely accepted as a group member. Again, the one-dimensional view of a professor's teaching style displays its inadequacy. Any picture of a classroom must take into consideration whether the instructor is *in* the group or *outside* it. If the instructor is not yet a member of the group and still represents a figure of outside authority, then certain roles he plays (as critic of a student's contribution, for example) will have a different impact from almost identical roles assumed by him after he has become a genuine group member. This is so because after he has become a member of the group, his contributions are both accepted and rejected about as easily as those of any other highly regarded member of the group. This matter will be further explored in Chapters Five and Six when we look at the student-centered teacher, Professor Stephen Abbot: the roles Professor Abbot chooses are determined by his sensitivity to his specific place in the group. He senses whether he is being listened to as a highly prized member of the group or as a figure who represents outside authority.

The third layer of meaning for the term *student-centered,* then, has to do with the group. It is neither the teacher as an individual nor is it the group member as individual around whom the learning process, as ideally conceived, revolves. At the center of the teaching-learning process is the group itself, a dynamic organism with its own life and with tremendous power.

The term *student-centered* means many things to many people, but generally these three layers of meaning encompass all the others: the term (1) emphasizes the student rather than the subject matter in the learning process; (2) puts the student rather than the instructor at the center of the class; and (3) sees the individual student and teacher as constituents of a larger and powerful organism, the total teaching-learning group.

Chapter 3

Distinguishing Features in the Portraits

Our analysis of evocative teaching styles has distinguished four prototypic models. It would be well, at this point, to give a brief summary of that analysis.

The most common of the four models is the Principles-and-facts Prototype. The teacher for whom this prototype serves as model focuses on principles, concepts, and other kinds of subject-matter; he is concerned with the systematic coverage of his subject. He believes the primary functions of a university teacher are to inform the student directly about certain topics and, above all, to provoke the student into additional learning through the processes of inquiry and discovery. The motto that characterizes the teacher using the Principles-and-facts Prototype as model is: "I teach what I know."

The second of the evocative modes is represented by the Instructor-centered Prototype model. The teacher who follows this model sets himself up before the student as a "model inquirer." He is not nearly as concerned as his Principles-and-facts Prototype colleague with coverage of subject matter. Instead of covering the field systematically, he is satisfied to sample the subject matter of his field, and he sees as his primary function the demonstration of the way an expert—namely, himself—deals with the problems selected for exploration. The motto for the Instructor-centered Prototype teacher is: "I teach what I am."

The other two prototypes among the evocative modes focus on student development. Teachers who follow these two prototypes emphasize not *what* a student knows—subject content—but *how* he acquires that knowledge. The teacher who follows the Student-as-mind Prototype does not attempt complete coverage of the subject matter (in this he is similar to his Instructor-centered Prototype colleague), but he samples selected areas of it, making certain to organize course content so that the material is suitable for helping students learn to perform complex intellectual operations. His goal is to encourage his students to develop ease in a variety of intellectual skills—verbal, analytic, rational, "scientific"—moving from the formulation of problems, to the analysis of data, to solutions. The motto for the student-as-mind Prototype teacher is: "I train minds."

The teacher who follows the Student-as-person Prototype focuses on student development in a different sense; he includes the totality of individual growth for the student. He treats the student not only as a "mind" but as an individual whose intellectual, emotional, aesthetic, and other developments are inseparable. The motto which characterizes this prototype is: "I work with students as people."

The four evocative teaching modes were illustrated in Chapter Two by four portraits of professors in humanistic disciplines. Each of these men—Professors Prince, Innis, Minter, and Persey—exemplified one of the four modes.

The four teacher prototypes are distinguished from each other by specific characteristics. There are thirteen of these distinguishing features, and we were able to identify them by professors' responses to thirteen key questions which were included in each interview. The distinguishing features can be divided into four groups: the professor's conception of student change, his conception of the nature of knowledge, his conception of the place of rational activity in the learning process, and characteristics of his classroom practice.

Student Change

Two of the thirteen distinguishing features concern the professor's conception of the changes he hopes will take place in his students as a result of his teaching. The questions which identify these two characteristics were designed to reveal the teacher's image of an ideal student (Question 1) and what the teacher believes to be desirable student change (Question 2).

Question 1: Think of the ideal student—the student who completes your course and, as a result of his studies with you, undergoes precisely the changes you hoped would take place. Do you have an identical image for all of your students? Is the image, in the last analysis, a *single* image for every student?

Three of the prototypic teachers—Prince, Innis, and Minter—answered yes, although they answered the question in different ways. Professor Prince's image of the ideal student is that of a young scholar with the commitments and behaviors that characterize the scholarly life. Professor Innis's image is of a student displaying attitudes, habits of mind, and an approach to the arts very much like his own. Professor Minter's ideal is a student who embodies the precept of man as a rational animal. In each case, the image of the ideal student is a single image. But for Professor Persey, the matter is more complicated. He does not have a single image of the ideal student because he emphasizes individual differences in students. He believes it is essential for professors to preserve and develop in students those qualities through which individuality is created. For Professor Persey, the ideal student is the person who has realized his own potentialities, who becomes everything he is capable of becoming. Since those potentialities vary from student to student, so must Professor Persey's ideal student reflect the pluralism of his conception of the mature person.

Question 2: Think of the changes you want to effect in your students. Imagine the kinds of changes and the direction of change. Do you believe that those students who reach the goals you have set for them change, basically, in the same way?

Professor Prince answered yes to this question and thus revealed the picture he holds of how each of his classes works. He believes that the process can be described quite simply. At the beginning of each term, a group of more-or-less ignorant students arrives, and as the term passes the students move from a state of ignorance to a state of knowledge. They learn the facts, principles, concepts, tools, and theories that make up the course content. The ignorance at the start of the term is generally equal, but the knowledge at the end of the term is markedly unequal. In Professor Prince's conception, it is this unevenness that is measured by the final examination and reflected in the course grade.

Professors Innis, Minter, and Persey all gave answers to this question which show that they hold quite different views from that of Professor Prince. Students who reach the goals these professors have set for them change in desirable but not necessarily similar ways.

When we combine the responses to Question 1 and Question 2, we obtain some excellent clues about views of student growth. The answers to both questions differentiate Professor Prince from Professor Persey. The answer to Question 1 distinguishes Professor Persey from Professors Innis and Minter. The answer to Question 2 distinguishes Professor Prince from Professors Innis and Minter. These relationships are shown in Table 1. (Table 1 organizes the responses to all thirteen questions, and has therefore been placed near the end of this chapter.)

The relationship between the responses to Question 1 and Question 2 is complex. One facet of that relationship can be illustrated by Professor Persey's freshman seminar in English, where one of his objectives is to increase the student's ability to read a set of facts fairly accurately. He wants to teach students how to avoid overreading and emerging with a questionable conclusion, but he also wants to teach them how to avoid underreading and thus failing to acquire the full meaning of the facts. Professor Persey knows from past experience that some students have been taught to be—or are by temperament—cautious when they are confronted by data, and they habitually underread them. But other students—perhaps the majority—are unrestrainedly impressionistic and tend to overgeneralize. Conceived in concrete, behavioral terms, the changes these two sorts of students need to undergo, as a result of their work in Professor Persey's seminar, are diametrically opposed: the two groups must move in opposite directions.

A major factor which complicates the analysis of responses to Question 2 is that the scales which psychologists and other researchers ordinarily use for measuring change in students are linear—that is, for any given characteristic, the scale allows only two possible directions in which change can take place: a given characteristic has either "increased" or "decreased" over a given period of time. When the problem is conceived in linear terms, we oversimplify an exceedingly complex process. In spite of this shortcoming, however, the responses given to both Questions 1 and 2—especially when they are analyzed together—serve to make useful distinctions between the four types of evocative teachers.

Nature of Knowledge

Two more of the distinguishing features among the four prototypes have to do with the way the teacher conceives of the nature of the knowledge that is to be gained by students. Our questions sought to reveal the professor's relative emphasis—if his conditions were exactly as he might wish them—on cognitive and affective knowledge (Question 3) and to discover whether he views knowledge primarily as product or as process (Question 4).

Question 3: Imagine an *ideal* class session in one of your courses. Does class activity focus completely, or nearly completely, on the transmission of knowledge that is primarily in the cognitive domain? Or does the class activity show that significant attention is given to knowledge in the affective domain? (The terms "cognitive knowledge" and "affective knowledge" were defined for those teachers who requested explanation. The terms are also briefly defined under "knowledge" in the Glossary of this book.)

Three of the prototypic professors—Prince, Innis, and Minter—showed by their answers to this question that they do not (or in any case do not intend to) pay more than incidental attention to noncognitive knowledge. Professor Persey, on the other hand, showed much interest in affective knowledge, although he also told us that he was certain a substantial proportion of his class time (probably well over half) was devoted to processes that concentrated on the acquisition of cognitive knowledge. When we asked Professor Persey whether he was unhappy about that large proportion, he replied that he was.

Question 4: As you help students acquire knowledge—including knowledge in both the cognitive and affective domains—do you conceive of that knowledge primarily as *product?* Or do you think of it as *process* as well?

This question, we discovered, usually required some explanation and discussion before it could be satisfactorily answered. As knowledge is commonly conceived, it is both an activity and a set of products which emerge from that activity. Some professors concentrate only on the products of knowledge, especially in their undergraduate courses. These professors ordinarily are concerned with rather complete and systematic coverage of the subject matter in the field. Other professors are content if the subject matter in the field is only sampled, and they devote their energy to helping students master the processes by means of which an individual learns the subject matter of the field. Their argument against teaching subject matter is that it changes as time moves forward. If the student is to become an educated person, they say, he cannot merely master subject matter; he must learn how to continue to keep subject matter updated in the years after leaving the university.

Professor Prince is the only one of the prototypic teachers who conceives of knowledge primarily as product. Professors Innis, Minter, and Persey all conceive, to a greater or lesser extent, of knowledge as process. Professor Minter emphasizes the acquisition of intellectual skills and abilities and, as we would expect, the concept of knowledge as process plays a central and explicit role in his educational philosophy and practice. The answers given to the question by Professors Innis and Persey indicate that they are also interested in the acquisition of skills and abilities, but for them the matter does not play such an explicit and central role. Still, their emphasis is clearly on knowledge as process. Only for Professor Prince, then, is knowledge as product central in the teaching style.

Place of Rational Activity

Another characteristic which distinguishes between the four prototypes is the view they hold of the centrality of rational, intellectual activity in the learning process. Question 5 was designed to obtain information on this subject.

Question 5: Imagine an ideal class session and then focus on the activities you would expect students to engage in as preparation for that class and, later on, for the final examination in the course. Are these activities almost always rational in nature? That is, are these activities characterized by the formulation of concepts and explanations, by reasoning, generalizing, particularizing, and other exclusively rational behavior? Or do you give specific attention to activities that are irrational, nonrational, and nonverbal? Remember, please, that we are speaking of activities that students are expected to *engage* in, not simply to talk about.[1]

Of the four professors, only Professor Persey showed any interest in the nonverbal and nonrational as actual means to be used by students in the learning process. The other three professors not only rejected such means but appeared annoyed that they might even be considered appropriate for college courses. Professor Persey expressed a conviction that students learn—that, indeed, everyone learns—the most important and most lasting knowledge through nonrational means. But he also told us that he was not quite sure about how to harness these means so that they could be controlled for pedagogic purposes. Nevertheless, he emphasized his belief that nonrational means should be central in the learning process, especially for the materials basic to humanistic studies.

Characteristics of Classroom Practice

The remaining eight of the thirteen key questions that identify distinguishing features deal directly with classroom practice.

[1] It is sometimes hard to make clear-cut distinctions. Some courses such as painting and musical performance are nonverbal in content, as are typing and sports, in areas outside the humanities. Responses to the question from professors teaching such courses had to be carefully analyzed to discover how such teachers fit into the four prototypic categories.

Question 6: As you think of an ideal class session that you are teaching, do you see yourself making all the decisions about the selection and sequence of topics and the general organization of the session? Or do you see yourself, at certain times, explicitly giving responsibility to the class, or a subgroup of the class, for any of these decisions?

Professors Minter and Persey responded to this question by saying that they seek advice from their students and give them responsibility for decisions which affect the organization of the class. Professors Prince and Innis said that they make all of such decisions themselves, and consider it appropriate that they should. It is interesting to note that both Professor Prince and Professor Innis, during our discussions on this question, became somewhat defensive about their views, and both denounced the "democratizing" that takes place nowadays in college classrooms. Professor Innis was particularly vocal on this point: "The process of democratization is just the other side of the coin of bureaucracy." He condemned classes in which, as he described it, "committees of students decide what is true and what is false." Professor Prince's views, in any event, are steadfastly conservative on the entire matter of student participation in decision making—except concerning dormitory life, where he believes that the student voice ought to be heard.

Question 7: In your class sessions, are you particularly and explicitly concerned with communication between each of your students and his classmates?

Professors Minter and Persey indicated unambiguously that they are concerned with the adequacy of communication between students. Professors Prince and Innis, however, are more concerned about communication between themselves and their students than between one student and another.

Question 8: Does lecturing, either by yourself or by guests, or do lecture-like presentations such as educational films, play a significant and continuous role in your class sessions?

Professors Prince and Innis answered yes to this question. Both of them devote a certain amount of time to nonlecture activities—discussions or question-and-answer periods—but lectures and lecture-like presentations dominate their classroom activities. Professor Minter and Persey answered no. They both deliver lectures from time to time, but these do not play a predominant role and are designed primarily to meet special student needs—needs either felt and expressed by students or perceived by the professors. Such lectures—unlike those of Professor Prince and Professor Innis—always focus on topics that present particularly difficult problems to students; and in the case of Professor Persey's courses, which are so highly personalized, such topics are different from one term to the next.

> *Question 9:* During discussion and question-and-answer periods, do you always, or almost always, initiate the dialogue by asking a question or setting a problem or soliciting a reaction? Or do your students often initiate the dialogue?

Only Professor Prince's classroom practice requires that he always, or almost always, serve as the initiator of instructor-student dialogue. In the cases of the other three professors, students are often the initiators in class discussion, and sometimes even present new problems to the teacher. Professor Innis, in particular, welcomes challenges by students which often take the form of accusations that he is inconsistent, that he is in conflict with one of the authors assigned for reading, or that some other authority in the field presents a more convincing point of view. Dr. Innis, however, is invariably victorious in the battles of wit which ensue.

Professors Minter and Persey have relationships with students that are, in any event, different from those of Professors Prince and Innis. Their dialogue with students is consequently of a different sort. Yet Professor Innis's response to this question is more similar to that of the two student-centered professors than to Professor Prince's, because only in Professor Prince's classes does a student actually feel restrained if he wishes to initiate dialogue during a discussion. We discovered that Professor Prince's students feel free to raise questions in class only when Professor Prince *asks* for them—which of course makes him the real initiator. Under such conditions, a student is led to feel that he is wasting his classmates' time if he himself raises questions that pose particular difficulty for him; the ethos of the class obliges him to save such questions for a time outside of class. Professor Innis's classroom atmosphere, during the question-and-answer periods, is not nearly so restrictive. Still, it is not as open as the atmosphere in Professor Minter's and especially in Professor Persey's classrooms, where students generally are free to initiate dialogue whenever they wish. These points are especially well illustrated in the three transcripts presented in Part Two.

> *Question 10:* Are you the kind of teacher who often models the learning process or the process of discovery? That is, do you often demonstrate the learning activity itself by actually learning with

your students, or by describing such an activity from your own personal experience or the experiences of other scholars and investigators in your field?

Three of the professors—Innis, Minter, and Persey—answered the question with an unequivocal yes, but Professor Prince found the concept behind the question foreign to his way of thinking about his role as a teacher. He found it inconceivable that a scholar, such as he, could learn anything in his own field from a discussion with an undergraduate student group.

Question 11: Do you frequently find yourself using pressures within your student group, and opinions expressed by the group, to motivate the individuals in it?

Professors Prince and Innis answered this question no; Professors Minter and Persey answered it yes. Ways in which student-centered professors typically use the student group to motivate individual students are well illustrated in the transcripts of the two student-centered class sessions which appear in Chapters Five and Six.

Question 12: Are cooperative projects, involving two or more students, often undertaken as an integral part of the work expected to be done in your courses?

Cooperative projects occur only in classes conducted by Professor Persey. For Professors Innis and Minter, the idea was not totally unattractive, but they felt that conditions in the academic setting did not permit them to encourage such projects. Professor Prince totally rejected such an idea. He complained that the projects would be impossible to grade because the instructor would not know what contribution had been made by each student, which would render him unable to judge either the quality or the quantity of the student's work.

Question 13: Are you generally satisfied with the standard testing and grading system used in colleges today?

The teaching styles of Professors Prince and Innis generally fit the standard grading system well, and they found it satisfactory. Professors Minter and Persey were not satisfied with it.

It should be noted, however, that almost all of the professors we interviewed had complaints of one sort or another about the grading system. Some pointed to features of the system itself while others objected to the ways in which the system has been abused by faculty colleagues, by students, and by persons outside the academic world. Almost all of these professors were in favor of reforming the grading system in some way. But there was little agreement about the nature or direction of changes thought to be desirable.

The replies given to the thirteen key questions enable us to make some clear distinctions between the four evocative teaching prototypes. In Table 1, the thirteen questions have been organized into three groups to show where the responses agreed and disagreed. Professors Prince, Innis, and Minter agreed in their answers to the four questions in Group I; Professor Persey's answers disagreed, showing that on these four questions he stands alone as a representative of the Student-as-person prototype. Similarly, the agreement between Professors Minter and Persey in answering the Group II questions marks them as followers of student-centered prototypes; and the agreement between Professors Prince and Innis in answering questions in that same group shows similarities in the relationships they establish between themselves and their students during the teaching process. But in his answers to Group III questions, Professor Innis agrees with the two followers of the student-centered prototypes; and Professor Prince stands alone, by his answers to those questions, as the representative of the Principles-and-facts prototype.

Reactions to a Hypothetical Situation

All of our interviews with teachers ended with the presentation of a hypothetical situation. Reactions to the situation also serve to differentiate the four prototypic professors. We described the hypothetical situation as follows:

INTERVIEWER: Let me ask you to imagine this situation. Suppose that a student comes into your office and makes himself comfortable in the chair alongside your desk—the chair in which visitors normally sit, the chair in which I am now sitting. And then, without saying anything he puts his feet up on your desk. When you look up, there he is—grinning at you good-naturedly. How do you think you would react?

Professor Prince's reaction to this situation stands in sharp contrast to the reactions of Professors Innis, Minter, and Persey:

P: I can't conceive of anything like that happening with one of my students.
I: Yes, but suppose it did happen.

Table 1

PATTERNS OF REPLIES TO THE KEY QUESTIONS

GROUP I (Questions 1, 3, 5, 12)

	Prince	Innes	Minter	Persey
Is your picture of your "ideal product" similar for all students?	Yes	Yes	Yes	No
(A) Do you focus mainly on cognitive knowledge or (B) do you give concerted attention to affective knowledge?	A	A	A	B
Is planned activity in your class always rational in nature, focused on concepts, explanations, reasoning, and generalizing?	Yes	Yes	Yes	No
Do cooperative projects, involving two or more students, play a significant role in student activity for your course?	No	No	No	Yes

GROUP II (Questions 6, 7, 8, 11, 13)

	Prince	Innes	Minter	Persey
(A) Are decisions about the course organization made completely by you, or (B) do you give responsibility to students?	A	A	B	B
Are you particularly concerned with communication between each student and classmates?	No	No	Yes	Yes
Does lecturing play a significant and continuous role?	Yes	Yes	No	No
Do you use group pressures to motivate individuals in the class?	No	No	Yes	Yes
Are you satisfied with the testing/grading system?	Yes	Yes	No	No

GROUP III (Questions 2, 4, 9, 10)

	Prince	Innes	Minter	Persey
Is your hoped-for change in students similar for all students?	Yes	No	No	No
(A) Is your focus on knowledge as product, or (B) are you also concerned with knowledge as process?	A	B	B	B
Do your students often initiate discussions during discussion periods?	No	Yes	Yes	Yes
Do you often model the learning process in class?	No	Yes	Yes	Yes

P: I would just stand up and quietly ask him to leave. And I would expect an apology of some sort.

I: Why would you expect an apology?

P: Because I expect to be treated with respect.

When we presented the situation to Professor Innis, we asked him
to assume this was a male student. Professor Innis appeared less certain
about his reaction than Professor Prince, but it is clear he would have
been displeased and would have wanted, in a gracious way, to show his
displeasure:

INNIS: You say this is one of *my* students?

INT: Yes.

INNIS: Frankly, I would be shocked.

INT: Why?

INNIS: Because my students don't treat me that way.

INT: I understand that. But suppose it did happen. What would you do
or say?

INNIS: I'm guessing, but I think I would just stand up. Then he would
have to stand up, too. And we would resume our conversation that
way—standing. And then I would sit down and say, probably,
"Please make yourself comfortable," and point to the chair. And
then I would make some joke—something that would keep him
from putting his foot on the desk again.

INT: What kind of joke?

INNIS: Any kind, so long as it would show him that I was displeased.

For Professor Minter, there was need, first of all, to understand
the reason why the student was behaving in this manner:

M: Let me get the situation straight. Is this student sticking his feet
in my face?

I: No, he just puts his feet on your desk in a perfectly casual way.

M: There is no sign of a confrontation, or anything like that?

I: No, it's a casual situation. He's smiling good-naturedly.

M: I don't think I would get too disturbed, in that case. I would probably let him know in some way that this sort of thing isn't done.
Maybe I would hand him a newspaper or a magazine and ask him
to use it to protect the finish on the desk. Or maybe I would just
tell him directly that I don't mind some unconventional behavior
but that what he was doing was interfering with our conversation.

I: But wouldn't that kind of response in itself interfere with your conversation? Wouldn't it be like shutting a door?

M: Oh, I wouldn't want to do that. I would want to figure out a way to use the incident to open the door. But I wouldn't be comfortable if he had his feet on my desk.

I: May I ask why?

M: I suppose it's because I can't tolerate such a casual attitude when a student is in my office to see me about his course work. After all, it's not a social visit.

I: It's the lack of formality, then, that would bother you?

M: Maybe not that so much. Maybe it's just that he would be assuming some kind of equality. That would be the thing I would find offensive. We *aren't* equals.

Professor Persey's reaction reveals his strong identification with his students and it shows, on another level, an even more interesting contrast between him and the other three prototypic teachers: unlike them, he is determined *not* to read the incident as an attempt by the student to "put down" the professor:

P: That is a very interesting situation. Of course, the student's just trying something out. He's probably trying out a new role.

I: And how would you react to that?

P: Whether he's trying out a new role, or whether it's something else, the thing I could least afford to do is become offended. For his sake, for the sake of his education.

I: You would not find his behavior offensive?

P: No. Why should I jump to the conclusion that this is a put-down? Of course, I would see right away that there was a message there, and I would try to figure out what the message was. I would say to myself that what he's doing is unusual, so there's probably a message. I would try to figure it out. But it needn't be a *bad* message.

I: What do you think his message might be?

P: That depends. It could be any one of several things. The most likely thing it might mean, I should think, is that it's a bid for friendship—a sign he wants to be a comrade. What it says is: "I've seen your colleagues do this. When they come into your office, they put their feet on your desk. I want to be a colleague of yours, so you should let me do what they do."

I: Let's assume that this is the student's message. Then what would you do?

P: If that's his message, then I have to decide whether I want to treat him like a colleague or not. Of course, even if I do, he and I both know that it's only temporary. Because his relationship to me isn't static, in any case—it keeps shifting. Sometimes I might treat him like a son. Maybe sometimes I treat him like a grammar-school child. But I suppose what he's asking for, really, is to be treated as a person, as an individual.

I: What would you actually do?

P: I wouldn't do anything. I would do the same thing I would do if he actually was a colleague. I just wouldn't call attention to it.

I: But what if you didn't want to treat him like a colleague?

P: Then I suppose I would have to call attention to his feet. But I'd want to do it in a nice way—some way that wouldn't hurt him. It would have to show him that I respect him as a person.

I: Let's go back to the beginning of the question again. What if you realized at once that the student's message was that he had no respect for you?

P: I would have to be really certain that was the message. That would be very important. If he was a student of mine and didn't have respect for me, then it's not likely I could teach him very much. It would be necessary to find out.

I: Could you ask him directly? Could you say, for example, to him: "Are you putting your feet up on my desk because you have no respect for me?"

P: Maybe I could, but I wouldn't. I would do it indirectly—something like, "I see you have your feet on my desk. Are you trying to tell me something?"

I: If I may make a personal comment, it impresses me how much thought you've given this question as we've been chatting about it. You find even such small things important.

P: There's *nothing* in a teacher's relationship with a student that isn't important. Unless of course you define education as just learning by heart the forms *amo, amas, amat* without ever learning their meaning.

*He seemed to hear the noise of dim waves and to see a winged
form flying above the waves and slowly climbing the air.
What did it mean? Was it a quaint device opening a page
of some medieval book of prophecies and symbols, a hawk-
like man flying sunward above the sea, a prophecy of the end
he had been born to serve and had been following through
the mists of childhood and boyhood, a symbol of the artist
forging anew in his workshop out of the sluggish matter of the
earth a new soaring impalpable imperishable being?*

James Joyce
A Portrait of the Artist as a Young Man

PART II

Portrait of a Teacher-Artist

The three chapters of Part Two show three stages in the career of a litera-ture professor who, from the time he first began teaching, was regarded by both students and colleagues as an excellent teacher. Transcripts of actual class sessions are presented to illustrate the development of Professor Stephen Abbot as a teacher-artist.

The first stage represents Professor Abbot's earliest years as a teacher; at that time, he followed the Principles-and-facts Prototype as his classroom model. These were the years before the Berkeley crisis of 1964, and the transcript that appears in Chapter Four comes from those tranquil days. Professor Abbot's teaching style at that time strongly re-sembled the style of Professor Prince, the art historian whose portrait we saw in Chapter Two. Professor Abbot, however, had much less experience as a teacher and was more naive in his relationships with students. But like Professor Prince, he was somewhat compulsive about covering the subject matter he had planned for each session. In Chapter Four, Pro-fessor Abbot plays the fairly standard roles of a professor who is more interested in teaching books than in teaching students. He is shown teach-ing a Moliere play to a group of students in Freshman English. He elicits from his students explanations of what the play is saying and how the dramatist succeeds in presenting his message. The transcript shows him engaging in a highly directive dialogue with his students, which he care-

57

fully controls throughout the session as he works toward goals that are centered on subject matter.

The academic revolution that was occurring in the early 1960s brought Professor Abbot's first stage of teaching to a close. New insights came rapidly; his concept of his goals and his sense of classroom roles for the college teacher changed drastically. By 1967, his teaching style was transformed. He had become a student-centered teacher. This second stage in his career is illustrated by the transcript presented in Chapter Five. Professor Abbot now bears a strong resemblance to Professor Minter, the humanities professor portrayed in Chapter Two: he is interested in students and concentrates on the training of their minds. His goals have changed radically, and the second transcript, where he is discussing *Hamlet* with another group of freshmen, shows that his teaching now focuses on the skills of critical thinking. He believes it is his task to train students to arrive at truth dispassionately and objectively, and he teaches them to work toward the solution of problems by using logic and reason.

Toward the end of the 1960s, Professor Abbot underwent further change. It was, in fact, a metamorphosis. Some of his colleagues began to view him as anti-intellectual because he abandoned many of the teaching objectives in which he had once so firmly believed. His educational philosophy and his teaching style came to resemble those of Professor Persey, the English professor of Chapter Two who follows the Student-as-person Prototype. Professor Abbot's goal now was to develop the student as a whole person. To this purpose, he became personally involved with his students during his class and conference sessions with them, and they began to call him Steve.

This most recent stage of Professor Abbot's development as a teacher-artist is exemplified, in Chapter Six, by a transcript of a class meeting that took place in 1971. His concept of teacher and student roles had been radically altered by the events of Kent State and Jackson State and the experiences he underwent in the spring of 1970 when his campus was "reconstituted" to meet what many of his colleagues and almost all of his students regarded as a major national crisis. The class session transcribed in Chapter Six is a wide-ranging discussion in which students report on certain readings and activities—some completed, some in preparation. Students express both conventional and outrageous views on Ibsen, Barth, Flaubert, Mishima, Shakespeare, a black arts workshop, a gay liberation poetry reading, comics as literature, and many other topics. Professor Abbot serves as catalyst and, sometimes, as victim.

In the first two transcripts, it is evident that Professor Abbot is working hard to become an artist at teaching; and he told us in recent interviews, as we studied the transcripts together, that he believes there were moments when he actually succeeded. The last transcript shows him imposing on himself an entirely different kind of discipline, and he feels he is more successful in his efforts at creating art. We wonder whether this will be his final stage as a teacher-artist—whether he will now continue to perfect his art within one of the modes that follow the Student-as-person Prototype. It is of course not possible to say. At this moment, Professor Abbot feels that this teaching prototype will continue to be the right one for him. But in offering this opinion to us, he also expressed concern about imperfections in his present practice.

The route through which Professor Abbot has moved thus far, in his attempt to become a teacher-artist, has probably been the right one for him. But we hope no reader will suppose that the same three stages would constitute the right progression for everyone. We interviewed several professors, for example, who started their careers as student-centered teachers of undergraduates but are now following the instructor-centered prototype and working entirely with graduate students; their own theories and research findings remain constantly at the center of their lectures and class discussions. Yet, in our view, they have achieved a high level of excellence and by our definition they are teacher-artists. Other professors with whom we talked during the course of our investigation tried student-centered approaches in their classrooms during the mid-sixties but found them uncongenial; their development as teacher-artists required a movement toward the prototype that focuses on subject matter. As with all artists, the pattern of development of the teacher-artist, too, remains unique. The progression that turned out to be inevitable for Professor Abbot—given his educational philosophy, teaching conditions, general personality, and the ethos on his campus—was from the Principles-and-facts prototype to the Student-as-mind prototype to the Student-as-person prototype. But our findings do not permit us to assert that the same three stages in the same order would constitute the right progression for every professor who wishes to become a teacher-artist.

Chapter 4

Before Berkeley:
Teaching Books

When Professor Stephen Abbot began his career, he quickly became a popular teacher, considered effective by students and colleagues alike. He had confidence in himself, understood that he was an excellent teacher, and had a clear picture of his goals and his teaching role. At this stage, he was a follower of the Principles-and-facts Prototype. Though he lectured occasionally, during those early years, he strongly believed in the value of the discussion class, and he saw his role, therefore, to be that of a discussion leader. It was his job, he believed, to keep the discussion moving without long and embarrassing breaks, and it was his responsibility to introduce new topics and to make statements to summarize the topics already discussed. He prepared the topics for discussion carefully, so that tangential issues could be avoided and so that he could maintain control. He never for a moment considered that the class as a whole, or any student in it, might wish—or should be asked—to undertake any of the responsibilities he had assigned to himself.

During these early years, it was Professor Abbot's practice to come to each class session with a list of topics he planned to cover during the hour. He had already distributed this list to his students at the close of the previous class session so that they could prepare themselves, because he believed they needed such a study guide in order to learn effectively. He regulated the discussion to make it conform to the study guide, allocating specific time periods to each point on the list and allowing longer periods to what he considered the most important topics.

Occasionally, as the transcript will show, he lectured to his class, but it was not his general practice. He believed that it was more effective to elicit conclusions from the students themselves, even when—as he told us in an interview some years later—"I had to put words into their mouths."

The discussion session presented in this chapter took place in a freshman course in literature. The book under discussion was Moliere's play *The Misanthrope*. According to Professor Abbot's study guide, three class sessions were devoted to discussing this play, and each session was given over to a different set of topics. The first session covered various formal aspects of the play; the second focused on the dramatic structure and plot movement of the play; and the third dealt with the general problem of the play.

The first session, mainly lecture but partly discussion, covered these topics: the history of the period in which the play was written; the life and background of the author; the language, style, and verse form in which the play was originally written; and comments about translation and related matters. The list of study topics for the second session contained questions about dramatic technique—for example, the handling of entrances and exits ("How does Moliere get a particular character on the stage when he wants him there?" "How does he get him off?" "Is the stage ever empty within a particular scene?"); techniques of exposition ("Of the many possible techniques of exposition, which one does Moliere choose?" "Is it cleverly interwoven with action, or is it obvious?"); the movement of the action involving "discoveries" and "reversals" (which Professor Abbot illustrated with a brief lecture on Aristotle's *Poetics*).

The third session, according to Professor Abbot's study guide, was to deal with "the general problem or conflict presented or depicted in the play." It is this session which is reproduced in the transcript that follows.

1. PROFESSOR ABBOT: At the last class meeting, we discussed the plot and something of the dramatic structure of The Misanthrope. *But we must not imagine that we have finished all there is to say about it. As a matter of fact, the most significant points haven't even been mentioned yet.*

You will remember that, when we began our course, we said that a good piece of literature can be appreciated on several levels. We have already discussed this play on the story level, and now—today—we are going to try to see what more there is to discover. It might be a good idea for you to take out your list of study topics, because some of these topics will be coming up in our discussion today. I hope you've had time to think about these topics and have even made some notes—with page references to passages in the play itself.

1. It is clear from the very beginning of this session that Professor Abbot, in this first stage of his teaching career—in the early 1960s—believes that the instructor should play the dominant role in a class discussion. His first speech shows how directive he is.

Professor Abbot's approach is also highly logical as he introduces the topic of the day. He sets the stage quickly, and then he goes at once back to "when we began our course," thus connecting the present session with basic course goals. He follows with a quick summary of the two previous sessions, because they, too, were devoted to the play under discussion, and he reminds the students about their responsibilities in preparing for the class discussion.

PROFESSOR ABBOT: [Continuing.] *But first I want to raise a general question: Is the dramatist just telling us a good story in this play, or is he using the story that he depicts on the stage as a means of presenting his ideas—his interpretation of some particular kind of problem?* [Professor Abbot pauses. There is no immediate response.] *I mean, how would you characterize the kind of problem the dramatist is portraying in this play?* [Pause. No response.] *Perhaps that's too big a question to start with. Let's try a smaller question first. Or, rather, let me ask an even more general question to start with. What kinds of problems have some of the works of literature we've read this semester dealt with?*

Professor Abbot raises a general discussion question to start off the session: he wants to know whether the dramatist's intention is merely to tell a good story or whether Moliere means to get some ideas across to his audience. The answer to the question must surely be obvious to the students. They have learned from their previous discussions that there are always ideas of some sort embedded in every literary work. (The professor who follows the Principles-and-facts Prototype, as Professor Abbot does at this stage of his teaching, typically believes that these are the ideas which he is able to discover but which his students do not yet see; the students take the course in order to overcome their ignorance in such matters.) But no one volunteers an answer—no one says, "In addition to the good story (or through the good story), the dramatist is making some kind of commentary about some problems."

Why is there silence? First, it is probable that the class has not yet warmed up, and since the students know that the class is being recorded, they may be nervous about speaking. Second, a professor who follows this prototype habitually asks a question only to follow it almost immediately with his own answer. Putting the question to the class in the first place is sometimes a kind of game that such a professor plays; he may not *expect* a response from the class. Even though Professor Abbot is not this sort of game-player, the students surely have experienced this type of classroom game, especially since this class took place during the early 1960s when the practice was almost universal. Third, the students are familiar with Professor Abbot's method of questioning (and it will emerge in this transcript): if a student *did* reply by saying that the dramatist is using his play as a vehicle for some comment about a human problem, he could be almost certain that his response would be followed by a second question asking what, in this particular instance, the nature of the problem is. The students probably do not feel ready to tackle such a large question. The student-gamesman who is in the class of a Principles-and-facts Prototype professor usually waits to be guided to an answer by the professor—that is, guided to the answer the professor considers to be correct. And that kind of student, in such a class, is not interested in any other answer. But although this is that type of class, the ethos somehow is different, and gamesmanship is pretty much discouraged.

When Professor Abbot sees that he receives only silence in response to his first question, he rephrases the question—or, rather, asks a second question which assumes that someone *has* offered the obvious answer to the first question. But still there is no response. Most teachers who follow this prototype, when confronted with such a situation, characteristically present "mini-lectures" which supply the answers to the questions. But Professor Abbot does not want to supply the answers. Even in the early years of his teaching career (as we later learned in our interviews), he had strong feelings about the value of overt student participation. His solution, therefore, is to change the level of his questioning, implying to the students that their lack of response is, in all probability, not their fault, but his own. He now begins to ask a series of short questions to *lead* the students to his answer, and so he ends his first speech by posing a practical question that is so easy it elicits an immediate response from one of the students.

2. *MISS ANDERSON: Well, religious problems.*
3. *PROFESSOR ABBOT: Yes, that's right. Like what?*

3. Professor Abbot rewards Miss Anderson by saying, "Yes, that's right." He confidently plays the role of expert; he is able to give the student an immediate positive feedback. As we shall see later in the session,

he also does not hesitate to give negative feedback when it is appropriate. When we discussed this point with him, he told us that, at the time this recording was made, only occasionally did a student defend himself if a professor's feedback was negative; it was not common, at that time, for students at his campus to disagree with professors during class sessions. If a student had a strong reaction to being criticized, he might bring up the matter after class or in an office conference, but as a general rule he would not do so in the class session itself. Later in the 1960s (as will be illustrated by the transcript reproduced in Chapter Five) Professor Abbot radically changed his conception of the way a discussion leader should overtly evaluate a student's contribution to the class discussion.

4. MISS ANDERSON: Well, Cur Deus Homo.

5. PROFESSOR ABBOT: Anselm. Yes. And what are some other kinds of problems?

6. MR. BAILEY: General social problems—economic conditions, and so on.

7. PROFESSOR ABBOT: Right. Like what? [Mr. Bailey hesitates.] *Mr. Clark?*

8. MR. CLARK: Areopagitica—*censorship.*

9. PROFESSOR ABBOT: Right. And what other problems?

10. MR. BAILEY: [Speaks without being recognized.] *Some of the plays dealt with philosophical problems, too. Like* Oedipus Rex *or* Job.

7. When Professor Abbot moves away from Mr. Bailey and calls on Mr. Clark, it is obvious that he does not mean to reject Mr. Bailey. And probably Mr. Bailey does not react as if it were a rejection (although it is not possible to make a true judgment about this matter from the transcript alone), because he speaks up—at *10*—without being recognized, and he presents a more complex response than the one Professor Abbot wanted to elicit from him at *7*. Perhaps Mr. Bailey's response at *10* also carries this message: "Professor Abbot, I would have been able to give you an answer at *7* if you had waited an instant longer." It is even possible that Dr. Abbot is, in some sense, aware of such a message; when, in *13*, he turns to Mr. Bailey and asks him a question, he does not call on another student when Mr. Bailey fails to respond immediately. And he elicits from Mr. Bailey, at *14*, an answer which he labels as "right" in *15*. Actually, Mr. Bailey is a key student in the class, for (as the transcript shows) he comes into the discussion on a number of subsequent occasions and almost always receives a positive reaction from Dr. Abbot.

11. DR. ABBOT: Yes. Many of the works we've read have dealt with philosophical problems. Well now, suppose we take these suggestions

and apply them to this play. Does Moliere treat a religious problem here?
[There is no immediate response.] *Miss Anderson?*

*12. MISS ANDERSON: [Hesitates.] I don't think so. I mean, I
know it's not the main problem, but I was just trying to think. There's no
mention of religion anywhere in the play, is there?*

*13. PROFESSOR ABBOT: No, there isn't. That's right. Now, let's
try the second category that was suggested. Is there a social problem of
some kind that the author wishes to make us aware of? Mr. Bailey?* [Mr.
Bailey does not respond immediately.] *Mr. Bailey, you mentioned social
problems a minute ago. What social problem does the dramatist wish to
call to our attention?*

11. When Professor Abbot returns to Miss Anderson at the close of
11, it is obvious that he is attempting to personalize the dialogue. This
technique can be contrasted with the techniques characteristic of many
instructors who follow models based on the didactic modes described in
Chapter One. In the didactic modes, questions or cues are directed to
students in an utterly impersonal way, the instructor either following the
order of seating, or reading names from a class list, or turning class cards
with students' names on them. Professors who follow the evocative prototypes rarely call on students in such an automatic way.

What has happened in *11* is this: Since it is Miss Anderson who
has first suggested religious problems (*2*), Professor Abbot turns back to
her (at *11*) to raise the possibility that the play might be illustrating a
problem that could, in some way, be classified as religious. When Miss
Anderson, after a slight hesitation, replies that this possibility is not in
fact acceptable, Dr. Abbot rewards her—at *13*—with his approval.

*14. MR. BAILEY: Doesn't the play give a picture of high society
in Moliere's time?*

*15. PROFESSOR ABBOT: Yes. That's right. This is a portrayal
of a segment of society. This is the high society of Moliere's time—that's
true. And maybe there is an equivalent to it also in our own day. I'll want
you to think about that, and if we have time, we'll talk about it later.
Now, Mr. Bailey, you said "high" society. How do you know that, exactly?*

14–15. Mr. Bailey here offers a tentative response to the question
Professor Abbot first posed in *1*. But Mr. Bailey does not want to make a
direct statement—he asks a question. Perhaps he is not certain this is the
answer Professor Abbot is looking for, or perhaps, as a gamesman, he wants
Professor Abbot to have the pleasure of confirming a student's "discovery." Professor Abbot shows, in his reply at *15,* that this *is* the answer
he is looking for, and he makes his approval clear.

15. But while Professor Abbot approves Mr. Bailey's answer—*14*—
he wants to bring up, at this point, the question of whether the play reflects only its own period or whether "there is an equivalent to it [the high
society of Moliere's period] in our own day." That is a purely *contemporary* issue, however, and many Principles-and-facts Prototype professors,
teaching a decade ago (the situation is different now), would have hesitated as Professor Abbot is hesitating here. But he clearly does think it an
important topic: "If we have time, we'll talk about it later," he says. But
of course that moment never comes. (See our comments for *108–118* and
for *122.*)

15–33. During this portion of the discussion, Professor Abbot plays
a kind of game with the class: he tries to get the students to give evidence to show that Mr. Bailey's tentative statement in *14* is correct. At
the close of *15,* therefore, he changes the immediate goal of his questioning. Up to this point, he has been trying to elicit a general formulation
about the play—a more positive version of Mr. Bailey's "Doesn't the play
give a picture of high society in Moliere's time?" (*14*)—and he does so
by proceeding through a series of relatively small steps from *1* to *14.* With
15, however, he changes his objective and places emphasis on another
important aspect of his teaching method, the "verification of evidence."
He asks students to present proof for their assertions. It should be noted,
in the segment from *15* to *33,* that the students are not building up evidence leading to a "discovery" (although this happens later in the session), but they are presenting evidence supporting an assertion that they
know Professor Abbot has already accepted as true.

*16. MR. BAILEY: Well, all the characters speak like highly edu-
cated men and women.*

*17. PROFESSOR ABBOT: That happens to be true, and ordi-
narily that would be good evidence. But in this particular case, that argument actually rests on rather shaky ground. Let me explain why. This is
something that I wouldn't expect you really to know about—but in this
particular period of literature, most writers, in French literature, anyway,
made all of their characters—and I mean all of their characters—sound
like well-educated people, even if they didn't come from the upper classes,
and even when they didn't have much education. I mean servants, and so
on. Of course we are involved in an even more complicated situation here,
in our reading of this play, because we are reading it in translation. But
my point is—I think we should look for better evidence than the language
that the characters use.* [Professor Abbot pauses and looks around the
classroom. He looks with expectation at Mr. Bailey. There is no immediate response.] *Well, what about the kinds of jobs these characters*

have? Wouldn't that give us a clue? [Mr. Bailey does not respond, but Mr. Davis asks for recognition.] *Mr. Davis?*

18. MR. DAVIS: Yeah. The people in the play don't have to work for a living.

17. The way Professor Abbot reacts to the evidence which is presented is interesting. He compliments Mr. Bailey on the relevance of his logic, even though, as he proceeds to explain, he must evaluate Mr. Bailey's argument as "shaky" for reasons that Mr. Bailey could not be expected to be aware of. (As he explains his point, one wonders whether he is parading his expertise; he does it in an obvious, although certainly not officious, way.)

Toward the end of *17,* Professor Abbot repeats his question of *15* and is met with dead silence. One of the reasons may be that Mr. Bailey's error of *16* makes the students cautious; they may fear other "traps." But then Professor Abbot, without hesitation, gives the class an obvious clue to the answer he is looking for; and, in *18,* Mr. Davis gives him that answer and is immediately rewarded with approval in *19.*

18–27. It should be noted that Professor Abbot does not actually put the answer, given in *18,* directly into Mr. Davis's mouth—as is so often the case during discussion sessions led by less skillful Principles-and-facts professors. He asks an "easy" question at the end of *17,* but it cannot be answered with certainty except by a student who has first-hand knowledge of the Moliere play. At the same time, Professor Abbot and the list of study topics have apparently occasioned here a genuine search for evidence, because both Miss Ellis *(20–23)* and Miss Fisch *(24–27)* make original contributions to the discussion. And although neither Professor Abbot nor the students make reference to it until the end of *31,* the list of study topics very likely gives the clues that enable Miss Ellis and Miss Fisch to find the passages in the text that they quote in *22* and *24.* Professor Abbot refers, in *31,* to "questions 7 and 8 on our list of study topics" which apparently have directed attention to these points and to the passages cited.

During an interview with Professor Abbot which took place some years after the class session was recorded, we asked him what kind of "discovery," and how much of it, he thought was being made here. He replied that he came to have strong doubts about the efficacy of this whole method for inducing "discovery." He pointed out that there was, however, a great insistence, both in the list of study topics and in the class session itself, that students present evidence to support assertions they make during the discussion. This characteristic emphasis appears also in the 1967–1968 transcript which is given in Chapter Five, but the matter is handled more subtly there, both by Professor Abbot and by his students. At the present time—as the transcript in Chapter Six shows—Professor Abbot hardly ever calls on students to support their assertions with objective evidence. An excerpt from our most recent (1972) interview with Professor Abbot is relevant:

> *A:* You ask someone to give you evidence, and if he believes what he believes strongly enough, he'll give you *something* even if he has to manufacture it. If he wants to persuade you, he'll just give you anything he figures will fit your brand of logic or will appeal to one of your biases. What I now believe I was teaching kids to do ten years ago was to practice the fine art of rhetoric. And I mean that in the good old Aristotelian sense: just persuading an audience by whatever means seems best. In the class we are talking about, *I* was the one to be persuaded, and those kids knew what I wanted, and they picked out enough little quotations from the play to satisfy me, and we all had a nice time doing it. But I don't really think they learned anything of any significance.
>
> I: But of course you thought so, then, didn't you? In the early 1960s?
>
> *A:* Of course I did.

We agree with Professor Abbot's characterization of his pre-Berkeley teaching style. It is questionable whether the process going on in this transcript—or the process that the list of study topics required students to undergo during their preparation for this class session—contributed very much to the development of their intellectual abilities. There is no doubt, though, that Professor Abbot, in this session, *is* imparting a body of information, which, as it builds up during the class hour, will give the students some sense of the way (as Professor Abbot understood it) an important seventeenth-century French writer conceived of a significant social problem of that period.

> *19. PROFESSOR ABBOT: Right. They don't work for a living.* [Miss Ellis asks for recognition, and Professor Abbot nods to her.] *Any other comments about that point, Miss Ellis?*
>
> *20. MISS ELLIS: Alceste has a lawsuit that he talks about, where he stands to lose a great deal of money. But from a financial point of view, he doesn't seem to mind losing it.*
>
> *21. PROFESSOR ABBOT: Yes. By the way, how do you know he doesn't mind losing it?* [He looks at Miss Ellis.] *Can you answer that question?*
>
> *22. MISS ELLIS: Yes. In the first act, he says to Philinte: "It*

does not matter what the cost/Just for the beauty of it, I'd prefer/To lose my suit."

23. PROFESSOR ABBOT: Very good. And there is an even better passage that's even more specific in the last act. Did anyone happen to notice it? [There is no immediate response.] *Miss Ellis?* [Miss Ellis does not respond.] *I was hoping you would have noticed it and marked it in your text.* [He looks around the room. There is still no response.] *It's on page 464 in our anthology, in the last act of the play.* [He reads.] *"The loss may run me twenty thousand francs,/But for that twenty thousand, I'll buy/The right to rail against the human race/And hate it always." That passage shows something about the character of Alceste. We're going to bring that topic up presently, but I don't want to interrupt our train of thought now. For now, I just want to point to this passage because it gives us additional evidence to underline what Mr. Davis said about the fact that the characters in the play don't have to work for a living.* [Miss Fisch asks for recognition.] *Miss Fisch, do you have something to add on this point?*

24. MISS FISCH: Yes. When Celimene asks Acaste and Clitandre if they're leaving, Acaste answers: "If my staying here's no burden to you,/Nothing calls me elsewhere." And Clitandre says: "I need to wait upon the king at bedtime, but/No other business asks for my attention."

25. PROFESSOR ABBOT: Yes. Miss Fisch has quoted some lines that add to the evidence before us. It shows that these people, of course, don't have to work for a living. And it throws additional light on the question before us—the question about their social status. What additional point in this passage tells us that they actually belong to the very highest type of French society? [Pause.] *Miss Fisch?*

26. MISS FISCH: Clitandre's reference to waiting upon the king at bedtime.

27. PROFESSOR ABBOT: Yes, right. You remember, at the last session, my telling you about the way the noblemen would come to the king's bedroom to participate in his getting up in the morning and his going to bed in the evening. [Pause. Miss Fine asks for recognition.] *Miss Fine?*

28. MISS FINE: No, you didn't tell us anything about that. You didn't talk about that.

28–31. The interlude that begins at *28*, where Miss Fine expresses her anxiety, and ends at *31* is amusing. It is significant, for it illustrates a subtle technique that is characteristic of only the best Principles-and-facts professors. Professor Abbot's response at *31* not only alleviates Miss Fine's anxiety but also gives him the opportunity to use her absence on the preceding Wednesday as an excuse for presenting to the class, in a little lecture, a summary of the points made during that class session. There is more here than meets the eye.

When we later asked Professor Abbot how he felt about devoting precious class time to this "lecturette," he pointed out that such a summary serves different purposes for different students. For those who, like Miss Fine, have been absent, it is a way of filling them in and preserving the continuity of the discussion. For those who were present, it reaffirms the major points covered and reasserts the emphases. But there is also an even more subtle point at stake here, Professor Abbot said: the class session is regarded with dignity; the class is considered important enough so that time can be taken from one discussion to clarify what took place at another discussion. (A personal comment: in rereading the transcript, we find impressive the fact that Miss Fine is treated so humanely. It would be ironic if, in a humanities class, above all, students were treated as nonpersons. But it happens in thousands of classes every day—and it probably occurred even more frequently in the early 1960s than it does today.)

Professor Abbot felt, at the time this class session was held, that a class session was extremely important in the lives of students. He believed, he said, that class sessions were like the towers of a bridge—central supports in the learning process—while the days between classes were significant only because they provided students with time to prepare for the next class session. By the early 1970s, his attitude had become quite different. Any really significant high points in student learning, he came to believe, occurred not *in* class sessions but *between* them.

29. PROFESSOR ABBOT: No, not last time. The time before last. Last Wednesday.

30. MISS FISCH: [To Miss Fine.] *That's right, Dorothy. You weren't here last Wednesday. Remember?*

31. PROFESSOR ABBOT: That custom was a rather interesting one. I guess it's an important point to make, too. So let me just state it briefly again for Miss Fine's benefit—and for the others who weren't here last Wednesday—if the rest of the class doesn't mind. I'll just give about a two- or three-minute summary of what we did on Wednesday. [Dr. Abbot summarizes the earlier meeting. It takes about ten or twelve minutes, and when he is finished he looks at the clock. Then he looks at Miss Fine and speaks directly to her.] *Now, Miss Fine, do you feel better about being absent last Wednesday?* [Miss Fine smiles and nods.] *Okay. Where were we?* [Pause.] *It was the passage Miss Fisch quoted about waiting upon the king at bedtime. Right? We were looking for passages from the play that show the social class we're dealing with here. Okay. Are there any other passages you have marked?* [Pause.] *If you had really thought carefully about questions 7 and 8 on our list of study topics, you probably would have marked several passages in your text. There is one in the third act that is extremely good. It illustrates the entire point we are making here.* [Mr. Bailey asks for recognition.] *Mr. Bailey?*

32. *MR. BAILEY: Yes, I have that. In the third act, Acaste gives a complete description. He describes himself this way: "I'm rich, I'm young, my family's old and noble,/And as that's the name I carry, any office/In the city could be mine, if I so choose."*

32. By the end of *31*, Professor Abbot is ready to stop discussion of the first major point of the session, and Mr. Bailey once again comes to his rescue in *32*, by quoting a passage from the play that Professor Abbot feels is pivotal in the entire argument thus far.

33. *PROFESSOR ABBOT: Yes. That's a very revealing passage. So we can see that Moliere takes pains to let his audience know the exact social status of his characters. Would we all agree with Mr. Bailey that this play gives us a picture of high society during Moliere's time?* [There is general assent.] *Then we are faced immediately with another question. Does this picture which the play presents also let us know whether the dramatist personally approved or disapproved of the things he portrayed? Or is he absolutely objective?*

34. *MR. GOODMAN: I think he disapproves. At least the main character disapproves.*

33–34. After he obtains general assent to Mr. Bailey's assertion of *14* (supported by various pieces of evidence that have been presented, *15–32*), Professor Abbot is ready to move on to his next question. Without hesitation, without the slightest doubt as to whose function it is to pose that question, he immediately puts it before the class. With Mr. Bailey's conclusion of *14* (that Moliere's intention is to present a picture of high society) confirmed, Professor Abbot now asks: Does Moliere's picture show approval or disapproval? He elicits a response from Mr. Goodman, a student who has not yet spoken during this session, but who, judging from his role during the remainder of the session, is an obviously bright student. Mr. Goodman, like Mr. Bailey, however, is willing to take his cues from Professor Abbot and to subject himself, more or less, to his domination.

35. *PROFESSOR ABBOT: Well, there's a difference. Are you saying that the main character represents the author's point of view?*

36. *MR. GOODMAN: I think—*

37. *PROFESSOR ABBOT:* [Interrupting.] *In any case, you're saying that Alceste disapproves, aren't you? What are some of the things Alceste disapproves of? Let's ask that first.*

38. MR. GOODMAN: The insincerity of the people, the way they gossip—their malicious gossip—and also their affectations.

37. Why does Professor Abbot interrupt Mr. Goodman at this point? As we read on in the transcript, we realize that he is not yet ready to move to an exploration of the question that he himself raised in *35*. Here is an example of an especially interesting technique: the discussion leader wants to raise a particular question at a certain point only to keep it hanging in the air, to be pulled into the discussion again at a later time when the group is prepared to answer it. It is obvious from the movement of the discussion which follows that the question of *35* will become central; Professor Abbot refers to it again at *67*, but it is not until quite a bit later in the discussion—actually not until *94*—that he allows a full discussion of it.

In *37*, Professor Abbot shows how completely directive he is as a discussion leader at this point in his career. He interrupts Mr. Goodman's answer to a previous question and substitutes another question. Yet Mr. Goodman is in no way irritated or resistant—or, if he is, he does not show it. He understands who is the leader and who is the follower, and he switches his attention from the question of *35* to the question of *37* with ease, giving Professor Abbot the reply he wants in *38*.

39. PROFESSOR ABBOT: And what about Philinte? Does he disapprove of these vices, too? [Pause.] Mr. Goodman?

40. MR. GOODMAN: Philinte seems to be on the fence. He's tolerant enough, but he doesn't indulge in these vices himself.

41. PROFESSOR ABBOT: But how about the event that occurred just before the play opens? Remember, when Alceste accuses Philinte of greeting someone with great warmth—and then it turns out that he doesn't even remember the man's name!

42. MR. GOODMAN: But in that case, wasn't Philinte simply trying to be nice? I think it was just the custom of the day to greet people that way. I don't think he was basically insincere.

43. PROFESSOR ABBOT: What do the rest of you think?

44. STUDENT VOICES: I agree with that. Yes, I agree. Right.

45. PROFESSOR ABBOT: Yes. I think most of us would agree with Mr. Goodman. Well, then, what may we conclude about Philinte's attitude toward these social vices?

46. MR. GOODMAN: I think he was just as much opposed to them as Alceste was, but he wasn't so loud and so extreme about it.

47. PROFESSOR ABBOT: Philinte is certainly conscious of these evils and he doesn't like them. He says so, remember, in the very first scene. But I'm wondering whether there isn't more to it than just that.

It's true what Mr. Goodman says. Philinte doesn't like these evils, but he's not so loud and extreme about it as Alceste is. But there's more to it than that. Suppose a person disapproves of certain practices—certain practices that are, say, prevalent in the community in which he is living. All right. Now, what are the possible courses of action that he might take? Just think what his possible courses of action are. [Pause.] *What are they?* [Slight pause. No immediate response.] *Well, first of all, such a person might try to reform the community he lives in—join some kind of movement to eliminate these practices, or alleviate them. Or second, he could leave that community and join another community that has a way of life more like the one he approves of. Okay. That's two possibilities. But there's a third possibility. It's also possible he might decide that actively fighting these evils would be useless, and there would be no point in going elsewhere to live, and therefore he might try to make the best of things right where he is. Okay. Now we come back to the question before us. We have Philinte and Alceste both disapproving of the evils of the society in which they live. And each one acts very differently on the basis of that same belief. Which solution does each one adopt?* [Pause. No immediate response.] *What about Philinte? How does he react?* [Mr. Goodman asks for recognition.] *No, I'd rather not call on you just now, Mr. Goodman. I'd rather hear from someone who hasn't spoken yet.* [Mr. Hatch asks for recognition.] *Mr. Hatch?*

39–47. There takes place here a series of short, leading questions in which Mr. Goodman and Professor Abbot perform excellently as a team; up to *47*, Mr. Goodman gives exactly the answers Professor Abbot is looking for. And when Professor Abbot asks the class, in *43*, whether everyone agrees with Mr. Goodman's conclusions, students speak right out, without recognition, in *44*, to show their agreement. It is quite probable that, in *43*, Professor Abbot's tone of voice and facial expression tell the students that he agrees with Mr. Goodman; they then follow his lead. In *45*, he explicitly expresses his agreement.

Still, Professor Abbot is not satisfied. Mr. Goodman has not characterized Philinte in exactly the way he wants. In *47*, he agrees that what Mr. Goodman has said is true, but adds "there's more to it than that." So in order to lead to the kind of contrasting statements that will characterize the difference between Philinte's behavior and Alceste's, he sets up an elaborate hypothetical question. It takes him a while to formulate it, and at first he is apparently thinking of using various members of the class to help him formulate it. But he is not encouraged in this direction by the class (his questions in the middle of *47* receive no response), and so he proceeds to formulate the question himself.

When the question is at last formulated, toward the end of *47*,

Mr. Goodman wants to answer it, but Professor Abbot does not allow him to speak. Mr. Goodman is very bright, and it is obvious from the transcript that he would monopolize the discussion if Professor Abbot permitted it. On the whole, however, Professor Abbot is able to control Mr. Goodman without being too obvious about it. Still, in *47,* he does not hesitate to refuse explicitly Mr. Goodman's request to respond.

48. MR. HATCH: Philinte tries to adjust himself to these conditions. He says you can't do anything about human nature, and he says behavior like Alceste's—that it's only going to lead to trouble.

49. PROFESSOR ABBOT: Did it actually lead to trouble?

50. MR. HATCH: It sure did. [Laughs.]

51. PROFESSOR ABBOT: [Laughing.] *Can you give us an example?*

52. MR. HATCH: The thing with Oronte and the sonnet.

53. PROFESSOR ABBOT: Yes. Would you comment further about that? [Pause.] *Describe what happened.*

54. MR. HATCH: Well, Oronte wrote a lousy poem and Alceste told him it was lousy, and Oronte got insulted, and by the standards of that period—according to those standards—he was justified in feeling that way. Alceste, you know, was ridiculous, and he—

55. PROFESSOR ABBOT: [Interrupting.] *Good. Okay.* [He looks around the room.] *Would you say, then, that Philinte is more practical than Alceste?* [Pause.] *Miss Anderson?*

56. MISS ANDERSON: Yes, he's more practical. So much so that he compromises with his principles. I personally like Alceste more.

57. PROFESSOR ABBOT: [To Miss Anderson.] *Well, how does he meet the problem? We've just said that Philinte's solution is—he makes an adjustment. But Alceste feels he really cannot exist in a society that is so corrupt. What is his ultimate solution? Does he want to work toward reforming it?*

58. MISS ANDERSON: No. He has given up the hope of reforming it, and he says he plans to leave society altogether.

59. PROFESSOR ABBOT: And what does that mean? Did he mean he was going to commit suicide?

60. MISS ANDERSON: Oh, no! He says he's going to leave Paris and live in a desert.

61. PROFESSOR ABBOT: [To the class.] *Are we to take that literally? Did he really mean a desert?* [Pause.] *No. In the seventeenth century, to a Parisian, leaving society meant leaving Paris. Living in the desert meant living, maybe, in your country home in the provinces.* [Pause.] *Let's pause for a minute here. From what we have said so far, can anyone express in a few words the social problem around which this play revolves?*

61. Professor Abbot has now completed the cycle of questions, and he is able to move on to the broad question which asks, basically, for the theme of the play: "Can anyone express in a few words the social problem around which this play revolves?" The next section of the session, *61–67,* is devoted to answering that question. At *67,* the discussion moves into the second major question: In what direction does Moliere's solution to the problem lie? The balance of the discussion, from *67* on, is devoted to this second question.

62. MR. BAILEY: The evils of high society.

63. PROFESSOR ABBOT: Well, yes. But that statement really isn't accurate enough because it doesn't include anything about the reactions of these particular individuals. You see? We ought to make it a bit more specific. We ought to relate it to individual people. I don't mean in particular—I mean in general. [Mr. Goodman asks for recognition.] *Mr. Goodman?*

64. MR. GOODMAN: That's what I was going to say. I think it's the relationship between one individual and another.

65. PROFESSOR ABBOT: Yes?

66. MR. GOODMAN: That's the theme of the play.

67. PROFESSOR ABBOT: Don't you think it's something that's really larger in scope than that, Mr. Goodman? You see, what we're concerned with here is not just society itself, and it isn't just the reactions of individuals to one another, or the relationship between one individual and another. The problem we're centrally concerned with here is the relationship between the individual and society. [To Mr. Goodman.] *Do you see that?* [To the class.] *Do you all see that? The relationship between the individual and society.* [Pause.] *All right. Now, is this a general topic treated by many thinkers during the period that we're studying?* [Slight pause.] *Yes, it is. The social sciences were coming into their own in the seventeenth and eighteenth centuries, and many thinkers were concerned with this very problem. They were all concerned about what they called the social contract, and the greatest thinkers tried to go back and reconstruct the origins of the relationship between the individual and the society. Let me take a few minutes here to explain this.* [Dr. Abbot continues this brief lecture on seventeenth- and eighteenth-century social thought for about fifteen minutes. He touches on such topics as the social contract, individual rights and the general welfare, self-interest and the public interest, and the development of a science of society, giving standard textbook information about these subjects. At the end, he returns to the theme of the individual's place in the social group.] *Now that we've established the general problem around which the play revolves, we can go back and ask Mr. Goodman whether Moliere himself indicates which attitude he agrees with—Alceste's or Philinte's.* [To Mr. Goodman.] *Do you think he indicates approval of Alceste's behavior?*

62–67. Mr. Bailey and Mr. Goodman both attempt to reply to Professor Abbot's question of *61,* but they do not make the point he wants made; he judges their answers to be inadequate. The students in the class know that he wants answers to his questions stated with appropriate precision, but they also know that he will not reject a response merely because it is not stated exactly as he himself would state it. In the short lecture he gives in *67,* Professor Abbot tries to show why his statement of the theme of the play is superior to the formulations made by Mr. Bailey in *62* and Mr. Goodman in *64.*

67. This is the second brief lecture that Professor Abbot presents during the session. The first, in *31,* summarizes a previous session. But the second, in *67,* is of a different sort. It is primarily a standard informational presentation of the kind that students might find in a textbook on social thought or in an encyclopedia; for this reason we have not reproduced it here.

Professor Abbot covers a number of topics in the mini-lecture, but he knows that he cannot hope to say everything that ought to be said on the subject in only a few minutes. He knows, too, that he runs the risk of losing his sense of time and continuing to lecture until the end of the period. A less skillful, or more egocentric, professor might succumb to this temptation, but Professor Abbot does not. He has obviously planned carefully what he wants to say on his subject, and he keeps in mind what must be covered before the period ends. The object of the mini-lecture is to connect the theme of the play to the history of social thought, to show that the play reflects in its theme the social problems with which thinkers of the time were concerned. Once this point is established, Professor Abbot is eager to return to the play.

68. MR. GOODMAN: *I don't think so. I think Alceste is right—in his ideas, I mean. But I feel about him that he's rather extreme in his behavior.*

69. PROFESSOR ABBOT: *You don't really care for him as a person, though you agree with his ideas. That's interesting, class, isn't it?*

70. MR. GOODMAN: *I don't care for him. I prefer Philinte, I think—as a person, I mean—as somebody I'd have to get along with, I mean.*

71. MISS ANDERSON: *Oh, I personally like Alceste a lot more. He's much more alive.*

72. DR. ABBOT: [Continuing his dialogue with Mr. Goodman.] *Do you think Moliere is making fun of that type of person? Of the type of person Alceste is?*

73. MR. GOODMAN: Oh, yes. [Pause.] *No doubt about that.*

68–107. To bring the discussion smoothly back to Moliere's "answer," Professor Abbot, at the end of *67,* uses the psychological device of returning to Mr. Goodman and the topic Mr. Goodman discussed earlier: Which main character appears to be speaking for the playwright himself? With this question we enter a new cycle of the discussion that continues until *107.* This cycle ends only a few minutes before the bell rings, allowing Professor Abbot just enough time to summarize the three class sessions the group has devoted to the Moliere play and to introduce the class to its next reading assignment.

68–73. Professor Abbot establishes, with Mr. Goodman's help, that Moliere "disapproved" of Alceste's behavior, since Alceste is portrayed in the play as ridiculous. We should notice that both Mr. Goodman, in *68,* and Miss Anderson, in *71,* express *approval* of Alceste. But Professor Abbot chooses at this point not to explore these reactions. Miss Anderson apparently is somewhat disturbed at this, and she raises the question again at the end of the period in *123.*

74. PROFESSOR ABBOT: [To the class.] *If we wanted to describe that extreme form of behavior in one word, how would we label it?* [He looks around the room.] *Mr. Ilgen?*

74. Dr. Abbot now begins a series of questions designed to lead to the conclusion that the play illustrates the Aristotelian conception of moral virtue, one of the central tenets of the so-called classical attitude toward life.

75. MR. ILGEN: Well, I don't exactly know. Alceste isn't very sociable. [Pause.]
76. PROFESSOR ABBOT: Okay. How about the label "unsociability"? Would you accept that as a label?
77. MR. ILGEN: Okay.
78. PROFESSOR ABBOT: All right. Let's say we have a quality or a characteristic in people that we label the quality of "sociability." And let's say it's possible to think of two extreme forms of behavior with respect to this quality—an enormous excess of this quality, so that it goes to a great extreme, and an enormous deficiency of this quality, so that it goes to the other extreme. Now, from what we've said, we can see that Alceste displays an enormous deficiency of this quality. He is excessively unsociable. Is there anyone who represents the other extreme, who overdoes it? [There is a strong response. Professor Abbot recognizes Mr. Jones.]
79. MR. JONES: All those characters in the court overdo it, and Celimene—she overdoes it, too. They all *represent the other extreme.*

80. DR. ABBOT: And these are the characteristics that Alceste—
[He stops, as though expecting Mr. Jones to complete the sentence.]
81. MR. JONES: Those are the characteristics that Alceste hates.

80–81. This interchange illustrates a device commonly used in "recitation" classes and generally by instructors who follow didactic teaching styles (see Chapter One). The device is not at all characteristic of Professor Abbot's style, not even during the period when this transcript was made. This is the only time that it appears in this transcript.

82. PROFESSOR ABBOT: Yes. [To the class.] *These are the characteristics—maliciousness, insincerity—that Alceste despises. What do you think about Alceste falling in love with Celimene? Mr. London?* [Pause. Mr. London does not respond. Mr. Goodman speaks up without recognition.]
83. MR. GOODMAN: Well, isn't that part of the fun that Moliere is poking at Alceste?
84. PROFESSOR ABBOT: Yes. Isn't it a masterstroke of irony that Alceste should fall in love with a person so completely different from himself? [Pause.] *Incidentally, in our discussion last time of the plot of* The Misanthrope, *there was one point that we didn't comment on—and that was Celimene's marital status. What is her marital status? Miss Kaplan?*
85. MISS KAPLAN: Celimene's marital status? [Professor Abbot nods.] *Yes, she had been married, and now she's a widow—a young, attractive widow.* [Laughs.]
86. PROFESSOR ABBOT: Yes. This point is part of Item 7 on the list of study topics for our last session, but we didn't get a chance to finish some of them up last time. So let's do this very quickly now because we don't want to lose track of the point we're on now—which has to do with this whole business about extreme forms of behavior. Miss Kaplan, why do you suppose Moliere made Celimene a widow?
87. MISS KAPLAN: Well, the fact that she had been married once— that makes it easier for us to accept her behavior, I imagine.
88. PROFESSOR ABBOT: That's right. And even more important, for her own society to accept her behavior. Widowhood gave her certain freedoms she could not have had as an unmarried young lady. Now, back to the main point. Celimene and Alceste, we just said, represent the two extremes with respect to this quality we have labeled "sociability." We've said that Celimene represents what we might call an excess of this quality and Alceste represents what we might call a deficiency of this quality. Now, what about the third major character, Philinte? What about him? [As Professor Abbot speaks, he goes to the blackboard and

draws a diagram. He draws a straight line which he labels "sociability," and then he writes the word "excess" at the right end of the line and the word "deficiency" at the left end of the line. He puts the name Alceste next to "deficiency" and the name Celimene next to "excess." His arm hovers over the central area of the line.] *Where would we put Philinte in this diagram?*

84–88. The discussion of Celimene's marital status is a digression. Apparently Professor Abbot is suddenly reminded, in the middle of *84,* that this topic was not covered in the preceding session. He explains it in *86.* When we discussed this transcript with Professor Abbot, we told him that we thought there was something compulsive about the way he brought in these points about Celimene because he interrupted the train of thought in order to do it. Obviously, he felt uncomfortable about doing it and, in *86,* he all but apologized to the class. Professor Abbot told us that he did, in fact, feel compulsive—at that stage of his career—about the coverage of subject matter. But he also pointed out to us that the digression lasted for only a few seconds and that he quickly got back on the track again at *88.*

89. MR. LONDON: He's a person who avoids both extremes. He's in the middle.
90. PROFESSOR ABBOT: So if Alceste and Celimene represent the extremes, what does Philinte represent?
91. STUDENT VOICES: The mean.
92. PROFESSOR ABBOT: Yes. Philinte's behavior represents the mean between the two extremes of conduct which we find in Alceste, on the one hand, and in Celimene on the other. I just want to say something more here about the theory of the golden mean. Do any of you remember where this comes from?
93. STUDENT VOICES: From Aristotle.

88–93. Professor Abbot's set-up is fairly obvious, and his direction is unambiguous. It should come as no surprise to us that the class moves right along with him into his little lecture on Aristotle's concept of the moral virtues (*94*); the whole class also follows Miss Marsh's thought pattern in *95* when she declares that Philinte represents the playwright's own point of view. (Philinte's behavior is characterized as illustrating the golden mean three times—in *91, 92,* and *94.*) As Professor Abbot makes clear later, the playwright's "official" view coincides with the view that is dominant among the members of the audience for which the play was written.

94. PROFESSOR ABBOT: Yes, it comes from Aristotle's Ethics. [Professor Abbot delivers a brief lecture on Aristotle's concept of the moral virtues, illustrating with a series of diagrams on the blackboard.] *So we see Alceste's behavior at one extreme and Celimene's behavior at the other extreme, and Philinte represents the golden mean. Now we come back to a question that we asked a little while ago, but we were not able to answer. Which type of behavior does the playwright himself approve of? Miss Marsh, what would you say to that? Whose behavior does Moliere himself approve of?*

95. MISS MARSH: Philinte's. I would say that Philinte represents the point of view of Moliere himself.

96. PROFESSOR ABBOT: Let me hear some of your reasons.

96. Professor Abbot insists on hearing Miss Marsh's reasoning for selecting Philinte in 95. Again we see how strong is his insistence that students present evidence for positions they take. Miss Marsh presents the grounds for her judgment in 97, but they are not acceptable to Professor Abbot, and he says so in 98.

97. MISS MARSH: Well, that's the most reasonable position. That's the most reasonable point of view of all. So I'm sure that was the point of view that the author approved of.

98. PROFESSOR ABBOT: But you seem to be arguing in a circle. [Mr. Goodman asks for recognition.] *Mr. Goodman?*

99. MR. GOODMAN: In the first place, Moliere called this play a comedy. So we would have to argue that if he wanted to show Alceste was in the right, he would have to have things turn out well for him in the end. But the play doesn't turn out well for Alceste in the end.

100. PROFESSOR ABBOT: Yes. That's a sound argument. You're resting your argument on the nature of the play itself—characterizing it as a comedy—which it obviously is intended as. [Pause. Mr. Bailey asks for recognition.] *Mr. Bailey?*

101. MR. BAILEY: Alceste is the object of ridicule. You wouldn't expect, if Moliere wanted to present his ideas sympathetically to the audience, that he would be ridiculing him. And, anyway, Philinte really doesn't have very much to do in this play, except to express the author's ideas.

102. MISS FISCH: Yes, he does. He is important. He's important for Alceste. Because he's always curbing Alceste's temper.

103. MR. BAILEY: That's not a very important part of the action.

99–103. Mr. Goodman and Mr. Bailey now return to the discussion, giving Professor Abbot other grounds to support Miss Marsh's conclusion of 95. He accepts these grounds, in 100 and 104, with solid approval.

104. PROFESSOR ABBOT: [Interrupting.] *Yes, that's right. That's not too important a part of the action of the play. We would have to say that Philinte has a more important function, and that is to express the author's own ideas. In fact, we even have a special word for that function. We say that Philinte is the dramatist's mouthpiece.* [Pause.] *Now, isn't there another character in the play who also stands for the same ideas—someone who has none of the qualities that Alceste condemns in Celimene? In fact, she's a good deal like Philinte in her behavior. Who is that?* [He turns to Miss Nakata.] *Miss Nakata?*

105. MISS NAKATA: That's Eliante.

106. PROFESSOR ABBOT: Yes, it's Eliante. Could we say that if Philinte is the male representative of the golden mean, Eliante might be taken as the female representative?

107. MISS NAKATA: Yes, the female representative.

108. PROFESSOR ABBOT: Now let me ask you another question. Does the basic difference in attitude between Philinte and Alceste appear at the beginning of the play—or is it only after the play has gone on for awhile that we come to realize this difference? [Pause.] *Miss Nakata, you still have the floor.*

108–122. Professor Abbot is aware that his time is growing short. At *108* he is beginning to wind down the session, and here begins a transitional portion of the discussion which will lead to his long closing speech at *122.*

109. MISS NAKATA: No.

110. PROFESSOR ABBOT: No what?

111. MISS NAKATA: No, it comes out at the beginning of the play. The very first thing they talk about in the first scene—that discussion about Philinte's warmth in greeting that person he didn't even know too well. That discussion there brings out to me this difference between them.

112. PROFESSOR ABBOT: But, let me ask—do they express their ideas explicitly at that time? Or do we simply deduce what their feelings are on the matter? [Pause. There is no immediate response.] *Let's look at our text, and I'd like to have you quote the appropriate lines for me.* [Miss Ellis asks for recognition.] *Miss Ellis?*

113. MISS ELLIS: Oh, Alceste and Philinte are quite explicit, even in the first scene.

114. PROFESSOR ABBOT: Would you quote the lines for us, please?

115. MISS ELLIS: [Reading.] *"That's all there is!/Flattery, treachery, selfishness, deceit./I can't endure it. I'll go mad! There is/No other way: I mean to break with all mankind!"*

116. PROFESSOR ABBOT: And what about Philinte?

117. MISS ELLIS: Yes. In the same scene, a little later, Alceste says: "Sometimes a sudden longing seizes me/To flee the human race—to live my life/In a desert." When Alceste says that, Philinte answers: It's the height of folly/To think your job is to reform the world./ I see a hundred things, like those you see,/ That could be better; but I quietly/ Accept men as they are, make up my mind/To tolerate their conduct."

118. PROFESSOR ABBOT: That's very good, Miss Ellis. So it's interesting how that very first scene states the main problem of the play and delineates the main characteristics of these two men. [Pause.] *Now I have another question along these same lines to ask: Would you say that there was much development of character in the course of the play?* [Mr. Davis asks for recognition.] *Mr. Davis?*

108–118. The discussion here tries to establish that during the short span of time that elapses from the beginning to the end of the play, no basic change of attitude takes place in any of the characters. Professor Abbot makes clear in *122*, however, that in the next play which the class is scheduled to discuss, significant changes *do* occur in the characters as the play develops; Dr. Abbot wants to prepare the students so that they will be looking for these changes as they read the play. This matter is connected (as he explains) with a formal feature: whether the work observes, or does not observe, unity of time.

Again, we see exemplified here Professor Abbot's great concern, during this early stage of his teaching, with his role as a guide to his students' thinking. He obviously regards his list of study topics as an extremely important document, supplying the students with the "right" questions to be asked. (Notice that, in *124*, he insists that all students remain seated until he has distributed the list of study topics. He seems upset, as if he fears that some students might leave the classroom without it.)

119. MR. DAVIS: No, there isn't. But there's no reason, you know, to expect any character development. The—

120. PROFESSOR ABBOT: [Interrupting.] *Why is that?*

121. MR. DAVIS: The whole play takes place in the same day. So you couldn't expect any character development.

122. PROFESSOR ABBOT: Yes, that's true. We will, however, be reading some plays which do not have unity of time, and we can expect to find significant changes taking place in the characters as the action of the play develops. [He looks at the clock.] *Now I notice that we have only a few minutes before the bell rings, and I just want to say, as a kind of summary here, that one reason we've read this play together in this course is that it represents the Classical attitude toward life. I want to distribute the list of study topics for our next class before the bell rings, but I want to finish my point first. You see, the golden mean—Philinte's point of view—the idea that there should be moderation in all things—this point of view represents the Classical attitude toward life. We said this was Moliere's point of view. We might put it another way—we might say that this was the dominant point of view of Moliere's age and of his audience. When we come to discuss our next play, which is a drama that was written during the Romantic era, I'll ask you to recall the Classical attitude toward life which we see reflected in* The Misanthrope, *and contrast it with the entirely different basic attitude that comes in our next play. And I think you're going to be able to see, also, why the audience of the late eighteenth and early nineteenth centuries didn't consider* The Misanthrope *a comedy at all—for they had this entirely different point of view toward life that made them look on Moliere's play as a tragedy and on Alceste as a great tragic hero.* [Pause.] *Are there any questions?* [Several students raise their hands.] *Miss Anderson?*

122. In this speech, Professor Abbot comments about the periods in which the two plays were written. We brought up this matter with Professor Abbot during a recent interview in which we discussed this transcript out of the early 1960s:

I: Of course you don't teach this way now. I mean, you don't ask students to read plays *because* they illustrate the periods in which they were written. Isn't that right?

A: No, I don't. Just the opposite! I would now maintain that if a play—or any work of art—doesn't *transcend* the period in which it was created, it should not appear on my study list for students. My emphasis now is on the "quality" in the work that makes it a meaningful experience for someone living in the world *today.*

I: But even in this transcript of one of your early classes, the perspective doesn't seem to me to be entirely historical. Except at those points where you suddenly feel that you have to be teaching some kind of content, when you suddenly become formal, when you begin to give lectures about the social contract in the eighteenth century or about Aristotle's ideas about virtue. Otherwise, don't you think you discuss the play in fairly contemporary terms?

A: All I can say is that when I read this transcript now, and when I compare that class with some of the ones you've recorded recently, I just can't believe that I was so naive.

123. *MISS ANDERSON: That's exactly what I was going to ask about. I really* like *Alceste. I don't think he's so ridiculous—not as ridicu-*

lous as you seem to feel. I really prefer him to Philinte. [The bell rings.]
I feel—

    124. PROFESSOR ABBOT: [Interrupting.] *I'm sorry, but our time is up. We'll have to delay discussion of that point.* [Some of the students are beginning to rise from their seats. There is considerable commotion.] *Please! Please don't leave before—* [Professor Abbot's voice becomes louder.] *Please, I want to ask everyone to remain seated until I have distributed the list of study topics. I'm sorry to keep you, but it will take only a few seconds.* [He distributes the lists.] *Okay. See you all on Wednesday.* [Some of the students leave; others go to the front of the room to speak to Professor Abbot.]

    123–124. Miss Anderson tries again, in *123,* to express the reaction to Alceste that she had tried to express in *71.* But conditions for pursuing her point are no better now than they were then. It is possible, of course, that Professor Abbot will raise the subject again (as he suggests in *124*) when the class discusses their next play, for Romantic audiences also preferred Alceste. But if the subject is to be brought up in that connection, the point will still be made in an impersonal way. That is the way Professor Abbot prefers it. It is obvious that he does not encourage the expression of personal reactions; none of the students, except Miss Anderson (and perhaps Mr. Goodman in *68*), ever express any ideas of a personal nature in this session. Everything is stated in objective, impersonal terms—which is obviously the way Professor Abbot, during this stage of his teaching career, wanted it. It is precisely this atmosphere that characterizes the style of the professor who follows the Principles-and-facts Prototype.

    There is an extraordinary difference between this class session from the early 1960s and the class session transcribed in Chapter Six, which takes place only ten years later. Professor Abbot has changed radically in those ten years: in the transcript made in the early 1970s, the air of the classroom is laden with personal messages. But we must remember that during those ten years—between the early 1960s and the early 1970s—an academic revolution occurred and a whole era in higher education came to an end.

Chapter 5

Late Sixties: Training Minds

During the middle 1960s, a number of changes occurred in American higher education. Events that were taking place on many campuses are now symbolized by the student revolt at Berkeley in 1964; and they led to a reevaluation of the objectives of university education and affected the teaching styles of many professors. Stephen Abbot was one of those professors. In the aftermath of the Berkeley revolt, he began to develop a new attitude toward his students and toward his own educational methods. He was on his way to becoming a student-centered teacher, a follower of the Student-as-mind Prototype, committed to the principle that the intellectual development of students should be the professor's major goal.

This second stage in Professor Abbot's development as a teacher-artist is illustrated by the transcript presented in this chapter. The class session transcribed here takes place in 1967. It is part of a general course in literature for freshmen, most of whom do not plan to major in literature. The subject of the discussion is Shakespeare's *Hamlet*. Altogether, six sessions were devoted to this play; the session presented here is the third of the six.

We interviewed Professor Abbot, both before and after the session, to talk about his objectives and methods. When we asked him what he hoped students would achieve in this class, he told us that he believed the most important thing students could acquire was a specific set of complex skills for reading literature. With these skills, he said, students would be able to continue their study and appreciation of literature long after they had left their formal study with him. Professor explained his method: "All of the students in the course are expected to formulate their own interpretation of each work on the required reading list. I ask some of the students to present their interpretations in class—in informal discussion, give-and-take with other students—and I expect them to defend their views by answering the objections of other students."

The word "interpretation" had a clear and concrete meaning for Professor Abbot and his students. It meant a statement about a play or a book (or any work of art) as a whole; the interpretation must explain what the work portrays or demonstrates. The "defense" that Professor Abbot expected consisted in showing how the interpretation illuminated ("fit") various parts and details of the work. As we shall see in the transcript, the session opens with a student named Albert telling his fellow students that he has tried to arrive at an interpretation of the play, but that he is afraid it doesn't "fit all the facts" given in the play. This use of the term "facts" was clarified by Professor Abbot: "Facts are any of the kinds of *data* that you find in a play or a novel or a short story. For example, what the characters do or say, what the narrator says, how a character thinks about another person or issue, the way events are presented as consequences of other events or particular points of view."

During this period in Professor Abbot's teaching career, he taught his students to use three steps in judging interpretations of a literary work. The first step was to reject any interpretation, however attractive it might appear, that contradicted the facts given in the work. The second step was to consider acceptable—and therefore deserving of further investigation—only those interpretations that satisfactorily accounted for all of the details given in the work. The third step was to choose from the various acceptable interpretations the one that gave the work the greatest richness and depth—although this choice, of course, would vary from one individual to another. Dr. Abbot believed, at this time, that a group of students—indeed, any group of people, whether young or mature—could discuss a work of art and come to general agreement about attractive interpretations which had to be rejected, and alternative (but also attractive) interpretations which would prove acceptable. He believed, in short, that the most significant aspects of the interpretation of a work of art could be discussed in a rational way following the usual tenets of logic. By 1971, as we shall see in Chapter Six, he no longer held this view.

Some other observations made by Dr. Abbot are included in the commentary accompanying the transcript which follows.

1. PROFESSOR ABBOT: Albert, would you begin today? Tell us about—Tell us the history of your thinking about Hamlet.

2. ALBERT: At first, I struggled about five hours to understand what he [Shakespeare] *was saying. Then, on the basis of our discussions in class, I attempted to formulate an interpretation. But I don't think it fits all the facts. As a matter of fact, I haven't even attempted to—*

3. PROFESSOR ABBOT: Would you rather not give it now?

4. ALBERT: I'll attempt to give it. It's a combination of—I think that—

1–4. We asked Professor Abbot why he opened the session in this way, and he said that it was one of the variants of his typical way of opening a class session. Ordinarily, he would ask a student to start the discussion, and the student could open the session as he wished. He suggested that Albert's concern here about whether his interpretation fits the facts is probably an attempt to protect himself in case his defense later proves inadequate. It probably is not an indication that Albert is reluctant to open the discussion, because he does not take advantage of the opportunity to withdraw which Professor Abbot gives him in 3. The tempo of the exchange in the recording, in fact, shows that Albert is eager to make his presentation.

5. PROFESSOR ABBOT: Shall we—

6. ALBERT: We can concentrate on Hamlet's character. First I want to [The remainder of the sentence is indistinct in the recording.]

7. PROFESSOR ABBOT: Can everyone hear Albert? Betty, would you move over and let Albert sit at the table? [Space is made for Albert to sit at the table.]

8. ALBERT: The significant trait of Hamlet's character, as I see it, is his idealism. [Pause. Professor Abbot and Albert speak at the same time, and then both stop.]

9. PROFESSOR ABBOT: Then you agree with Charles on that point?

8–9. Since this is not the first session devoted to the discussion of *Hamlet,* Albert is not the first student in the class to present his interpretation to the group. Charles has presented his interpretation in the previous session. Thus, Professor Abbot's first substantive comment about Albert's interpretation is to make a comparison with another student's interpretation. It is, we should note, neither acceptance nor rejection of Albert's statement; it is an attempt to establish agreement or disagreement between the student who has the floor and a student who has previously spoken.

10. ALBERT: Entirely, yes.

11. PROFESSOR ABBOT: Entirely?

12. ALBERT: I mean as far as this is concerned. As far as idealism is concerned. Hamlet's decision is shattered by the hasty marriage of his mother.

13. PROFESSOR ABBOT: Shattered.

13. Here Professor Abbot simply repeats, without comment, what Albert has said. One reason may be that Albert is a foreign student and speaks with a strong accent. He also speaks rather softly, and Professor Abbot may be worried about whether everyone in the class has heard him. (Aside from his strong accent, Albert's English is generally good; the transcript has only occasionally been edited to correct errors in his syntax.) Professor Abbot's own observation about the repetition was given to us in an interview we held with him shortly after this session was recorded: "I often do it, but not always for the same reason. In this case, Albert had paused, and maybe that was just my way of telling him to go on. My repeating what a student says doesn't mean that I agree with it— as my students well know."

Professor Abbot felt, at this stage of his career, that it was his function to help students clarify what was in their minds, and if possible to help them expand and refine what was beginning to take shape. He does not (here or elsewhere during the session) evaluate students' comments or render judgments about them. Later on in the semester he assumes the role of critic (he told us), but he does it only after enough of the semester has elapsed to allow him to establish rapport with the students. Rapport, he believed, was necessary for *effective* criticism. For he did not want the students to accept his ideas because they wanted good grades or were afraid of him; and he did not want them to reject his ideas because they saw him as an authority figure. He told us: "I have to work toward a relationship that will permit students to accept or reject my ideas in a relaxed, natural way." Were there ever times when he came to the end of the semester without establishing the rapport he considered essential for effective criticism? "Unfortunately, yes," he said. "But I always try again the next time."

14. ALBERT: Shattered. So when he realizes that his father was killed by the uncle who is now married to his mother, he decides that he is—he is supposed to avenge this. Then comes the ethical conflict, and this delays the murder. He really has only a single opportunity, and he tries to rationalize. He doesn't want to kill the king if the king is going to heaven.

15. PROFESSOR ABBOT: He rationalizes? That isn't his real reason?

16. ALBERT: No, that isn't his real reason. [Pause.]

17. PROFESSOR ABBOT: He's motivated by some other force.

18. ALBERT: Yes. I think the ethical conflict within him is just because he wouldn't—well, the assassination of Claudius at this moment would just be killing in cold blood. It wouldn't be an act of self-defense, as it was against Polonius and Rosencrantz and Guildenstern.

19. PROFESSOR ABBOT: But you're saying that this moral conflict is not on a conscious level. Is that correct?

19. Professor Abbot had told us in interview: "In order to help the student clarify what is in his mind and expand and refine what is beginning to take shape, the instructor has to be careful about putting words into the student's mouth. He has to be careful about putting his *own* ideas and words into the student's mouth. It is a real danger, and it takes a lot of self-control." So we asked him whether his question at *19* was not perhaps a violation of this principle. After he reread the transcript, he expressed dismay: "I was claiming that Albert had said something he actually hadn't said. The statements in *14* and *18* don't justify what I say in *19*. The question is significant, but I should have led up to it differently." We asked him how he would do it, if he had it to do over again. "I might say, 'As you see it, Albert, is this moral conflict on a conscious level or not?' In that case, Albert probably would have said no. But my question would have given him a chance to express his interpretation in his own way."

At this point in the transcript, there is no outward sign that Albert is frustrated by Professor Abbot's interruptions, but of course it is not possible to know what Albert actually felt. Albert is a patient and serious student, and he is accustomed to a more authoritarian atmosphere in the classrooms of his native land, so perhaps his threshhold for such interruptions is quite high.

20. ALBERT: I would think that—

21. PROFESSOR ABBOT: [Interrupting.] *Do you know why I am asking the question?*

22. ALBERT: Yes.

23. DR. ABBOT: Why?

24. ALBERT: Because if it is on a conscious level, it would appear in one of the soliloquies.

25. DR. ABBOT: In the soliloquies.

26. ALBERT: I think there is some evidence, where he says—

27. PROFESSOR ABBOT: [Interrupting.] *Let's not cite evidence just yet. We want to be a bit clearer about your interpretation of the play. Okay, how do you go on?*

27. In connection with Professor Abbot's views concerning a professor's criticism of students and his rapport with them (see comment at 13), we asked whether it is possible for a professor unwittingly to reveal positive or negative reactions to student comments by such subtle clues as tone voice, gesture, and even tempo of utterance. For example, could the abrupt stopping of Albert at 27 imply rejection? Albert's withdrawal from the dialogue at 28 might be interpreted to mean precisely that. "It sounds that way on the tape," Professor Abbot said, "and I was astonished when I heard it. But I wasn't aware of it during the class session, although it appears now as a possibility."

28. ALBERT: I think that's the basis of it.
29. PROFESSOR ABBOT: Hmmm. [Pause.] Well. [He looks around.] David, what do you take to be Albert's central point?
30. DAVID: [He sounds confused.] Well, I'm just putting it all together.

29–30. Is Professor Abbot also rejecting David? David is confused, but Professor Abbot makes no attempt to pursue a dialogue with him, help him clarify his ideas. David does not rejoin the discussion at any later time during the session, so it is conceivable that he sees the exchange at 29–30 as rejection. Dr. Abbot commented: "I believe that students must try to follow what other students are saying, and if they don't understand what is being said, it is their responsibility to interrupt the discussion and ask for clarification. Also, I am not in the habit of restating a student's statements for the benefit of the rest of the class. I know that many instructors do—especially when they agree with the point. But that means that some students will be passive all through the class, and listen only to the instructor. I want the students to learn from each other."

31. PROFESSOR ABBOT: It would be good to have a restatement. Evelyn, would you restate it?
32. EVELYN: I can't restate it. I've been looking up a point in the text. [Laughter.]

32–35. Professor Abbot does not leave Evelyn abruptly the way he left David, even though she is not able to restate Albert's point, either. He explained: "She was participating. She couldn't restate the point because she was looking up something in the text in response to what Albert said."

33. PROFESSOR ABBOT: In order to question Albert about something?

34. EVELYN: No, just to get it clearer in my mind about these self-defense killings.

35. PROFESSOR ABBOT: [To Evelyn.] Yes. What exactly—

36. ALBERT: [Interrupting.] I would be able to restate it.

37. PROFESSOR ABBOT: You want to restate it yourself. But I wonder whether there's been any communication at all during the last five minutes. [Pause.] Frank, could you restate it?

37. Professor Abbot is explicit here about his concern with adequacy of communication. As students become conscious of what is expected of them, he told us, such explicit expressions of concern usually are less frequently necessary. In his words: "The instructor's total method of inquiry—including a conception of the various roles that students and instructor play—become second nature to the group. If successful sessions are to happen in the future, it takes some hard training during the beginning sessions in a course. What that means is that, at the beginning of a semester, I am almost compulsively concerned with problems of methodology and procedure. I keep asking the class: *How* do intelligent people discuss such problems? That is the central point. But as the semester moves on, these things become less important, and substantive questions get the attention." In view of these remarks, it should be remembered that the session transcribed here took place just before the middle of the semester; while many of the students appear to have accepted Professor Abbot's methods and expectations, Professor Abbot himself is still concerned with adequacy of communication—indeed, almost more so than with substantive questions.

Since Dr. Abbot insists upon having students restate what other students have said, another of his observations in interview with us is relevant: "It's an eye-opener to the student if he discovers—as he often does—that *no* one can really restate—to his own satisfaction, at least—what he has just said."

38. FRANK: Yeah. Al says that before the action of the play begins, Hamlet was an idealist. And that his idealism was shattered by the marriage of his mother with his uncle. And he said that during the action of the play it was largely a moral conflict. No, he said "ethical conflict"—

39. PROFESSOR ABBOT: [Interrupting.] Any difference in your mind between a moral conflict and an ethical conflict?

39. This question about the difference between "moral" and "ethical" comes up again, several times, later in the session.

40. FRANK: Yeah.

41. ALBERT: There's no difference.

42. PROFESSOR ABBOT: [To Frank.] Albert says that for him there is no difference.

43. FRANK: All right. Then it's a moral conflict—whether Hamlet should kill Claudius or not.

44. PROFESSOR ABBOT: Whether he should kill him or not. Is that where the conflict lies? [Frank nods.] Okay. Go on.

45. FRANK: I think that's all.

46. PROFESSOR ABBOT: Well, he went on to say that there was only one opportunity, and Hamlet didn't take that one, but rationalized.

47. FRANK: I don't accept that.

48. PROFESSOR ABBOT: Well, you aren't—

49. FRANK: [Interrupting.] I know. I know. That's what I say. But I probably forgot it in my mind.

50. PROFESSOR ABBOT: Oh, I see. Then you're inquiring into your own motives? Your behavior?

51. FRANK: Yeah. [Hesitates.]

52. PROFESSOR ABBOT: [To Frank.] Please go ahead.

53. FRANK: Well, I think that's all.

54. PROFESSOR ABBOT: [To Albert.] Has Frank restated your point adequately?

38–54. It takes time for Albert's point to be restated sufficiently for Professor Abbot to ask Albert whether he is satisfied with the restatement. During this time, while Frank and Professor Abbot are cooperating on the job, an interesting thing happens: when Professor Abbot reminds Frank of an important aspect of Albert's statement that he has omitted in the restatement (*46*), Frank says (*49*) that he has forgotten the point because he does not agree with it. This is an insight, made by Frank, into his own behavior, and Professor Abbot is quick to point it out to him (*50*).

54. This question seems to be typical of the technique used in this class. Professor Abbot explained: "The group should not expect that the instructor will consistently restate a student's point. In most discussion classes, instructors not only restate the point, but immediately tell the class whether they think it's a good point or not." It is our observation that students commonly expect the restatement to come from the instructor, especially when the instructor follows the Principles-and-facts Prototype. We asked Professor Abbot why he does not immediately evaluate a student's point. "I don't think anybody can learn anything that way," he said. "At least anything significant. I don't think anybody can learn anything important to his development by having it told to him by an authority figure."

55. ALBERT: Yes, I think so. I would like to add this: Because Hamlet has this ethical conflict, he doesn't even look for his opportunity like the others. Laertes, for instance—

56. PROFESSOR ABBOT: Hamlet doesn't—

57. ALBERT: But Hamlet doesn't want *to, because—because he doesn't want to create the opportunity.* [George asks to be recognized.]

58. GEORGE: I'd like to ask you, Mr. Abbot, what is the difference between an ethical conflict and a moral conflict. Is there a difference?

59. PROFESSOR ABBOT: In my vocabulary? No. The terms are interchangeable in this context. [Henry asks for recognition.]

59. Professor Abbot is not in the habit of giving direct replies to questions addressed to him. He usually turns the question back to the group, sometimes rephrasing it or refining its wording or syntax. Nevertheless, he answers George's question, which refers back to *39–42*. Apparently this matter has been bothering George, even though he says nothing about it until *58*, and the likelihood is that he has not heard all of what has happened between *42* and *57*. Professor Abbot told us that he answered George's question directly because "this was an incidental point. It needed immediate solution, and it should not have been permitted to hinder the progress of the discussion."

60. PROFESSOR ABBOT: Henry?

61. HENRY: I'd like to ask Albert to clear up a little bit of this ethical conflict. Just what is the conflict in Hamlet's mind? It's evidently whether he should kill Claudius or not. But what is the pro and con of it?

62. ALBERT: Whether to kill a person.

63. HENRY: To kill a person?

64. ALBERT: Yes.

65. HENRY: It's nothing—I mean, would he have the same conflict if he were to kill anybody? *I mean the fact that it's Claudius, his mother's husband, and it's his uncle, King of Denmark. Now, that has nothing to do with it?*

66. ALBERT: It has something to do with it, I think. It makes it even stronger, simply because Claudius is the husband of his mother. So I think there is a variety of elements, but it is primarily the fact that he shouldn't kill a person. I mean assassinate *someone.* [Pause.]

67. PROFESSOR ABBOT: [To Henry.] *You have nothing further?*

68. HENRY: No.

69. PROFESSOR ABBOT: Are there any other points that need clearing up before we put questions to Albert? Idelle?

69. A new section of the discussion is about to start. Professor Abbot will now invite the students to ask Albert to explain various parts of the play within the framework of his overall interpretation. This is a normal part of the procedure after a student's general view has been presented to the class.

70. *IDELLE: Yes.*

71. *PROFESSOR ABBOT: Any questions?*

72. *IDELLE: Well— [Pause.] No. I just— [Pause.]*

73. *PROFESSOR ABBOT: [To the class.] Any questions you want to ask Albert? [Jane asks for recognition.] Jane?*

74. *JANE: [To Albert.] Would you clarify the relationship between Hamlet and his mother? Was it purely an idealization? Was that the relation? Of respect for an ideal she presented in his mind?*

75. *ALBERT: She was to him a mother, and he probably didn't know her too well because he wasn't at home too much. He was away at college, so he may have some infantile conception about her, as every child has about parents. He idealizes them, but when he comes back and sees what the situation at home really is— [Pause.]*

76. *JANE: Then?*

77. *ALBERT: Then he's disillusioned.*

78. *JANE: Disillusioned.*

79. *ALBERT: Yes.*

80. *PROFESSOR ABBOT: You agree with Charles on that point.*

81. *ALBERT: Yes. He is disillusioned.*

82. *PROFESSOR ABBOT: Disillusioned. [Pause.] Are you using this disillusionment to explain— [Pause.] Is the disillusionment connected with the moral conflict?*

83. *ALBERT: It can be connected with it.*

84. *PROFESSOR ABBOT: But I'm asking is it?*

85. *ALBERT: I think there is a relationship because— [Pause.]*

86. *PROFESSOR ABBOT: Is there—*

87. *ALBERT: Because it induces a certain melancholy.*

88. *PROFESSOR ABBOT: Melancholy. Does the melancholy have anything to do with Hamlet's delay in the murder of Claudius?*

89. *ALBERT: Yes. It impaired the power of action.*

90. *PROFESSOR ABBOT: It impaired the power of action. What about the moral conflict you described earlier? Is the melancholy a second factor, but the moral conflict the* primary *factor?*

91. *ALBERT: I think the moral factor is the more important one, but the other— [Pause.]*

92. *PROFESSOR ABBOT: The melancholy.*

93. *ALBERT: But the melancholy adds to it. And his suicidal impulse can be explained by this—*

94. PROFESSOR ABBOT: Uh huh.

95. ALBERT: This melancholy. Yes.

96. PROFESSOR ABBOT: But not by the moral conflict?

97. ALBERT: No.

98. PROFESSOR ABBOT: The moral conflict can't be the basis for the suicidal impulse—

99. ALBERT: No, it can't.

100. PROFESSOR ABBOT: Because the suicidal impulse appears before the cause of the moral conflict. In your interpretation, the moral conflict cannot come until after Hamlet has spoken with the Ghost. Is that correct?

101. ALBERT: Yes. But I wanted to say something about Hamlet's decision to put on an antic disposition. This shows a mental instability. A man who decides to feign madness is not, in other words, a stable person, and he probably realizes himself that he will not be able to control himself in all situations. Therefore it is the way out for him.

102. PROFESSOR ABBOT: Uh huh. A kind of release.

103. ALBERT: Yes. Under the mask of pretending madness, he sometimes can just be mad, really.

104. PROFESSOR ABBOT: Uh huh. Well, but—

102–104. Professor Abbot's "Uh huh" means "I understand what you mean." It does not mean "I agree with you" or "You are right."

105. ALBERT: And the other reason for putting on an antic disposition is a matter of security. There is an old custom at that time not to kill mad people. And he wouldn't be taken seriously by the others, and the king wouldn't consider him dangerous. [Betty asks for recognition.]

106. PROFESSOR ABBOT: Betty?

107. BETTY: [To Albert.] I don't see where you have any evidence at all, whether in psychology or anyplace else, for saying that putting on this antic disposition shows a trace of madness. I think the sole reason for putting on the madness is the security you mentioned as the second reason.

108. ALBERT: A sane man doesn't make such a decision. [The group reacts audibly. Betty and other students are speaking at the same time. Words are indistinguishable in the recording.]

109. BETTY: I don't see how—

110. PROFESSOR ABBOT: [To Betty.] A man who has complete psychological security, Albert is saying, would not ever come to that plan.

111. BETTY: I disagree. I mean I agree that Hamlet is emotionally unstable, but I don't see—

112. PROFESSOR ABBOT: [Interrupting.] Well, but this is almost a side issue in Albert's view, anyway.

100–112. It is obviously difficult for an instructor to make split-second judgments about the degree to which a student needs or wants his help in formulating responses to questions or statements he might wish to make. Professor Abbot, while listening to the tape, said that he did not believe he had helped Albert by telling him, at *100,* something that was already obvious to him. Albert responds to Professor Abbot's intended help by making a point, in *101,* that is largely irrelevant. Later on, at *112,* Professor Abbot tells the class that he believes the subject is a side issue, but he already sounds unhappy at *104.* "I was just beginning to feel uncomfortable," Professor Abbot said, "without knowing whether I should do anything about it. At *112* I decided to do something."

> *113. BETTY: Yes, a side issue.*
> *114. PROFESSOR ABBOT:* [To Albert.] *Isn't that true?*
> *115 ALBERT: Well—* [Many students are speaking at the same
time. Albert is interrupted by Kevin.]

115. Albert is clearly not prepared to accept Professor Abbot's view that his statements in *101* and *105* are a side issue. But Professor Abbot does not want the discussion to continue in this direction, and an explosive moment has been reached. The impasse gives Kevin a chance to present his interpretation.

> *116. KEVIN: I think the whole crux of Hamlet's action is the fact that—*
> *117. PROFESSOR ABBOT:* [Interrupting.] *Are you offering an alternative to Albert's interpretation?*

116–117. Professor Abbot does not give Kevin a chance to complete his sentence. He gave us his reason: "I had tried to instill in the members of the class the habit of always beginning a comment by stating its relevance to what had previously been said. And I wanted Kevin to do that here. I think everyone could tell that Kevin was not speaking to the point, and I interrupted because I wanted Kevin to make clear how his comment related. I expect students, by this point in the semester, to do this for themselves and not have to be reminded. It's a matter of mental habit, and it ought to carry over to discussions outside of class and after students leave college."

> *118. KEVIN: It's not an alternative. But I think it goes just a little bit deeper. You see, I don't believe it's a moral conflict or that he's debating whether it's right or not to kill—*
> *119. PROFESSOR ABBOT:* [Interrupting.] *So you are disagree-*

ing, really, on a very basic point? You said it was the same hypothesis but probed more deeply. But it sounds as though— [Kevin nods in assent while Professor Abbot is speaking. Then he interrupts.]

120. KEVIN: I think Hamlet knows in his mind that he should kill the king, but the reason he does not do so, the reason he is capable only of rash and impulsive acts, is because he doesn't know in his own mind whether " 'tis nobler to suffer the slings of fortune, or by opposing to take arms against them." For this one very good reason—

121. PROFESSOR ABBOT: [Interrupting.] I'm not sure I understand. Could you explain in twentieth-century American English prose what it is that Hamlet doesn't know?

122. KEVIN: Well, he doesn't know whether to take positive action against injustice because— And you've got to remember that he's thirty years old and not an immature child— [George interrupts.]

118–122. Kevin has no sooner begun his answer to Professor Abbot's question of *117* than he is interrupted by George at *122*. This interruption makes the transcript difficult to follow because Kevin's central point has been made only in a fuzzy, preliminary way (*118, 120, 122*) when an additional point from the end of *122* is challenged by George. Kevin, however, has stated in these passages what will emerge later as the central point in his interpretation—that Hamlet's delay in killing Claudius stems from a real doubt in Hamlet's mind about whether there is any point—whether it is worth it, after all—for men to fight injustice. Albert had woven his interpretation around a quite different explanation of Hamlet's delay—that is, a strong doubt as to whether the circumstances in which he found himself could really justify murder.

It is surprising that Professor Abbot and the students in this class seem so good-natured about being interrupted. But the atmosphere in the class appears to allow it; there is a general air of freedom and informality.

123. GEORGE: Hey, how do you know he was thirty years old?
124 KEVIN: We find that out in Act V.
125. GEORGE: But that's in Act V. The "To be or not to be" speech is in the Second or Third Act. [A student makes a humorous remark, but it is indistinguishable in the recording. The entire class laughs.]

126. PROFESSOR ABBOT: Well, George, how much of a time lapse is there between Act III and Act IV?
127. GEORGE: I don't know. That's why I asked.
128. PROFESSOR ABBOT: Is it, in your mind, so long that—that your question becomes significant?
129. GEORGE: I don't know. I'm doubtful. That's why I asked.

130. PROFESSOR ABBOT: You weren't here at our first session when we discussed that point—the lapse of time. [George nods in assent.] *Well, our conclusion was that it must be less than a year between the First Act and the last Act. So, he's about thirty years old. But this may or may not be important to Kevin's point. It's perfectly possible for a man to be thirty and yet display immature behavior. Isn't that right?*

123–130. The discussion goes off on a tangent, started by George's question. At *130* Professor Abbot attempts to bring it back to the subject of *122.* He is not successful, however, in returning the discussion to specifically the place where it was left. He told us: "I probably could have got it back there by asking Kevin another question like 'Why, as you see it, isn't Hamlet able to take positive action against injustice?' " As things stand, Kevin's view on this matter does not emerge until later.

131. KEVIN: Yeah. And it ties in with what I wanted to say. From the evidence I got about the behavior of his mother—toward what he thinks of his mother—it seems to me that he was a man who never acted directly on his own, as a boy and as a young man. He never made any direct action and he was completely dominated by his mother. And he was unhappy, because he enjoyed the feelings of his mother toward him. He got his happiness from—[Long pause.]
132. PROFESSOR ABBOT: So there is this dependency on his mother, you're saying.
133. KEVIN: And he cooked up the theory that his mother and his father had an ideal love.
134. PROFESSOR ABBOT: You say that, in fact, isn't true?
135. KEVIN: That's right.
136. PROFESSOR ABBOT: Uh huh. [To Charles.] *You see, Charles? We're all thinking along the line you laid out last time—but branching off. I mean your point about idealization. That's the way Albert began, and now that's the way Kevin is going.*
137. CHARLES: That's the way we all begin. But we diverge, and—
138. PROFESSOR ABBOT: Uh huh.
139. CHARLES: And there's really quite a difference. Albert's interpretation— [Pause.]
140. PROFESSOR ABBOT: What is your reaction to Albert's interpretation? That it's not really a integrated? Hm? [Charles nods in affirmation.]

140. Professor Abbot's question is surprising. We asked him about it during our interview:

I: The question at *140* doesn't seem to be characteristic of your style.

A: When I heard the tape, it came as a surprise to me, too. Actually, you'll find that there aren't many occasions during this session when I make a definitely evaluative statement about a student's hypothesis. I won't say that I feel I must never do it—but I've not yet worked with this group long enough to have their confidence. At least not to the point where they would accept in more than a superficial way any evaluation I might make. When I gain their confidence, then I can act more like one of them—more like a peer, criticizing freely and saying what I feel. Then I can expect my criticism to be listened to with respect.

I: But how do you explain your having rendered this judgment in *140?*

A: Well, I think it's just a hangover from traditional classroom techniques. The sort of device where the instructor puts the answer into the student's mouth and then agrees with it.

I: You didn't really *intend* to do it here?

A: No, I didn't. That's right.

141. ALBERT: [Several students are talking at the same time, and only the last word of Albert's statement is distinguishable.] *Loosely.*

142. PROFESSOR ABBOT: [Apparently Dr. Abbot was also speaking simultaneously with the students.] *But continue, Kevin.*

143. KEVIN: I forgot my point. [Laughter.]

144. PROFESSOR ABBOT: You were speaking about Hamlet's dependency on his mother, and the relationship between his mother and his father.

142–144. We asked Professor Abbot whether he would have been embarrassed if he had not been able to remember Kevin's point himself. "No," he said. "In a group that is well-oriented in my method, the students feel it's their responsibility, too, that the class session should go well. If I couldn't have remembered Kevin's point, I would have asked if anyone else could remember it." Would this kind of behavior be different in the more traditional kind of discussion session—for example, for a teacher following the Principles-and-facts Prototype or the Instructor-centered Prototype? Dr. Abbot said: "In the traditional kind of discussion session, if the instructor asked the class to remind him of Kevin's last point, the students would suppose that the instructor was up to something sneaky. Or maybe on the spot."

145. KEVIN: Yes. Hamlet believes that anyone who smiles sweetly and is nice is a good person. And all the world is made up of such people,

146. PROFESSOR ABBOT: Uh huh.

147. KEVIN: And he has never met anyone to the contrary.

148. PROFESSOR ABBOT: I see. There's a line in the play where he says that it's important for him to put this down: a man may smile and smile, and still be a villain.

149. KEVIN: The important thing is that—is the fact that he is close to thirty, and that a man who has lived like that all his life does not change overnight. And in addition to that—he is a sensitive, idealistic person—the hatred he feels toward Polonius and the king is not merely because— [George is talking to another student in a loud voice, although what he says is not distinguishable in the recording.]

150. PROFESSOR ABBOT: George, could you wait until Kevin has finished!

150. This sort of comment does not appear consistent with Professor Abbot's teaching style of this period. In any case, by the early 1970s, it would have been impossible for him to make such a comment, as we shall see in the transcript reproduced in the next chapter.

151. KEVIN: The way he feels toward Polonius and the king and his mother is not because they weren't what he thought they were, but because they broke up this dream world. He hated them for it. But when he acts, his situation is forced upon him. When he kills Polonius, he uses—First of all, he has this frustrated aggression in him, and then Polonius makes a move behind the curtain, and right away Hamlet thinks the man is playing the fool again—all these people are just rotten—and he runs him right through.

152. PROFESSOR ABBOT: When you say "he thinks," do you—

153. KEVIN: Well, it's a split-second decision. But that's what motivates him. That's what rubs him wrong. That's what sets him off. And the reason he doesn't kill Claudius is because Claudius is not playing the fool. Hamlet has no real justification. He has no real hatred toward Claudius. He does not see how revenge can bring him any possible happiness. [Quotes.] *"Whether tis nobler in the mind"—*

154. PROFESSOR ABBOT: [Good-naturedly.] We're back to your quotation again.

155. KEVIN: We have to come back to that. It's not a conflict of ideals. Which will make him happier? That is, I think, the simplest way to put it.

156. PROFESSOR ABBOT: Uh huh.

157. FRANK: But— [Pause.]

158. PROFESSOR ABBOT: Frank?

159. FRANK: But the king smiles at him. [Pause.]

160. PROFESSOR ABBOT: [To Kevin.] *Frank says, "But the king smiles at him."*

160. Again, as at *142–144,* Professor Abbot's behavior contrasts with the behavior that is typical of the teachers who follow the Principles-and-facts Prototype and the Instructor-centered Prototype. Frank, in *159,* addresses a comment to the instructor, instead of directly to Kevin. Professor Abbot, then, in *160,* readdresses the comment to Kevin. He told us that he hoped to accomplish two things: "First, I want to encourage students to get out of the habit of expecting I will comment on everything said to me. Second, I want students to have dialogue with each other." Thus, in *160,* Professor Abbot acknowledges Frank's comment without engaging in a dialogue with him. In this instance, however, his stratagem does not work: as *161–164* reveal, he does become engaged in a dialogue with Frank about Kevin's interpretation.

161. FRANK: That's right. But Kevin says Claudius isn't important here.
162. PROFESSOR ABBOT: But Hamlet makes the discovery during the course of the action that not *everybody who smiles is good and sweet.*
163. FRANK: But Kevin said that Hamlet thought everybody who smiled was all right.
164. PROFESSOR ABBOT: Right. Then Kevin said that a change had taken place. Kevin believes that during the course of the action of the play, a change in Hamlet's attitude toward the world about him takes place.
165. KEVIN: Yes, he now has a new outlook on life. Before, he believed that everybody was fine and the world was a lovely place to live in. Then he changes. And at the end, he believes things come in the destiny of a man—no matter what a man may do, it makes no difference. Now, I think the play—before this change of attitude and afterwards— he is an individual who has never been able to assume responsibility and act by himself. [Pause.]
166. PROFESSOR ABBOT: Uh huh. [To the class.] *Interesting, isn't it?*

165–166. It is clear that a high point in the session has been reached. The printed transcript cannot convey the pitch of excitement that is obvious in the recording. Professor Abbot, in *166,* turns to the group with a neutral and uninformative—and also unevaluative—comment about Kevin's view of the play. And the questions which the students want to ask Kevin start immediately. Professor Abbot does not even have to ask for them.

167. *EVELYN:* [To Kevin.] *I'd like to see if I understand what you mean here. Do you mean that Hamlet doesn't kill Claudius because— well, because he didn't like Claudius from the beginning? In other words, he doesn't discover that Claudius was not living up to his ideals, but he hates all these other people because he* thought *they were virtuous?*

168. *KEVIN: I think he hates Claudius very, very intensely, be-cause— In the beginning of the play, in order to explain his mother's marriage—in order to explain his wife's—his mother's marriage—*

169. *PROFESSOR ABBOT:* [Commenting on Kevin's mix-up between wife and mother.] *Wow!* [Laughter.]

170. *KEVIN: Hamlet tries to rationalize his mother's action. That's why he says to the Ghost: "Oh, my prophetic soul." He hates Claudius very much, but still cannot act. And if he would come upon him doing something true to his real character, he probably would run him through without hesitation.*

171. *EVELYN: What do you mean by your term "playing the fool"? You said Polonius was "playing the fool."*

172. *KEVIN: Being hypocritical, being two-faced, being his own ambitious self—*

173. *PROFESSOR ABBOT: Being—*

174. *EVELYN:* [Interrupting.] *Well, then, while Claudius was praying, that could have been seen as a moment of hypocrisy.*

175. *PROFESSOR ABBOT: But recall that Hamlet at this point sees Claudius not as a hypocrite but as a sincere person whom a moment of piety had struck.*

176. *BETTY: I don't see how that follows.*

177. *PROFESSOR ABBOT: Pardon?*

178. *BETTY: I don't see how that follows. If he thought that Claudius was a hypocrite, then—*

179. *PROFESSOR ABBOT: But even—*

180. *BETTY:* [Interrupting.] *He could have killed him right there. Or he could have believed Claudius was sincere.* [Kevin asks for recognition.]

181. *PROFESSOR ABBOT: Kevin?*

182. *KEVIN: No. Hamlet can only act impulsively when he can forget himself. And the only way he can act impulsively is for somebody to set him off—some outer irritation, some outer stimulant.*

183. *PROFESSOR ABBOT: Some immediate stimulant.*

184. *KEVIN: That's right. Immediate. And he just does not have*

that at this time. You see— [Several students interrupt. One of them mentions Rosencrantz and Guildenstern.]

185. *PROFESSOR ABBOT: Does Hamlet have such a stimulant in the case of Rosencrantz and Guildenstern?*

186. *LEWIS:* [Without recognition.] *Yes, I believe so.*

187. *GEORGE:* [To Kevin.] *That's not right. He tells his mother in the closet scene he is going to try something like that. At the end of Act III, he even says he is up to some trickery. There is no outer stimulant right there.*

188. *KEVIN: There's a lot of aggression he's got to get rid of.* [A number of students speak at the same time.]

189. *PROFESSOR ABBOT: Just a minute. Just a minute. George?*

190. *GEORGE: Well, I say that Hamlet* plans *to kill them.* [Again a number of students speak at the same time.]

191. *PROFESSOR ABBOT: Would you give George a chance to continue?*

192. *GEORGE:* [To Kevin.] *I'd like to ask you one question.*

193. *KEVIN: Well, let me answer your other point first. When Hamlet speaks to Horatio—*

194. *MORRIS:* [Interrupting.] *Say, Mr. Abbot, is this a duet?*

195. *PROFESSOR ABBOT: Morris wants to know if this is a duet.* [Laughter.]

196. *KEVIN: I just want to make this one point. When Hamlet speaks to Horatio and explains how he got up there on the deck and went into the cabin, he says that it was a rash act and—* [Hesitates.]

197. *PROFESSOR ABBOT: "Indiscretion sometimes serves us well/When our deep plots do pall."*

198. *KEVIN: Yes. If it was a planned action to kill Rosencrantz and Guildenstern, they why does he say that?*

199. *GEORGE: "Indiscretion" means that it wasn't right. That's all.*

200. *KEVIN: No, it means a rash, an unplanned action—* [Kevin and George are speaking at the same time.]

201. *PROFESSOR ABBOT:* [To George.] *"But rashness be the better for it,/Indiscretion sometimes serves us well." I'm not quoting accurately, but it's clear he means that a rash act has succeeded where a deep plot has not succeeded. And that's why he says, "There's a divinity that shapes our ends/Roughhew them how we may."*

202. *GEORGE: I think you can build a case on both sides, but that's not the question.*

203. *PROFESSOR ABBOT: I'm just trying to understand how—* [Professor Abbot and George are speaking at the same time.]

203. When Professor Abbot first listened to the tape recording of this class session, he became agitated at this point. Our conversation:

A: I was really frustrated here. You see, right here I was trying to explain to George that he's got to try to understand the specific event, for the moment, in terms of the total framework Kevin was presenting. Now, clearly, George wasn't making this effort. This is a very difficult principle—or rather, habit of mind—to build in students. You see, if a student doesn't make this effort, he does two things: he obstructs the progress of the discussion, and he's not taking the appropriate steps by which to acquire this particular mental habit.

I: Does George realize that you're disapproving of him here? Or to be more exact, does he realize the grounds of your disapproval? It's one thing to be corrected by the instructor because your point is unsound, but it's quite another thing to be corrected because—as in this case—you're going about your task in the wrong way.

A: I'm sure he doesn't. That's why it's so important for an instructor to have patience. Because it will take time, even with a bright student like George.

I: You say you were frustrated. But I can't see that your patience has run out, because you permit George to continue.

A: Well, you should remember that I'm concerned about Kevin's education, too. What's happening at this point is important for Kevin's process of discovery, and George is the central instrument at this point.

204. GEORGE: [To Kevin.] *Can I ask you one question? That "To be or not to be" scene—what do you make of it? He doesn't know whether it's right to kill the king, or—?*

205. KEVIN: No, not that. "Whether 'tis nobler in the mind"— that's *my big line.* [Laughter.] *You see, he doesn't know in his own mind which will bring him more reward, and that's the only thing he can—*

206. GEORGE: [Interrupting.] *What? What will bring him more reward?*

207. KEVIN: "Whether to suffer the slings and arrows of outrageous fortune, or take up arms against a sea of troubles and by opposing end them"—

208. GEORGE: [Interrupting.] *What do you mean by "a sea of troubles"?*

209. KEVIN: Whether to suffer the injustice of having his father killed by his uncle and having his uncle marry his mother, or whether not to suffer it.

210. GEORGE: You say it's whether to suffer all these things—

*everything his mother has done and his uncle has done—or—what's the
alternative you have?*

    211. KEVIN: The alternative is to kill the king. [Everyone appears
to be talking at the same time, apparently in protest against Kevin's
interpretation of the "To be or not to be" soliloquy. Professor Abbot at
last brings the group to order and recognizes Morris.]

    211. The noise in the recording is very loud. We suggested to Pro-
fessor Abbot that the students were perhaps justified in raising such a
storm of protest, and he agreed that Kevin's interpretation of the soliloquy was "to say the least, peculiar." He went on to explain: "The generally accepted literal meaning of the lines is this: Hamlet is contemplat-
ing suicide. He asks himself whether it is better to accept the pains of
outrageous fortune and live with them, or whether it is better to take arms
against his troubles and end them by destroying himself. Kevin wants to
turn the soliloquy around and make it say what he believes Hamlet's
problem to be. In Kevin's version: Should a person accept and live with
the horrors of the world—symbolized by Claudius—or should he attempt,
by taking arms against them—that is, by assassinating Claudius—to rid
the world of them?"

    We asked Dr. Abbot why he didn't correct Kevin, and he replied:
"What would that serve? He is already getting all the disapproval he can
handle from his classmates. I accept the principle of learning by discovery
—so what would be the point? Kevin will be okay."

    212. MORRIS: [To Professor Abbot.] *I only wanted to humbly
ask Kevin a question.* [Laughter.] *Kevin, in the light of your interpretation, I wanted to—I'd like you to explain something to me which is not
clear.*

    212. Professor Abbot told us: "Watch out for this character Morris.
He's the one who needs to be watched!" No one listening to the recording
could have missed the mockery in his voice at *194,* and the other students
seem much amused by his remarks. Morris is nervous and jumpy, but he is
bright. He is also very talkative, and his sentences are sometimes difficult
to untangle. During our visits to Professor Abbot's classes, Morris sought
us out to give us his views and to volunteer help with our project. He
told us that Professor Abbot was "the only decent teacher" he had ever
had. But Morris's admiration for Professor Abbot manifests itself in a
strange array of behaviors during this class session: hidden compliments
(234), mocking tone *(194, 212),* baiting *(219, 223).* The relationship
between Morris and Professor Abbot appears highly acceptable to the
other members of the class, however, and the students seem to find

Morris more attractive than irritating. For our part, we found him immensely likable but also somewhat hard on the nerves.

> *213. KEVIN: Okay.*
> *214. MORRIS:* [To Kevin.] *If accepting that Hamlet idealized his mother and was dependent upon his mother and saw his father replaced by his uncle, and upon suspecting that his uncle murdered his father and then married his mother—how could there be a moral or ethical conflict? Because if that were the case, there would be no ethical conflict in that he should avenge his father.*

214. Morris speaks with a dialect which Professor Abbot described as "one of the accents of New York City," and we had difficulty understanding the question. Professor reworded it for us: "Given all of the circumstances in which Hamlet found himself, there is no reason for him to feel doubt about his *right* to avenge his father's death. Where, then, lies the conflict?"

> *215. KEVIN: I agree with you. That's not the conflict that I tried to—*
> *216. GEORGE:* [Interrupting.] *You have more or less—*
> *217. KEVIN:* [Disregarding George.] *He knows full well that he has justice on his side, as far as whether he should kill his father. That's not his conflict.* [Pause.]
> *218. PROFESSOR ABBOT:* [To Morris.] *Kevin is saying that justice is on Hamlet's side. But is he going to be any* happier *if he kills the king?*
> *219. MORRIS: But there is something else. There is the fact that the fellow is a soldier. He was a soldier also. I read that in the introduction to our edition of the play.* [Laughter.]

219. From our interview with Dr. Abbot:

I: Why is the class so amused? What's so funny about Morris's remark in *219?*

A: Morris is joshing. There has been so much stress on "giving the evidence" in our previous discussions that Morris is just probably waiting for someone to ask him to give it. His reference to the introduction is just meant as a provocation. As you know, one of the basic principles of this method is that evidence coming directly from the text is worth far more than some critic's opinion.

I: But you don't think it might be an expression of hostility toward you?

A: It's possible. But I doubt it, actually. Morris and I have a close, father-son type of relationship. We often joke around with one another.

220. PROFESSOR ABBOT: Oh?

221. MORRIS: The editor says they gave Hamlet a military funeral.

222. PROFESSOR ABBOT: What exactly is your point? As a soldier, he was accustomed to sticking swords through people, and therefore shouldn't have hesitated in case of Claudius? [Laughter.]

223. MORRIS: I certainly think so. [A number of students are speaking at the same time.]

224. PROFESSOR ABBOT: Are you trying to understand Hamlet, or are you trying to show the way you would have acted in such a situation? [Laughter.]

224. We asked Professor Abbot whether his comment is humorous or hostile. "Surely the tone is completely humorous," he said. "Morris and I often joke around this way, as I told you."

225. MORRIS: No, I'm trying to say—happiness. If we can say there is a moral conflict or ethical conflict—I don't think the word "ethical" is proper because it is not a question of ethics, because he sees that justice is on his side—

226. PROFESSOR ABBOT: The term "ethical conflict"—

227. MORRIS: [Interrupting.] Well, I'd like to ask you, Kevin, just one corollary—in that how, by nature—I mean, after your study of Hamlet's character, how will he not be satisfied or not happy by avenging his father's death?

227. No doubt the reader will find this speech as inarticulate as we do. Yet it is obviously not unintelligible to Morris's classmates. Kevin, at any rate, immediately grasps Morris's meaning and restates it without hesitation in *231*.

228. PROFESSOR ABBOT: Kevin, do you understand the question?

229. KEVIN: Yes. From all the evidence I can gather—

230. PROFESSOR ABBOT: [Interrupting.] Excuse me, Kevin. Some of us may not have understood Morris's question. Would you restate it?

231. KEVIN: Well, Morris would like to know why, from my study of Hamlet's character, I think he could get no happiness in avenging Claudius's action, Claudius's murder of his father. Well, from what I can find out about Gertrude and her character, her actions in the play, it seems to me that Hamlet never had the opportunity for determining whether or not he should perform a certain action. He never received any kind of joy or satisfaction from successfully completing an act which he thought out himself.

232. *PROFESSOR ABBOT: Uh huh.*

233. *KEVIN: He just didn't have any practice in making decisions.*

234. *MORRIS:* [Humorously.] *He just didn't have a good education. He didn't go to the right college.*

234. Morris is obviously, but good-naturedly, making fun of Professor Abbot's concern with training students' minds for decision making. Professor Abbot has been explicit about his goals in previous class sessions, and the subject now enters into class discussion in this natural and humorous way.

235. *GEORGE:* [Humorously.] *That's right!*

236. *KEVIN: He seems to be completely passive. When his mother asks him to do something, he always says yes. In Act I, Scene 2, Hamlet wants to go back to college, and the king makes a long and impassioned speech asking him to stay. Then the queen makes a speech—only two lines—in which she injects herself on a personal level. She says, "Do not go back to Wittenberg, lest my prayers fly away"—or something like that—and without hesitation, he says, "I will obey you." And the second time, she does the same thing—in the speech with Rosencrantz and Guildenstern, after the king again makes a long and impassioned speech. And there, she has less reason to speak than before, but nevertheless she injects herself on a personal level.*

237. *PROFESSOR ABBOT: Uh huh.*

238. *KEVIN: She's not a bad person. She doesn't do anybody any harm. She's just egocentric.* [Pause.]

239. *PROFESSOR ABBOT: Nancy, you've been listening to this discussion. What do you—*

240. *NANCY:* [Interrupting.] *Well, a while ago when he was trying to make his point, he called it "ethical," and he objected.*

241. *PROFESSOR ABBOT: Who is that? Who is "he"?*

242. *NANCY: Kevin, there.*

243. *KEVIN: I objected because Morris meant "ethical" in the same sense, whether or not—*

244. *NANCY:* [Interrupting.] *And you're arguing whether or not it would do Hamlet any good. I think Charles made that point at the last discussion. That's why he asks whether it's better to suffer in silence. Right is on my side so far as that goes, but my ideals are shattered. Will*

that bring back my ideals? Do you see? Will it do me any good to kill the king, really? Will it solve the problem? In the case of Rosencrantz and Guildenstern, in the case of all the foreign combat and everything, it wasn't that *question, you see. So, in some ways, you and Charles are both right.*

245. *CHARLES: But we aren't saying the same thing! Kevin stated a corollary of my interpretation, and then worked back to a different hypothesis altogether.*

246. *PROFESSOR ABBOT: Could you show us what the differences are between yours and his, Charles?*

247. *CHARLES: Well, I made the point that he didn't want to kill the king because that wouldn't set things right. The thing he really wanted was his old world of youth restored. Therefore, my main hypothesis is his idealism. I think I can work out rather scientifically all the action of the play from that. But Kevin's interpretation seems to be—I don't know whether I'm getting it right or not; there are so many points he brought up—that there was indecision on Hamlet's part because—*[Hesitates.] *Well, I'll leave go the point "Whether tis nobler to suffer in the mind" and so forth—because of a dominating tendency in his mother, and he had never done anything on his own, on the spur of the moment. And I think that point can be thoroughly disproved.*

248. *PROFESSOR ABBOT:* [Puzzled.] *He had never—*

249. *CHARLES:* [Interrupting.] *Had never committed an impulsive action, and it was an impulsive action—* [A number of students are speaking at the same time.]

250. *KEVIN: Hey, Chuck, I never said—* [Kevin's voice is lost in the hubbub. Nancy's voice is heard. Professor Abbot's voice is heard, but the first part of his statement is indistinguishable.]

251. *PROFESSOR ABBOT: He explains that on the basis of an impulsive action, but he's saying Hamlet never commits a major action that demands a thought-out decision.* [To Kevin.] *That was your point, wasn't it?* [Kevin nods in assent.] *What were you saying, Nancy?*

252. *NANCY: When he does stop to think it out, he never gets anywhere—when it comes down to Claudius. He could think it out when it came to Rosencrantz and Guildenstern. He could think it out because he could explain the situation in the one case. He didn't apply, you see, except personally, this self-protection business that—he was still toying with the situation.* [A number of students ask for recognition, and some begin to speak. After a moment, Professor Abbot brings the group to order again.]

253. *PROFESSOR ABBOT: Now, let's give Olive a chance to talk.*

254. *OLIVE: Do you think—*

255. PROFESSOR ABBOT: [Interrupting.] *Are you asking* me *or are you asking—*

256. OLIVE: No; Kevin. Now this impulse, right after he has seen the Ghost—why couldn't he have killed the king after that, rather than waiting around? Certainly I think he had enough outside stimulus to kill the king.

257. KEVIN: Why didn't he kill the king when he had the most wonderful opportunity in the world—when he was praying?

258. OLIVE: Well, you see— [Olive, Kevin, and several other students are speaking at the same time. Their words are indistinguishable. Then Olive's voice is clear.]

259. OLIVE: He could have killed him on impulse then.

260. KEVIN: He has got himself riled up. It was all anger. It isn't that he's an idealist. [Several students are speaking at the same time.]

261. QUENTIN: No, that's not *the conflict at all. Not* his *idealism.*

262. KEVIN: I know.

263. QUENTIN: He does not want to kill the king at all. He does not want to kill the king. [Several students are speaking at the same time.]

264. KEVIN: The world was a very fine place, and now the world is no longer a very fine place. I don't see where idealism fits in.

265. NANCY: His idealism has been shattered. That's why he doesn't want to kill the king. [Almost everyone is speaking at once.]

266. PROFESSOR ABBOT: Now wait a minute. Now wait a minute.

267. GEORGE: I want to ask Charles to give me evidence of Hamlet's idealism. [Pause.]

268. DR. ABBOT: Charles?

269. CHARLES: All right. I think there is plenty of evidence. On page 92— [Members of the class are looking up the reference. George takes advantage of the momentary lull.]

270. GEORGE: On this point of Hamlet's never having to act on his own, he was away at college, so you might be able to assume that he acted there once in awhile on his own.

270. From our interview with Professor Abbot:

I: I was interested in that comment of George's about college.

A: It's a revealing comment. It shows the quest for self-sufficiency and the breaking down of dependency on parents, and all that. And it's also revealing of George, who is a more aggressive kid than the others.

I: Yes. That's obvious from the recording.

A: I don't mean just his classroom behavior. George would be the very one, I mean, to imagine Hamlet—or anyone—acting independently, especially away from home and away from parental influence. Obviously George has been wanting to express this idea since way back—perhaps as far back as *123*, when he opposes Kevin. Of course, it's hard to say when an idea first comes into one's mind. The stimulus might have been something Kevin has said more recently—say, at *231*. Maybe that's what George is reacting to. It's hard to know. But what is interesting to me is that George is an aggressive kid and is projecting onto Hamlet some of his own reactions to the world. He wants to think of Hamlet as a person capable of acting on his own, at least when he's away from his parents and at college.

I: Is there, in fact, any evidence in the play as to whether Hamlet did act on his own when he was at Wittenberg?

A: I don't think so. Except the general evidence that Charles quotes here in the next passages in the transcript.

> *271. CHARLES:* [Ignoring George's comment.] *There is evidence for idealism in two different elements in the play. There is evidence in the thought of Hamlet as it comes out in the soliloquies, and there is also evidence in his actual behavior toward other characters.*
>
> *272. GEORGE: I'd like to see it in his soliloques. I don't see—*
>
> *273. PROFESSOR ABBOT:* [Interrupting George, sounding severe.] *Okay. Give him a chance to reply!*
>
> *274. CHARLES: On page 92, Hamlet says, "I have of late, but wherefore I know not, lost all my mirth, foregone all custom of exercise," etc., etc.*
>
> *275. PROFESSOR ABBOT: Well, what does that show?*
>
> *276. CHARLES: That reveals how his previous view of the world has disintegrated.*
>
> *277. PROFESSOR ABBOT: Uh huh.*
>
> *278. CHARLES: And then his relations toward Horatio and toward Laertes. He overidealizes them tremendously.*
>
> *279. GEORGE: How do you mean, he—*
>
> *280. CHARLES:* [Interrupting.] *He always conceives of Laertes as a "noble youth." You see, I started out with the notion that he overidealized relations between his mother and his father. He did more. He overidealized the world. He overidealized his acquaintances. I think there is proof that he overidealized his acquaintances.*
>
> *281. PROFESSOR ABBOT: What about Rosencrantz and Guildenstern?*

282. *CHARLES: Rosencrantz, Guildenstern, Horatio, Laertes—
all of them.*

283. *PROFESSOR ABBOT: Uh huh.*

284. *CHARLES: He's been entranced with both Rosencrantz and
Guildenstern since early youth. It says that in the play.*

285. *PROFESSOR ABBOT: Uh huh.* [Henry asks for recognition.]
Henry?

286. *HENRY: I'd like to make one more point about his idealism.*

287. *PROFESSOR ABBOT: Okay.*

288. *HENRY: It's about Ophelia. I agree that Hamlet is idealistic.
I won't say anything further about that now, because I've got practically
an entirely different idea of the whole play which might come out—*

289. *PROFESSOR ABBOT: Would you like to present it in class
during the next session?*

289. Professor Abbot, no doubt aware that his class hour is almost
at an end, takes advantage of Henry's comment at *288* to structure the
opening of the next class session. He followed up his offer after class: see
the comment following *308.*

290. *HENRY: Okay. But what I want to say now—a good example to show the idealism of Hamlet in his relationship with Ophelia.
Ophelia, in my interpretation, and I think in practically anybody's interpretation, was above-board in practically the whole play—except that her
father asked her to help him, and she was a conspirator just because she
had Hamlet's interest at heart. She wanted to know what was wrong with
the fellow, and so forth. Anyway, Hamlet loved Ophelia, and then for
practically no reason at all, he breaks off this terrific relation with
Ophelia and calls her a whore and makes all those remarks to her to show
that his whole concept about everybody, so far as he's concerned, has
gone down about six notches, for no reason.*

291. *QUENTIN: He still loved her.*

292. *HENRY:* [Ignoring Quentin's comment.] *To me, it's a general indication of depression.*

293. *RALPH:* [Interrupting.] *He goes from idealism to—* [Pause.]
Materialism.

294. *PROFESSOR ABBOT:* [To Ralph.] *I don't think "materialism" is the word you want. You mean "oversuspicion"? This is, suspecting
people of motives they don't have, of base motives that don't exist?*

294. Professor Abbot rejects "materialism" as the opposite of
"idealism" in this context. Ralph is probably, here, misapplying the op-

position of idealism and materialism that he has learned in a history of philosophy course. But Professor Abbot does not make an issue of it.

295. *QUENTIN: I can't see that. He still loves Ophelia.*

296. *FRANK:* [Agreeing with Quentin.] *Because in the last act, when Laertes—where Hamlet was mad because Laertes was acting up like that, he says, "Well, what about* my *love for her?—"* [Several students are speaking at the same time.]

297. *PROFESSOR ABBOT: Uh huh.* [Pause.] *What do you do with the fifth act, Charles? What do you do with Hamlet in the fifth act?*

298. *CHARLES: Well, a change has taken place.*

299. *PROFESSOR ABBOT: In what direction?*

300. *CHARLES: I would say Hamlet is coming back more towards normal.*

301. *PROFESSOR ABBOT: And how would you specifically characterize the change in his attitude towards Ophelia?* [As Charles attempts to answer this question, Frank and George also begin to speak. George's voice is heard quoting something from the text about Hamlet lying between a maid's legs.]

302. *PROFESSOR ABBOT: George, I don't think the microphone picked up your comment.* [Laughter.]

303. *GEORGE: That's what it says in the book.* [More laughter.] *There is a point I would like to make about Ophelia. Polonius had given Ophelia instructions to reject Hamlet, and Hamlet knows that the king has seduced his mother. Polonius wants to solidify himself with the king, so he tells Ophelia not to give her favors to Hamlet. Now Hamlet, in that case, can infer that she is giving them to the king. And that's why he calls Polonius a "fishmonger" and tells her to go to a nunnery.* [He reads from the text.] *"Conception is a blessing, but not as your daughter may conceive." He thinks she is going to conceive by the king. That's why he calls Polonius a "fishmonger."*

304. *PROFESSOR ABBOT: So you're presenting more evidence for the point of view that Hamlet suspects base motives where base motives—*

305. *GEORGE:* [Interrupting.] *No, I'm really trying to say—you see, Ophelia is rejecting him and therefore he has grounds for being suspicious. I mean, he was* justifiably *suspicious.* [Henry and Nancy are speaking at the same time.]

306. *HENRY: That's just the point. He thinks that everything is a cause.*

307. *GEORGE: The fact that the king has seduced his mother naturally makes him suspect that the king is also having an affair with*

Ophelia. How should Hamlet know that her father has given her instructions not to see him? [Many students are commenting at the same time, resisting George's point.] *You've got to take into account that her father was a big shot in the government.* [The bell rings.]

308. *PROFESSOR ABBOT: Oh-oh, time's up.* [Many students are speaking simultaneously.]

308. There is so much noise on the tape at this point that it is not possible to transcribe what is being said. Many separate conversations are apparently taking place. But a few details can be supplied from the observer's notes.

Professor Abbot turned to Henry to ask if he would start the discussion at the next session, and Henry confirmed what he earlier said at *290.* "Maybe you can start with a kind of summary of what Charles, Albert, and Kevin have said," Professor Abbot suggested. "It might be good, if you have time, to get together with them in advance and go over their points of view with them, so you can represent them fairly in your summary." Henry nodded and said he would; then he walked over to where Kevin was surrounded by a group of students, who were arguing angrily. Morris, then, jangling his key chain, half-seriously and half-laughingly began to complain to Dr. Abbot that he was not getting a chance to express his views in the class. David (who had not said a word since early in the session, when Professor Abbot had seemed to reject him, but who had sat listening intently ever since) moved over to join Evelyn, who was pointing out something in the text to Charles.

Many of the students seemed reluctant to end their discussion. But other students were already beginning to enter the room for the next class, and Professor Abbot's students eventually moved slowly toward the door.

Chapter 6

Early Seventies: Working
with Students as People

The spring of 1970 was a time of crisis for American universities. It was the spring of the Cambodian invasion, of the killings at Kent State and Jackson State. On many campuses, students and faculty members worked together to develop "reconstituted" curricula, hoping to define more carefully the role of the university in American society. Stephen Abbot, in this spring of crisis, faced a crisis of his own: it centered on his role as a university professor and his interest in his undergraduate students.

The reader last saw Professor Abbot in 1967–68, the year of the Columbia University crisis, which had also caused him to reevaluate his goals and reshape his teaching style. He then followed the student-as-mind Prototype, taking as his goal the training of students' minds. But as time passed, he gradually moved away from the highly logical, rational frameworks of aesthetics, pedagogics, and metaphysics that characterize professors who follow that prototype. His vision of the ideal teacher now came to resemble the student-as-person Prototype. He emerged from the crisis of spring 1970 with new attitudes toward students, literature, and educational goals. He was a new man with a new view of life. In the words of one of his students, "Steve joined the human race."

115

The man and his career are inseparable. The new Stephen Abbot no longer felt that his classes supplied the peak experiences in the intellectual lives of his students. "I used to feel that my class was the center of things," he told us. "What students did outside of class, I thought, they did as preparation *for* the class. But I know now that isn't true. It's what happens out there—*between* classes, not *in* them—that is the center of things, and what happens in class is preparation for *that* experience." He now saw his students as people. He was no longer a fountain of knowledge and he was much less certain about his views. "I don't feel so certain about my knowledge of things," he told us. "I no longer say that everybody ought to have read *The Iliad,* for instance. Who am I to judge? I still don't take astrology seriously—except as a kind of poetry— but I no longer think people are being ridiculous when they do. It's what people *are* that matters."

When we visited some of Professor Abbot's classes during this most recent stage in his development, we were at once impressed by the transformation—in him, in his teaching style, in his students. Sometimes it seemed (although that is not the case in the present transcript) as if he would sit in his place at the table and say almost nothing for an entire class period, only occasionally adding an "uh huh" or a "yes" to the discussion. He always took notes during the sessions, in an unobtrusive way, keeping them for two or three weeks and then using them as the basis for lectures which, when he gave them, would take up the whole class period. These lectures also represented a departure from his former style: he lectured now about what the students were reading and thinking and what they were doing, and he related to those central concerns his observations about literary subject matters or methods. We saw in his new style a strong resemblance to the style of Barton Persey, the student-as-person Prototype professor whose portrait is given in Chapter Two; and it turns out in fact that Professors Abbot and Persey are friends.

The transcript reproduced here was made during a class session in a general literature course for lower division students, a course designed to meet the "distribution" requirement in humanities. As the printed transcript shows, Dr. Abbot no longer delivers mini-lectures of the sort that were characteristic of his earlier teaching method. He is no longer an information dispenser. However, he plays many other kinds of roles in the classroom as he becomes totally involved with his students as people.

[Dr. Abbot has not yet arrived. Students voices are heard. There is noise of chairs moving, doors opening and closing.]

1. ALICE: Well, yes. Right. [Alice's voice is high-pitched, rather nervous. A male voice is heard but the words are undistinguishable.] *Yes. I did, too. And also, I wanted to ask—*

2. PROFESSOR ABBOT: [Entering the room and interrupting.] *I'll be right back. I want to pop into the control room for a minute.* [He leaves. Student voices are heard again.]

2. Professor Abbot goes to the control room to double-check about arrangements he had made for recording the class session. The class is meeting during the present term in a small seminar room adjacent to an observation room and recording studio. A one-way mirror allows observation of the class without interruption. The students know about the observation room, having toured it during the opening class session. They are also aware that this session is being recorded.

3. ALICE: Oh, no. Right. Well, are you able to? I don't think Steve can really be serious about this. I'm going to ask him. [The male voice is heard once again, but again the words are not distinguishable.] *I don't think Steve is serious when he tells us to discuss these books with our parents and family—* [Other voices are heard.] *No, I've tried, and it's just impossible.* [Other voices.] *Right. Me, too. See, in my case, there's no way. My father—he thinks all poets must be fags. My mother—*

3. "Steve," of course, is Professor Abbot. He had asked the students to try to discuss with their parents and other members of their families, whenever circumstances allow, the activities undertaken for the course— books read, plays attended, other events. Alice and her classmates are complaining that they have not been successful in their attempts. There is so much noise in the room, however, that most of what is being said cannot be transcribed.

Alice is a highly verbal young woman who, as we shall see, takes the course and herself very seriously. We learned that she is married and has a child, is a full-time student on the campus, holds a part-time job, and has an almost compulsive need to "succeed" as a student. The pressures in her life, along with her resentment, emerge later during the discussion.

4. A STUDENT'S VOICE: Yeah, Steve is here. [Other voices.] *No, he just went into the control room.* [Voices.] *No, he's wearing a sweater.*

4. Apparently a student who has just arrived has asked what Professor Abbot is wearing. The question is significant because it was Professor Abbot's custom at this time to wear a suit, with dress-shirt and tie, on days when he planned to deliver a lecture. Since he is wearing a

sweater, the students know that a regular class session—that is, a discussion session—is in store for them.

5. *ALICE: All* she *wants is to keep the Chinese from bombing San Francisco. And my husband—he's just interested in four things—* [Voices.] *Only four things: baseball games, hockey games, football games, and basketball games.* [Laughter.]

6. *PROFESSOR ABBOT:* [Entering the room.] *Sorry. I just stopped by the control room for a second. We're being recorded again today.* [Pause.] *Well. Good to see you all. We were all here just the day before yesterday, but it seems like really a long time ago. So it's good to see you.* [Pause.] *I have memos for some of you.* [He calls out names and distributes memos.]

6. The "memos" to which Professor Abbot refers are actually individual notes to students in response to "memos" they have given him. The students are not required to write papers or to make any written reports. The activity for the class consists of reading (novels, plays, poetry, other books), attending events (poetry readings, plays), and participating in literary "happenings." Each student works out his own reading and activities plan at the start of the term, and Professor Abbot makes suggestions for modification and refinement. Twice a month, each student gives him a "memo" which tells him in an informal way what the student has been doing. These "memos" are not returned to the students, but Professor Abbot usually prepares some kind of answers or comments, also called "memos"—which he distributes at this time.

7. *ALICE: Steve, are you really serious when you tell us to discuss the books we're reading for the course with our family?*

7. Professor Abbot's students do not wait for him to start the discussion. Here Alice speaks out without asking for recognition, and she brings up the subject of her earlier concern. It will occupy the discussion until *18*.

From the very beginning of this transcript, we are aware of the high degree of personal involvement on the part of the students. There can be no doubt but what this course is an integral part of their lives: they cannot separate what they do for this course from what they do as part of what college catalogues used to call "student life." It is this quality of personal involvement which sharply distinguishes this transcript from the two we have previously seen. The change is no doubt due, in part, to the changing times, but the crucial factor is the change that has occurred in Professor Abbot and in his teaching style since the spring of 1970.

> 8. BERNIE: *That's right, Steve.*
> 9. ALICE: *For me, that's just impossible. Really.* No *way.*
> 10. PROFESSOR ABBOT: *Yeah. Well—*
> 11. BERNIE: [Interrupting.] *She's right, Steve. Would you have been—I mean, did you do that? Did you discuss books with your parents when you were at college? Books you read for your courses?*
> 12. PROFESSOR ABBOT: *Well, I—*
> 13. BERNIE: *Or maybe you didn't live at home.*
> 14. PROFESSOR ABBOT: *No, I* did *live at home. And I hardly ever discussed with my parents the books I was reading at school. I did, sometimes, with my brother. But my parents—well, I reported to them about my academic progress. I told them about my teachers, and they always wanted to know about my grades. But it never occurred to me to discuss the books with them. No one ever suggested it. But if the idea had been suggested to me, I think I would have done it.*

14. In response to Bernie's question (*11*), Professor Abbot does not hesitate to speak about personal events in his own life. This behavior stands in sharp contrast to the instructor roles he has previously played.

> 15. BERNIE: *Well, it wouldn't be easy for me to share my experiences in this class with my parents. You see, my background is from an Italian working-class family. My father is retired now, and—*
> 16. PROFESSOR ABBOT: *What sort of work did he do?*
> 17. BERNIE: *He worked in real estate, and he drove trucks and a jitney, and he's done factory work and worked in produce. Anyway, I don't live at home. There would have to be a special occasion—I mean some real reason—for me to bring up with my dad what's happening here at school. I mean, there normally just wouldn't be any reason to.*
> 18. PROFESSOR ABBOT: *Make a reason. Try it. You may be surprised! I mean, try it, but if it doesn't go, don't push it. If your parents read English easily, get them to read some of the novels and other things you're reading for this class. Get them to share your life with you. Don't withhold from them.* [Students' voices are heard.] *Well, try it. And let me know in your memos how successful you are.* [Pause.] *Any other comments or questions? Cheryl?*

18. Professor Abbot is unusually insistent about this matter, considering his generally casual attitude throughout the session.

19. CHERYL: Yes, Steve. I just wanted to say that I really didn't appreciate your comments last time against physicians. I agree with you about the AMA, but not about physicians in general. Unless you know a lot of physicians—which I don't think you do, since you seem to be so prejudiced against them—I don't think you are qualified to make statements like that. Perhaps you have reason to be prejudiced against some of them, but I don't think that you can lump all physicians in one big group, which you practically did, any more than I would say all professors are liberal fanatics.

19. As we learned from Professor Abbot, he had made some remarks about doctors during a discussion of Ibsen's *An Enemy of the People,* although he could not afterward remember what the remarks were. He understood, however, that Cheryl might have misread tongue-in-check comment as hostile attack. In the tape, she sounds quite angry at *19,* but somewhat appeased at *21.* What is significant about this interchange is that the free atmosphere of the class allows her to express her anger.

20. PROFESSOR ABBOT: Yes, that's right. I meant my comment to be a criticism of the AMA as an institution, not of its individual members. Just as you've often heard me criticize American higher education as an institution in American society—but there are many wonderful professors. You're right, and I'm glad you brought that up, to give me a chance to say what was actually in my mind.

21. CHERYL: Yeah. Well, I was really P-O'd about that comment, and when I told my boyfriend about it—he's in medical school—he was, too!

22. PROFESSOR ABBOT: But when you see him again, discuss it again with him—I mean the difference between the individual physician and the institution. The AMA, for one thing, and on an even larger basis the whole institution of medical practice in the United States—

23. CHERYL: Yeah, well, he's really against the AMA himself.

24. PROFESSOR ABBOT: And also make clear that it was just a personal opinion I expressed. I even forget now how it came up or what the connection was.

25. A STUDENT'S VOICE: An Enemy of the People. [Several voices are heard.]

26. PROFESSOR ABBOT: What?

27. A STUDENT'S VOICE: You remember, when we were talking about the doctor in An Enemy of the People.

28. PROFESSOR ABBOT: Oh, yes. By the way, how many of

you saw it this past weekend? [Some of the students raise their hands.] *How did you like it?* [A number of students speak at once.] *What? What did you say, Dan?*

    29. DAN: I said I ushered. I finally ushered at ACT. It was the first time I'd ever seen a real play. I really enjoyed it. I could actually understand what was going on!

    30. PROFESSOR ABBOT: That's good. Remember that we want to devote some time to talking about An Enemy of the People. *So be sure to see it before the end of the month. Or, if you can't get to ACT, be sure to read it. It might even be interesting to do both, but if you do read it and see it—both—don't be disturbed if you find some of the lines are different because of different translations.* [Pause.] *Okay. Who would like to start today?*

    25–30. Professor Abbot is reminded to mention to the class that all of the students are expected to see or read the Ibsen play before the end of the month so that he can schedule a discussion of it. At the time of this class session, the play was being performed by the American Conservatory Theater (ACT), a professional company resident in San Francisco. Professor Abbot has made an effort to tie in the work for the course with literary experiences available in the area. For some of the students, this is a new experience (as Dan indicates in *29*)—not only to see a performance of a play, but also to gain admission by ushering. The ACT cooperates in the attempt to make live theater available to students: in addition to its opportunities for ushering, it offers "student rush tickets." Students, for a minimal charge and with proper identification, are permitted to occupy all available seats at curtaintime.

    30. Professor Abbot, at the end of *30,* asks who would like to start, suggesting that what has so far taken place is "pre-class rap." From the point of view of formal structure, the class discussion actually begins at *31.*

    31. ERIC: I want to ask about what Fred was saying last time— what Fred was saying at the end of the period last time. [Pause.]

    31. Here begins a long dialogue between Eric and Fred which lasts until *58.* Eric begins by restating a point Fred has made in the previous session about Barth's *The Floating Opera,* but it takes him until *41* to complete the restatement. Then when Eric is about to ask the question he mentions in *31,* Fred takes up the subject again in *42,* and Eris does not get a chance to ask the question. But perhaps the actual asking of the question is not necessary: communication between the two students seems firmly established. The Barth novel is on Fred's personal reading list for the course, and his discussion of it at the previous class session has obviously made Eric interested in it; and he wants to hear Fred say something more about it. Perhaps that is Eric's real question, and so he obtains the answer he seeks.

32. *PROFESSOR ABBOT: Okay.*

33. *ERIC: Fred was talking about* The Floating Opera. [*Pause.*]

34. *PROFESSOR ABBOT: Yes.*

35. *ERIC: Do you remember, Fred, you said the main character there—*

36. *FRED: Uh huh.*

37. *ERIC: He refers to notional assent as opposed to real assent, and you said that notional assent is like just an intellectual acceptance of circumstances—*

38. *FRED: Uh huh.*

39. *ERIC: While real assent you get through contact, through involvement with the circumstances.*

40. *FRED: Yeah. It's sort of like moving from passive to active.*

41. *ERIC: Now, I've been thinking about that a lot and— Well, you didn't get a chance to finish what you wanted to say, and—*

42. *FRED:* [*Interrupting.*] *No, I didn't.* [*Pause.*] *I thought more about it, too, when I got home, and I told my wife about our discussion, and I realized I probably didn't explain too well what I meant. I should have given you a personal example, right from my own life, to make it clear. My wife is eight months pregnant. This will be our first child. Now, the changes that have occurred in my mind in the last seven months, due to this coming birth, are staggering. You see, the thoughts that are modifying my mind are simply the change of direction from notional assent to real assent. As I say, it's sort of like moving from the passive to the active. The fact that I'm going to be responsible for the bringing up of a human being brings about a whole mental shift.*

43. *PROFESSOR ABBOT: Uh huh.*

44. *FRED: You know Bob Dylan's "It's All Right, Ma, I'm Only Bleeding"?* [Several students are speaking simultaneously.] *He says there that the one who's not busy being born is busy dying. So you see, with regard to my own life, the realization of being a father, of being responsible for the early life both physically and mentally of a human being is an impact that I really can't explain. It has brought the question of life and death closer to my reality. It has acted like a catalyst in the processes vital to me. I now see life and death as real entities.*

45. *PROFESSOR ABBOT: Uh huh.*

46. *FRED: Before this pregnancy, my mind would give notional*

assent to the life process, but now I have been thrust into the reality of the life process. And I also look at my own parents in a different light. I see them as projections of what my wife and I will soon become. Eventually and inevitably, there is death. This circle—this life and death process—has always, to me, bordered on fantasy. I've never seen myself involved with this pattern as much as I do now. [Pause.]

47. *PROFESSOR ABBOT:* [To Eric.] *Is Fred's point clear to you now?*

48. *ERIC: Uh huh.*

49 *FRED: You see, it's possible for you to say, automatically, "I understand—yes, I see the problem and can feel what he's going through." This is what I mean by notional assent. You can follow the reasoning and intellectually join in, but you can't share my emotional experience. Added to this mental anguish is an emotional ecstasy—that's almost unparalleled. I say unparalleled because it's so entirely different from any other emotion I have ever felt.*

50. *PROFESSOR ABBOT: Uh huh.*

51. *FRED: So my adjustment to the baby, mentally, has brought me closer to life. You see, I'm really very lazy and tend to drift whatever way I'm headed, but this event has put me on a definite path. I don't really mean definite—I guess it's definite, but it's yet undefined. I've become more sensitive to life because I need answers.*

52. *ALICE: You mean—you need answers. Like what?*

53. *FRED: Well, in the beginning the baby needs mostly love and comfort, which isn't hard to provide, and this part of his existence doesn't trouble me. When the child begins to want to understand what is around him—that's what I find to be the problem. My wife and I will be the main contributors to the basic personality of a human being. This thought just overwhelms me. My wife and I have to make this child's life meaningful to him until he takes over. What do I teach him? What do I tell him to prepare for? I don't understand life myself, so how can I prepare another human being for it?*

54. *PROFESSOR ABBOT: Are there any models you've set for yourselves? I mean, like in some cultures, an adult member of the family, perhaps parents themselves—*

55. *FRED: Oh. Well, my parents and also my wife's parents brought us up in the usual middle-class, illogical way, but with plenty of love. Both my wife and I have rejected practically all of their bullshit ideals and ideas, but we have appreciated their love. I guess love is the answer to many problems. This has got to be the basis for any family. It doesn't do any good to talk about it and intellectually confirm it, but the idea has to be put to action. Well, I have really failed to convey the changes I've gone through, but really no one but myself could under-*

stand them, anyway. I'm not— [Several students are talking at the same time.]

56. GERTRUDE: [The first part of her sentence is not clear.] *. . . would be happening, sort of, anyway, even without the baby. My wedding anniversary is tomorrow, and my husband and I have been reminiscing about the past and all the changes we have gone through since being married. We have been married for three years now, and if I met myself as I was three years ago, I would probably not recognize myself. But not only have both me and my husband changed, but also our relationship. I get confused sometimes when I talk to some married couples we meet, and I tell them how we've changed being married, and they don't understand what I'm saying, as if it hasn't happened to them. It makes me think we are unique in this, although I know we're not. I think living with someone is one of the most complex, difficult, and rewarding experiences that I or anyone else could have. It's really exciting to see how you react to things and how your husband reacts to things and how uniquely the two of you as a unit react to things. It's too fantastic for words.* [Several voices are heard, one of which is Dr. Abbot speaking to Eric.]

57. ERIC: I want to think about it some more. And I'm going to read The Floating Opera *because Fred really turned me on to it.*

42–57. Except for Alice's question at *52* and Gertrude's rather long statement at *56*, Fred has done most of the talking since *42*. He is a tall, thin, serious young man with shoulder-length hair, and he speaks so eloquently that the class is unusually quiet when he talks. It is significant that, during this dialogue, Professor Abbot says almost nothing. At the end of *55*, there is a kind of climax, and many students, stimulated by Fred's statements, wish to speak. It is Gertrude who is heard, but the other students still want to speak when she has finished. But Professor Abbot manages to get Eric back into the dialogue, and he supplies the closure for this portion of the discussion.

58. PROFESSOR ABBOT: Okay. And maybe you'll want to say something more after you've finished reading it. And others, too. I think there are others here who plan to read the Barth novel. Right? [Several hands go up.] *Okay.* [Pause.] *Harlene?*

58. Professor Abbot reinforces the closure of the dialogue Eric initiated at *31*. Then he waits to see if any member of the class wants to add anything. We asked him what he would have done, at this point, if Harlene had not volunteered. "I know what the students are doing from the memos they turn in," he said. "So I probably would have turned to somebody who hadn't spoken recently. I might have said something like: 'You mentioned in your last memo that you were doing so-and-so. I found your comments interesting, and I wonder if you would like to share them with the group.' " As we shall see later in the transcript, this is precisely the way Professor Abbot elicits contributions from Opal in *160* and Saralou in *191*.

> *59. HARLENE: I wanted to share my—*
> *60. PROFESSOR ABBOT:* [Interrupting.] *This is about the lecture you went to?*

59–86. This part of the discussion amounts to a report from Harlene about a lecture she has attended as part of her activities for the course. The lecture has been given by a visiting professor from Japan. For reasons that emerge in *72* and *74,* Professor Abbot wants to postpone Harlene's presentation, as he begins to say in *64.* But he apparently feels something in the class atmosphere which makes him change his mind. During Harlene's report, Dr. Abbot frequently interrupts her, attempting to keep her on her subject. Harlene has begun, early in the term, to read some novels of Mishima, but others in the class also want to read Mishima, and it has been agreed that a discussion of his works will be delayed until more students have read him. But it was because of Harlene's familiarity with Mishima's novels that Professor Abbot had suggested she attend the lecture. He hoped, he told us, that she would be able to supply some background information for students who had not yet read Mishima, as well as some stimulus for those students not yet decided about reading him. But Professor Abbot was not pleased with Harlene's report: "She was too effusive. Her ideas weren't organized. And that remark about *The Sound of Waves* [83] turned me off."

> *61. HARLENE: Yes, the lecture I went to last week. I was supposed to tell about that today. Well, I went—*
> *62. DR. ABBOT:* [Interrupting.] *You remember that Harlene went to hear the lecture on Yukio Mishima last week by the professor who was visiting from Japan. I've forgotten his name—*
> *63. HARLENE: Dr. Tomoichi Yamada—*
> *64. DR. ABBOT: And we want to hear from her about what he had to say. But I was wondering whether we shouldn't wait until—* [Pause. He appears to change his mind.] *Well, do you want to hear about it now? Okay.*
> *65. HARLENE: Well, last week, you remember, I left class early*

to catch that lecture by Dr. Yamada. Ian was supposed to go with me, but he wasn't here, so I—

66. *IAN:* [Interrupting.] *You know, I just forgot all about it. It just slipped my mind.*

67. *HARLENE: Well, I really can't say you missed an awful lot. See, the lecturer had a terrible time with his English. It was just incredibly hard to understand him. I know I missed a lot of what was going on. Dr. Yamada talked about how Mishima was a bridge between East and West because though he's very Japanaese, also he knew Western culture very well and was influenced by the West.*

68. *PROFESSOR ABBOT: Yeah. Uh huh.*

69. *HARLENE: And he talked about his ideas of beauty and art and how it was all connected to his ideas about discipline. He didn't talk much about Mishima's weird ideas—well, I think they're weird, anyway— his ideas about physical power and the discipline of the body, and that's all connected with his ideas about military strength.*

70. *PROFESSOR ABBOT: Uh huh.*

71. *HARLENE: And he detested intellectuals. You know, people with big brains and soft bodies who're always thinking and can never make decisions or really act on anything. And some of the characters are like* that. *Like, in this novel* After the Banquet *that I've been reading, there's this politician—*

72. *PROFESSOR ABBOT:* [Interrupting.] *Oh, I thought we would wait until everyone had had a chance to become acquainted—*

73. *HARLENE: Oh, sure.*

74. *PROFESSOR ABBOT: —with one thing of Mishima's. Then we can all talk about him together. Okay?*

75. *HARLENE: Oh, sure.*

76. *PROFESSOR ABBOT: Some of the critics talk about Mishima as though he were kind of a bundle of contradictions. His work seems to display strong sexuality and strong asceticism, nostalgia for the past, but it's also future-oriented in certain ways, excitement about being alive and enormous fascination with death. Things like that. Did Dr. Yamada say anything along these lines? Did he see Mishima as—*

77. *HARLENE: No, he didn't. He talked about his life only a* little bit. *He was at his best, he said, like when his writing was based on facts in his own life. But Dr. Yamada said—let's see, I have this in my notes—that Mishima's weakest point was his excess of imagination and expression when not based on factual circumstances in his life. Like,* Forbidden Colors *has a lot to do with the gay world in Japan, and Mishima himself was supposed to be gay. But with Yamada's comments in mind, I wonder if some of the things in the book are all the way true.*

78. PROFESSOR ABBOT: Okay. When we—

79. HARLENE: Yes. I haven't finished Forbidden Colors *yet, so I shouldn't say anything about it yet, anyway.*

80. PROFESSOR ABBOT: Okay. Let's—

81. HARLENE: I forgot to mention that Dr. Yamada did refer to Mishima's disgust with modern Japan and his longing to return to the ancient morality and ways—you know—honor, samurai warriors, and that kind of thing. Dr. Yamada also touched upon surrealism and dadaism in Japanese literature and made comparisons between literature and some painting, which I couldn't really follow. [Pause.]

82. PROFESSOR ABBOT: Uh huh. Okay.

83. HARLENE: Oh, I wanted to say something about The Sound of Waves, *another book by Mishima. It's a short book, easy to read. I found I got rather bored. It's one of those books where you can predict exactly what's going to happen. It's a very sweet little story, but I'm just not into that type of thing at this stage.* [Several students are speaking at the same time.]

84. PROFESSOR ABBOT: But do you feel some others here around the table might— [Several voices are heard.] *It might be interesting to see how others react.*

85. HARLENE: Yes, I would. That's why I brought my copy of The Sound of Waves. *It's only seventy-five cents, but I thought I would pass on this copy. I want to hear what somebody else thinks about it, too.*

86. PROFESSOR ABBOT: Okay. Thanks, Harlene, for your comments about the lecture. [To Ian.] *Are you sorry you missed it?*

87. IAN: Oh, I was going to say— [Pause.] *There's an article about Mishima by Gore Vidal in the* New York Review of—

88. A STUDENT'S VOICE: Oh, Gore Vidal! Phooey! [Laughter.]

89. IAN: No, I don't particularly like Gore Vidal, either. But honestly, this article of his on Mishima is really pretty good. [Many students are talking at the same time.]

84–89. Professor Abbot expresses some of his irritation with Harlene, in *84*, when he asks her whether other students might not have a different view of *The Sound of Waves.* But Harlene good-naturedly offers, in *85*, to share her copy of the novel with the class. Harlene is quite young. She is not stupid, but she is somewhat childish and undisciplined. For some reason, her naivete and her eagerness irritate her classmates as well as Professor Abbot. But whatever bad vibrations are in the room are dispelled by the unidentified student who reacts to the mention of Gore Vidal (*88*). With Ian's comment in *89*, the portion of the session dealing with Mishima comes to a close.

90. JANET: [Voice emerges from hubbub.] *This was the Gay Liberation poetry reading I went to. I had to cut my history class, but I'm so glad I did. It was a very enlightening thing for me. I was most impressed by Alta. It never occurred to me before to associate anything good with lesbians. I can accept made homosexuality easily enough, but female homosexuality—that's a different story. I always think of highly butch types, but Alta changed my head. Her poetry was so moving. She sounded almost as if she would cry. You could tell she was real. Didn't you think so, Steve?*

91. PROFESSOR ABBOT: Yes, I did. That was the first time I'd ever heard her, though I believe she's read on campus before. She was impressive. But the most important poets there were Robert Duncan and—

92. CHERYL: I heard it, too. I really didn't like Robert Duncan at all. I didn't understand him, I guess. And by the time they got to Thom Gunn, I was so tired of sitting, I couldn't really appreciate him. But I liked the way he looked, anyway. [Laughter.]

93. JANET: Was this the first Gay Liberation reading they've had on campus?

94. PROFESSOR ABBOT: I don't know. I think it is. I think this is the first year that gay students have an official campus organization. It's really astonishing. Couldn't have happened, even a few years ago.

95. BERNIE: I don't think it would have happened yet, except the ACLU sued the university—or threatened to, or something.

96. DR. ABBOT: But it's a good thing, don't you think?

97. BERNIE: Oh, sure it is. [Long pause. Everyone seems to be waiting for someone else to speak.]

98. KEITH: Maybe this is the time for me to tell all—[dramatic pause]—*about Batman and Robin.* [Laughter]

90–98. Janet's comment, at *90,* does not constitute a report to the class—that is, it is a sharing of an experience with the group but it consists of no more than superficial information-giving. Professor Abbot, in this instance, chooses not to turn it into a report, which he might have done by eliciting more details about the poetry reading from Janet or from other members of the group. The conversation about it ends, then, at *97.* At *92,* Cheryl's comment about Thom Gunn—"I liked the way he looked" —is ambiguous, as she probably meant it to be. Professor Abbot, who also attended the reading (as he reveals in *91*), told us that Gunn, on that occasion, was rather spectacularly dressed in leather.

The long pause at the end of *97* suggests that Professor Abbot is waiting for comment from some of those students who were eager to speak at the end of *89.* But everyone hesitates, and the air seems heavy. Keith's remark in *98,* however, breaks the tension as the class bursts into laughter.

99. DR ABBOT: [To Keith.] *Oh, from your last memo, I didn't think you were going to be ready for some time to present your—*

100. KEITH: No, I'm really not—yet.

101. DR. ABBOT: Keith is doing a special project on the comic strip—the comic strip as art. Not as sociology, but as art.

99–101. Obviously, Keith's comment in *98* has taken Professor Abbot by surprise. He explains Keith's project, in *101*, because the class, apparently, has not heard about it before. Although Keith says, in *100*, that he is not yet prepared to talk about the project, he proceeds to do so. The report continues until *118*.

102. KEITH: Yeah, comics as a form of folk art. I have re-stricted this to humor drawings in either a strip or single panels, so I have ignored editorial cartoons and animated films and things like that. The films were too hard to see in bulk and the others too dependent on current events. Steve, I'd like your reaction to my decision about that. I also ignored most action strips and most love-story comic strips.

103. IAN: How come?

104. KEITH: Well, I find them slightly ridiculous and slightly nauseating. I began in the campus library, reading all the collected volumes of cartoons, which was about five long shelves' worth and comprised mostly of selected cartoons and anthologies.

105. IAN: I don't get it. Are those actually in volumes over at the library?

106. KEITH: Yeah. For example, The Classic Cartoons, *edited by Cole and Thaler, and others by other editors whose names I don't remember. Also I read a long print-out on twelve California cities who at one time or another censored comic books or banned them altogether.*

107. IAN: Where do Batman and Robin come in?

108. KEITH: Yeah. Well, one of the most important books about the effect of comics on children is by this guy Wertham. Well, I read Wertham's book. I didn't much agree with most of the things he says. I think he overstates his case. Like his statement about "clear, inferred homosexuality"—that's an actual quote—regarding the characters of Batman and Robin. I bought several of them from my little brother. In only one was I able to find a single instance where they even touched each other.

109. A STUDENT'S VOICE: When was that?

110. KEITH: Well, that was when they were tied back-to-back, being lowered into a vat of bubbling ink by one of the villain characters. I also decided to go to a bookstore over on MacArthur Avenue where dirty comic books line the whole right-hand wall when you come in.

There were about thirty different magazines, ranging from mild and truly very funny ones, like Fabulous Furry Freaky Brothers, *to about fifteen soft- to hard-core pornography, featuring various and sundry things. Like, on one cover, a nude couple copulating on the street, subtitled "Telephone Booth Style." Or a smiling middle-aged couple was shown pointing to the pool of fluid formed from the dripping couple— not sweat—saying, "Gee, there's just no stopping newlyweds, is there?" This was varied by another which promised a homosexual encounter with a beheaded corpse. The body was ignored—the head was used. Wertham would have loved it. [Laughter.]*

111. PROFESSOR ABBOT: [Laughing.] I would think—

112. KEITH: Actually, the proprietor of the shop said he sold very few of the really raunchy ones. Mostly to tourists, he said. I also talked to a man about twenty-five, named Harry, who works for a comic book company on 72nd Street. It deals in collector's items and current books ranging from twenty cents to thirty-five and forty dollars. He didn't want to spend very much time with me, and he said he'd already been interviewed just a few days before. There's an article, an interview, that appeared in the Sunday magazine section. It appeared a few days after I talked with him. [Pause.]

113. PROFESSOR ABBOT: Uh huh. Does anyone want to put any questions to Keith?

114. KEITH: Well, I've come to some tentative conclusions already, but they have to be tested out.

115. DR. ABBOT: Let's hear what they are.

116. KEITH: Well, for one thing, I have come to the conclusion that the breadth, complexity, and plain variety of drawing and style makes cartooning, in my opinion, an art—based on a mere art-as-art criterion. Like, Krazy Kat *is nearly in some space-distorted ways, like a huge fire hydrant outlining the moon and stars—is as much art as Dali's limp watches. Comic drawing is art by humorous intent and is just as artistic as soup cans on canvas.*

117. PROFESSOR ABBOT: Uh huh.

118. KEITH: Another conclusion that I have come to—but this still has to be tested some more—is that both style and humor have changed, both as time and nationality have changed. As time in American cartooning—humorous, I mean, not political—as time passed, it became more sophisticated in humor. That's just a tentative conclusion. And then, I am coming to some conclusions about national and ethnic differences, but I don't think I'm prepared yet to state exactly what that conclusion is. So I'll wait until later. Maybe next month when I give my next report to the class. Okay?

119. PROFESSOR ABBOT: Okay. Fine. [Pause.] *Okay. What now?* [Long pause. Professor Abbot is making notes.]

110–119. When Keith completes the two long speeches of *110* and *112,* it looks as if he has come to the close of his progress report. But Professor Abbot obviously feels a lack of completeness, and he asks the class, at *113,* to put some questions to Keith. This is a device that he used frequently during the earlier stages of his teaching career, as the transcript in the preceding chapter illustrates.

At *114,* Keith indicates that he has more to say, but he apparently believes that further presentation is premature. Professor Abbot, at this point, could postpone further discussion, but he chooses, in *115,* to encourage Keith to continue. The subject is closed in *118* by Keith, and Professor Abbot reinforces the closure in *119.*

119. Professor Abbot seems completely passive. He waits for the class to choose the next topic.

120. ALICE: You often ask what we're reading or what we've seen that we would recommend to others in the class or to our other friends. Well, I'm reading something I don't *want to recommend.* [Laughter.]

121. PROFESSOR ABBOT: What is that?

122. ALICE: I'm reading Krishnamurti's Think on the Things. *Well, I'm still thinking.* [Laughter.] *I have absorbed some very logical and interesting ideas from him which I hadn't seen before, particularly about competition and love. But I'm not ready to accept his complete philosophy. He offers a plastic-bubble world filled with joy where no one or nothing can ever hurt you again. I'm sure I would have once found that marvelous. But, confronted with the promise, I find it terrifying. Whether his pretty, trouble-free existence is truly possible or not is irrelevant—the point is I don't really want to stop crying or throwing things in jealous rages or fighting the good causes or saying the word "I."* [Pause. Everyone is very quiet.]

123. PROFESSOR ABBOT: Uh huh. Does anyone else know Krishnamurti? Heard him on KPFA or read anything of—

124. ALICE: [Interrupting.] And while I have the floor, I want to get something else off my chest. I've done very little for this class so far, I must admit. Why? Well, I have a job that I hate, along with my family responsibilities, and the work for other classes, plus moving into another apartment, plus my rotten dentist, plus marital problems, and a five-year-old son determined to destroy me. Now, the fact that this is an unstructured course requires so damn much initiative. You almost feel as though work for this course is a luxury you can't afford, that you should use every moment productively instead of in a leisurely pursuit of enjoyable experiences with literature. Anyway, I've just been putting things off, and I feel guilty as hell. I haven't even started a project of my own. I don't even know what I want to do.

    125. PROFESSOR ABBOT: You make it all sound so serious!

    126. ALICE: Well, it is! It's tragic!

    127. PROFESSOR ABBOT: It isn't, and you know it! Let's make an appointment right now so you can get going, and let's make it today. [He takes his appointment book out of his pocket.] *When are you free? How about right after class?*

    128. ALICE: Okay. But you know, Steve, I might as well tell you now—I'm terrified of you.

    129. PROFESSOR ABBOT: [Astonished.] *Terrified of me? Why? Why should you be?*

    130. ALICE: I— Well, I just can't believe that people can be motivated at school by anything except grades. I mean, in the last analysis. There has got to be some reward.

    131. PROFESSOR ABBOT: Of course. But there are rewards and there are rewards. We've talked about this before. But I still don't understand. Why should that make you afraid of me?

    132. ALICE: Well, I expect you to spring out at me at the end of the term with a big fat F. [There is laughter, which Alice has encouraged by her gestures and her intonation.] *Oh, I know I'm completely irrational about this. But what can I do?* [Many students are speaking simultaneously. Fred's voice is heard: "Aw, Alice, come on!"]

    133. PROFESSOR ABBOT: Okay. Okay. Let's get back to Krishnamurti. It would be interesting to have someone else's reaction to him, too. Anyone heard him on KPFA, or listened to him on record, or read him?

120–133. The lull in the conversation at *119* gives Alice the opportunity she has been waiting for. It is clear from her remarks at the very beginning of the session that she has been having considerable anxiety about her work for the course (see comment at *3*). This anxiety emerges in full force at *124,* and she appears to be only postponing it at *122.* It seems likely that her mention of the Krishnamurti book—toward which she displays enormous hostility—is merely the means by which she is able to arouse interest and attract the attention she obviously needs in order to launch into her complaint of *124.* Even the charming preamble of *120* subsequently looks as if it is intended to ward off suspicion and to seduce Professor Abbot and the rest of the group.

    Professor Abbot makes it manifestly clear at *127* that he does not want to pursue, as part of the class discussion, the problem that Alice raises. "She was gameplaying," he later told us. For that reason, he suggests that she see him privately and he offers to make an appointment with her. His behavior shows the degree to which he takes her seriously, and it should have allayed her anxiety. (Such behavior, for a professor in the middle of a class session, is unusual. But Professor Abbot proceeds with ease, and apparently no one is disturbed by what he says and does here.)

Alice, however, is not to be put off so easily. She has the floor, and she means to keep it. She does not respond to Professor Abbot's suggestion of *127*, and in *128* she tricks him into continuing the dialogue in class. Her device is clever: she tells him that she is terrified of him—and it is then clear to him that he cannot break off the conversation. Alice wants to have the class for her audience.

The members of the class must know, as Professor Abbot does, that Alice is playing with all of them. But it is also clear that her anxiety about grades is genuine. Still, enough is enough—and at the close of *132,* there is an outburst of student voices directed against Alice. At *133* Dr. Abbot quiets the class and steers the discussion back to Krishnamurti.

134. LOWELL: Yeah, my parents used to listen to him a lot on KPFA last year or the year before. I don't think he's been broadcast recently. I saw a display of some books of his over at the bookstore and glanced through them—

135. ALICE: Yes, that's where— [The end of the sentence is not distinguishable.]

136. LOWELL: I'm doing my project on Hesse and Eastern literature, and I suppose I could— [Several students are speaking at the same time.]

137. PROFESSOR ABBOT: Okay, Lowell, fine. That'll be good. Do you want to say anything more about your project, or your other activities?

138. LOWELL: No, I'd prefer to wait.

139. PROFESSOR ABBOT: Okay. Have we set a date yet, for the big discussion—the big discussion on Hesse that you're going to lead?

140. LOWELL: Well, we said right after the holiday.

141. DR. ABBOT: Okay. Let's make that firm. The first class session, right after the holiday. For that session, everybody will have read Demian *or* Steppenwolf *or* Siddhartha. *Or if you've read one of them before, you can either reread the same one or read another one. But you should have at least one freshly read for that class session. Okay? And the topic is— What's the topic, Lowell?*

142. LOWELL: We're going to try to figure out why Hesse is just

*about the number-one author among college kids today. That's the topic
for the discussion: Why is he so appealing?*

134–142. The subject of Krishnamurti, originally introduced by
Alice at *122,* does not take hold, but it serves to bring Lowell into the
discussion. Lowell is a Hesse "expert," and arrangements have previously
been made for him to lead a discussion on Hesse on a date not yet fixed.
Professor Abbot fixes the date in *141* for the first session after the holiday.
Lowel announces his topic in *142:* Why should Hesse be such an appealing
author to college students today? We asked Professor Abbot if he had
any objection to the discussion of topics that are outside of literature, and
he replied: *"Outside* the field of literature? Who says it's outside?"

143. PROFESSOR ABBOT: Okay. Please—

144. LOWELL: [Interrupting.] *Oh, just one more thing. For the
kids who live at Malcolm X Hall, we're planning to have a sort of preliminary discussion. That's planned the evening before, for the kids who
live at Malcolm X. But anybody from the class who wants to come, you're
welcome. And if you're married, you know, bring your husband or wife.
We haven't had much response before from those who are married, but
we really want you all to come.*

145. GERTRUDE: Is Steve going to be there?

146. PROFESSOR ABBOT: No.

*147. LOWELL: No, we aren't inviting faculty to this discussion.
You see, part of the purpose is to prepare for the discussion we're going to
have in class. So we want to do it by ourselves. Steve understands. Right?*

144–147. A number of students in the class, including Lowell, live
at Malcolm X Hall, an "experimental," coed dormitory on campus. We
asked Professor Abbot about this arrangement for a discussion away from
the classroom, specifically excluding him. "It wasn't my idea," he said.
"When I first suggested to Lowell that he lead a discussion on Hesse, he
came up with this idea about a 'preliminary discussion' at Malcolm X
Hall. I have no way of knowing what kind of discussion it will be. I can
only guess that Lowell wants to have some kind of dry run, a rehearsal,
before the class discussion, and he wants to do it his own way. Which is
to say, no faculty members present."

148. PROFESSOR ABBOT: Oh, yes. No problem. [Pause.] *Well,
where were we? Alice has made a nonrecommendation. Does anyone
have something he wants to recommend?*

148. There are about twenty or so minutes left in the session, and from this point Professor Abbot plays two major roles. First, he attempts to elicit from the students "recommendations" for their classmates—literary works or activities they believe are worth sharing. Second, he approaches students who have not yet spoken during this session, offering them an oportunity to tell what they have been doing, or at least trying to make sure that nothing has gone wrong with their current projects.

149. MARY: Yes. Little Big Man, *with Dustin Hoffman.*

150. PROFESSOR ABBOT: The film Little Big Man. *It just opened a few days ago.*

151. MARY: Yes, we saw it last night. It's strange, funny, terribly sad—I think a very good film. I was shaken up from the violence, though. I had an identity link with an Indian girl in the film—she was played by a Chinese girl—and it was quite unsettling.

152. PROFESSOR ABBOT: Do you know the novel, Little Big Man, *by Thomas Berger?*

153. MARY: No, I don't.

154 PROFESSOR ABBOT: It's available in paperback. Only ninety-five cents, I think. [Pause. Nick raises his hand.]

155. NICK: I read it, and I saw the movie, too. [Pause.]

156. PROFESSOR ABBOT: Do you recommend the movie?

157. NICK: Well, I was disappointed in it. Not only was I disappointed with the amount of the story that the film left untold, but there were a number of places where the filmmaker's interpretation and mine differed greatly. After reading the novel and seeing the movie, I was shocked to see that they had taken some of the more serious moments of the novel and turned them into roaring comedies. In reality, what they did was to show what happened and omitted the reasons behind the action. They left out almost all of the ideas, that the book explained, about Indian tradition and custom.

158. PROFESSOR ABBOT: Uh huh.

159. NICK: In spite of all the shortcomings, I did enjoy the film. The character of the old chief is my favorite—probably because the author uses him to explain the majority of the Indian lore and attitudes. The Indian idea of everything being alive as opposed to the white man's idea of everything being dead—that's very striking. Their beliefs and what happened are so closely related that it's amazing that the Indians didn't win the conflict. What I mean is—the theory that everything is alive seems to be so powerful that one would think it could overcome anything.

160. PROFESSOR ABBOT: Uh huh. Does anyone want to ask Nick anything? [To Nick.] *Let's wait till some of us have seen the film or read the novel, and then maybe they'll have some questions to raise.*

Anyone else? [Pause.] *Opal, you're reading* Madame Bovary. *How are you finding it?*

160. Since Nick has expressed a highly personal view about the film, stressing what he regards as its shortcomings, Professor Abbot makes an opportunity here for other members of the class to ask Nick some critical questions. But evidently few of the class members have seen the film, since it has just opened.

Professor Abbot now turns to Opal, another student who has not yet spoken. Opal is younger than most of the other students in the class, and she is rather shy. But she feels comfortable in the class, and as *161* and *163* show, her reticence vanishes as soon as she begins to speak and realizes the others are sincerely interested in what she has to say. It is also significant that Opal was led to her reading of *Madame Bovary* by a comment made by Professor Abbot during one of his lectures. She told him, in a memo following the lecture, that she wanted to add the novel to her reading list, and he gave his approval.

161. OPAL: *I'm just about halfway through. Most of the other kids read* Madame Bovary *before. But I never read it. And I didn't even know the plot. Two weeks ago, when you mentioned it in your lecture that day, that was when I decided to read it. And then last week, I mentioned it before class to Eric, and he told me that she commits suicide in the end, and I didn't even know that, and somehow the book hasn't been as fascinating since. I knew some tragedy had to happen, but to be quite honest, I really didn't give it much thought. I knew the plot was leading to something dramatic and horrible, but I left it at that. But I guess it's still interesting to watch how it will lead up to that point.*

162. DR. ABBOT: *Uh huh. What about Emma Bovary herself? I mean, as a woman. As a person.*

163. OPAL: *Madame Bovary, as a woman, really fascinates me. In the beginning, when the reader sees the story from her husband's side, I developed a fondness for her, probably because I was seeing her from his eyes. She seemed very countrylike, excitable, pleasant, cheerful, and eager to venture into a new life. But as the book continued, my feelings changed from fondness to pity, shock, anxiety, and just plain being annoyed. I was annoyed with her manner in which she treated her husband, not so much overtly as in her mind. I was also annoyed by her fantasies. Of course we all fantasize, but because hers didn't come true, she blamed it on her husband. She was also extremely materialistic. I realized her situation was not that great, but she seemed to want to live in such a romantic world, rather than accepting reality. Her marriage was very romantic at the beginning, but after the excitement and newness wore*

off and the boredom set in, it seemed as if she didn't want to work at anything. The honeymoon was over. [Professor Abbot's voice is heard, simultaneously with Opal's, but the words are not distinguishable.] *Yes, but I also pitied her. I thought it was great that she read and sewed, played the piano, and did a lot of creative things, but after awhile she was bored with that. I was shocked at her reaction to her boredom— becoming sick, throwing up, and so forth. The reason I was shocked is that when I'm bored, which does happen to everyone, and after I just can't take it any more, I try to get myself out of the situation instead of accepting it. I guess I shouldn't try to relate to the book, being that it took place in a different era and country. But also, because I was getting bored along with her, and I kind of wanted her love affairs to start developing, especially with Leon. But he left. If he comes back, I'll have to wait and see.*

164. PROFESSOR ABBOT: Okay. I imagine a number of us want to react to what you're saying, but why don't we hold our thoughts until you've finished, and then we'll talk more about it. Maybe even next week. You'll have finished the novel by then, won't you?

164. Professor Abbot does not want to pursue the discussion of *Madame Bovary,* partly because Opal's ideas about it may change when she has finished reading it, and partly because the class period will be ending soon and he feels that he must encourage several other students to speak before the session is over.

165. OPAL: Oh, yes. Probably in just a couple of days.
166. PROFESSOR ABBOT: Okay. Good. [Professor Abbot surveys the table.] *Pete, how are things with you?*

166. Pete is a biology major who has never had an interest in literature. This course with Professor Abbot is, in all likelihood, his last formal academic contact with literary works. Professor Abbot told us about Pete: "Since I found out that he's attracted to Janet, I've been trying to use that attraction to stimulate his interest in the course and in literature. But I'm not sure what good it will do. Janet is pretty heavily into the women's liberation movement, and her reading list for the course is made up exclusively of women writers. Maybe that isn't what Pete needs for motivation."

167. PETE: Oh, okay, I guess. I had a real treat watching the tube a few days ago. I wonder if anybody else—
168. PROFESSOR ABBOT: What was it?
169. PETE: Well, you know, it isn't often that I feel this way

about the shows. Most of the time they just fill time. But this time, I heard Marcel Marceau speak! I really enjoyed his comments, how ancient dances incorporated mime to say things about life that couldn't be verbalized. But what was really exciting was the films of him in action. He's really incredible. That night was a good night for the tube. Before Marcel Marceau, there was a program about the Don Christiansen Puppet Theatre. They showed some of their performances. Most of them were very hard to intellectualize, and at first I found myself trying to do that. But after letting myself go, which is something I find hard to do, because of lack of practice, I began to feel the emotions they were trying to send out.

    170. PROFESSOR ABBOT: Uh huh.

    171. PETE: You remember when we read that passage from Virginia Woolf, when Janet gave her report on modern women writers. I was very impressed by her success to verbally express an emotion. Marcel Marceau and the Don Christiansen Theatre do the same thing through the use of mime and also use various stage techniques to express emotions that are seldom verbalized. You know how much I enjoy this course, but I'm not a very avid reader, and when I do read I don't know what makes for good writing—except, some things I enjoy and others I don't. Janet's comments about Virginia Woolf made sense to me. I realized that if you can verbalize pure emotions, you're more able to understand them. And also if you can understand your emotions, you can verbalize them. Anyway, I realized I really enjoy that type of writing, and I've been meaning to ask Janet about what to read. Like, where should I start?

    172. PROFESSOR ABBOT: You and Janet haven't had a chance to talk about this yet?

    173. PETE: No.

    174. PROFESSOR ABBOT: Well, get together on this as soon as you can. [Pete nods in agreement.] *Okay. That's good.* [Pause.] *Anyone having difficulty on his course project?* [Professor Abbot looks at Peggy.] *You know, Peggy, you haven't said anything about yours, and I haven't received a memo from you in a long time. Let's get together for a conference. Okay?* [Pause. Peggy nods. Professor Abbot turns to Rhoda.] *Rhoda, I keep wondering if anything is wrong. You've been out of class for awhile, and—*

    174. Peggy is a problem student. She has done very little work for the course, and Professor Abbot is putting some pressure on her here. The situation is quite different with Rhoda, however, and he asks directly if something is wrong. His suspicion is confirmed by Rhoda's statement in 175.

175. RHODA: Oh, it's just my life outside of school is too de-
manding, and school has become secondary. I have a problem with my
sixteen-year-old sister. [Several voices are heard.] *My sister Ellen has been*
living with me for the last few months. Things were going pretty well
until a couple of weeks ago. She left on a Saturday night and didn't come
home until Monday morning. We talked a long time, and I thought we
had things pretty well straightened out. But evidently not. I dropped
her off at school last Wednesday morning and haven't seen her since.
I'm worried about her, and I've just about exhausted my ideas to deal
with her problems.

176. PROFESSOR ABBOT: Wow, that sounds serious. Is there
any office on campus where—

177. CHERYL: [Interrupting.] *I think she ought to go over to the*
Counseling Center. I don't know whether they can help directly, but
they'll know where to go.

178. PROFESSOR ABBOT: Uh huh. The Counseling Center.
[To Rhoda.] *You know—*

179. CHERYL: [Interrupting.] *I really think the Counseling*
Center is the place. [To Rhoda.] *Because the problem may be more than*
just your sister. I mean—you know—it could be yourself, too. And the
people over at the Counseling Center are really wonderful.

180. JANET: Well, also there are a couple of terrific therapy
groups on campus. There's—

181. PROFESSOR ABBOT: [Interrupting.] *Okay. Maybe some of*
you could talk about this with Rhoda—[Several voices are heard simul-
taneously]—

181. Professor Abbot makes a suggestion which he hopes will close
the discussion of Rhoda's personal problems, but he is not successful.
Janet continues, in *182* and *184* to say what she has started to say in
180. It is interesting that Janet compares the free atmosphere in the
therapy groups with the atmosphere in Professor Abbot's class, with the
class (in her opinion) coming out the loser. Professor Abbot makes no
comment about Janet's conclusion.

182. JANET: I belong to two groups here on campus. A women's
consciousness-raising group and a therapy group on campus. The two
groups have been really great. Somehow, in the two groups, there's a level
of honesty you just don't find anywhere else. I mean—you know—much
as things right here aren't— I mean, right here, in this class, things—

183. PETE: [Interrupting.] *We're pretty honest with one another*
in this class.

184. JANET: Yes, but it's still a class. I'm still judged, and I'm still competed with. But with the two groups I mentioned, I have two places of refuge where that doesn't happen. I've reached a point in my life where I have to either share my love with other human beings or turn to God. And I don't believe in God, so I've got to find some way to share with people and help them share with me. [Pause.]

185. *PROFESSOR ABBOT: Uh huh.* [Pause.]

186. *BERNIE: Say, I wanted to ask about this before. Has anybody seen* No Place to Be Somebody? [He looks at Saralou, who nods.] *I saw it, and I really recommend it. I'd be interested to hear from others, when you see it. I feel that everyone should go see it. The play deals with the blacks and the Mafia in the lower East Village of New York, during the past fifteen years.* [Pause.] *The first two scenes were extremely funny. but the last one makes such a statement that you can't help but be depressed when you walk out.* [Pause.] *It was just tremendous. I don't want to say too much about it because it will ruin it for you.*

186. Bernie returns the discussion to the subject of literature. He looks at Saralou because she is the only black student in the class. She joins the discussion, after some initial reluctance, and gives her opinion of the play starting at *192.* Her response is interesting because, as we learned from Professor Abbot, she never participates in the discussion—or, in any case, had never done so up to the time of our interview—without being asked. Professor Abbot, knowing she has seen *No Place to Be Somebody* and has written a long, thoughtful, and analytic memo about the play, wants her to share her ideas with the group; hence his direct invitation in *187.*

187. *PROFESSOR ABBOT:* [To Saralou.] *In your last memo, Saralou, you mentioned—*

188. *SARALOU: Yes. I saw it when I was in Chicago, just before it came out here.*

189. *PROFESSOR ABBOT: Tell us what you thought about it.*

190. *SARALOU: It was the best play I have seen in a long time.*

191. *DR. ABBOT: Do you want to say a word or two about it?*

192. *SARALOU: Yes, I do. In the play there were four dominant roles. Firstly, Johnny, who was the hero and the loser—and a pimp. The second was Gabe, who was a playwright who was too light to be black and too black to be white. The third was a homosexual that I don't remember his name. And last but not least, there was Sweetcakes, who who was Johnny in his young days. There were* [a word indistinguishable in the recording] *meanings to the play, and all the characters were synonymous of the black man in America today. If that man chooses the road of crime or easy money, would he lose? Of course. Or if he chooses*

the so-called honest approach—like getting into the theater—he was still a loser. The only alternative, as shown in the play, was to be a very passive in-between role, such as the one played by the homosexual. The homosexual was accepted by the largest theater in the city, and resigned himself to being homosexual, and accepted roles as a dancer and other feminine roles to make it. And he always got work. Gabe in the play wanted to play very masculine roles and could never get work. I think of this play and associate this type of role-playing to Flip Wilson.

193. PROFESSOR ABBOT: Uh huh. How is—

194. SARALOU: Flip has been able to remain on the media, whereas Sammy Davis, Bill Cosby, and others have failed. I'm sure it is not a question of talent alone that keeps Flip on the media. But he plays down the black male-female roles or the black male-female relationship. To me this says that the person is no threat to the white pure ladies in the audience. By threat I mean that, at the base of racism in terms of black men, the fear is that they all want to climb in bed with Miss Anne. So Flip is like the homosexual in the passive role in the play. He is a people pleaser—white folk pleaser.

195. PROFESSOR ABBOT: Uh huh. Have you—

196. SARALOU: I also saw a movie in Chicago that I thought was very disgusting, and that was The Great White Hope. *To me this was just saying that there's only so far a black man can go with a white woman, and so on. All the old rehashed shit that all black people are aware of and don't really appreciate seeing reinforced on the celluloid.*

197. JANET: Saralou, did you happen to go to the Black Cultural Festival about a month ago here on campus?

198. SARALOU: No, I spent that weekend with my family in L. A.

199. JANET: My roommate and I went to it. There were only about ten to fifteen white people there, including myself and my roommate, and I was the only blonde. Boy, was that an experience! The program consisted of several black poets who gave fantastic readings to the beat of bongo drums, a group of black dancers, a group of black singers, and a black jazz band. One of the poetry readings was done by two black guys.

200. PROFESSOR ABBOT: Uh huh.

201. JANET: The people in the show were putting down white boys. They talked of revolution, and that the black will rise, and how important black women are to the race. But at the same time, they knocked their own black brothers by calling them whores, pimps, junkies, murderers, and so on. The dancers were really loose. I could never dance as beautiful as they did. Even this one black guy who was at least six-five and 230 pounds was graceful. The whole program was really an experience for me.

202. PROFESSOR ABBOT: I heard about what a good program that was. I'm sorry I missed it. [Professor Abbot looks around the table.] *Let's see. Mary, you've been quiet today.*

202–208. During these last few minutes of the session, Professor Abbot wants to be sure that he has given everyone an opportunity to speak. Mary has spoken only briefly earlier (*149, 151, 153*). In *208,* Professor Abbot asks directly whether everybody has been heard from. He mentions Dan, who has spoken only once (*29*), and Terry, who has not spoken at all.

203. MARY: Well, I've been listening to everyone.

204. PROFESSOR ABBOT: Aside from Little Big Man, *what have you been doing?*

205. MARY: Oh, lots. I've been reading The Great Gatsby *for my English class.*

206. PROFESSOR ABBOT: Enjoying it?

207. MARY: Oh, yes. But, you know, when I read anything I take it quite personally, and I react quite personally, but I can't get any of that over in the required essay for the English class. It's frustrating. My mind goes completely blank when I sit down to write. I look at the suggested topics for The Great Gatsby *and can't see how they relate to the book. I discovered after the first paper that the English class was purely for composition, which I didn't know or want. It was upsetting to get my paper back graded on the grounds of exposition. Exposition I'm not interested in! Perhaps I need it, but I've discovered being conscious of form completely inhibits me.*

208. PROFESSOR ABBOT: I know what a problem that can be. [To the group.] *You know, the point Mary's making deserves a whole discussion. There's a lot to say about it. Let's do that sometime soon.* [He looks at his watch.] *It's almost time to break. Let's see, have we heard from everybody? Dan? Terry? Who else?*

209. TERRY: Well, as you know from my last memo, I've started reading Portrait of the Artist as a Young Man. *That was because you read someone's memo from your other class who said it was the most important book in his life. That sounded promising. I'm about a quarter of the way through.*

210. DR. ABBOT: How are you finding it?

211. TERRY: Well, I like it. The first pages have a bit of the feeling of Dylan Thomas's A Child's Christmas in Wales. *But now I'm in a part where it's getting pretty heavy.*

212. IAN: You know, I started reading it earlier this quarter. But I found the reading very slow, and I didn't stick with it.

213. PROFESSOR ABBOT: But it's amazing what happens sometimes when you go back to something six months or a year later. You wonder where you were the first time around. Well, you know my philosophy about that. If you aren't ready for something or if it isn't right for you, there's no point in forcing it. But also, I should add, if it's too much for you now, remember to try it again some months later—or a year or two later.

213. At the close of the period, Professor Abbot repeats a point that he hammers away at continuously—that no one should reject a work forever on the basis of one negative experience.

214. IAN: They're getting ready to fold up in the control room, Steve.

215. PROFESSOR ABBOT: What makes you think so?

216. IAN: Well, somebody in the control room just lit a cigarette. I just saw it through the mirror. They know we're going to break up in a minute. [He faces the one-way mirror.] *Okay, you guys, we're just about finished here.* [Laughter.]

217. PROFESSOR ABBOT: [Looking at his watch.] *In fact, I've kept you overtime, and I apologize. Peggy, could I see you for just a second? And by the way, Diana wasn't here today. Will anyone see her? She lives at Malcolm X, doesn't she? Would you tell her to telephone me, please?* [There is noise as the students prepare to leave.]

217. As the class ends, Professor Abbot remembers to ask Peggy to make an appointment with him, as he has suggested in *174*. He is also concerned about a student, Diana, who has been absent, and asks those who live at Malcolm X Hall to get a message to her. Even details as small as these reflect the fundamental principle governing Professor Abbot's work as an artist during this stage of his teaching career: his insistence on dealing with students as people.

And Minos imprisoned Daedalus in the laby-
rinth. Now the labyrinth was a chamber that
with its tangled windings perplexed the outward
way. But Daedalus constructed wings for
himself and his son and made his way safely
to Sicily.

Apollodorus, *The Library; Epitome*

PART III

Inside the Labyrinth

Unlike the artist who works alone in his loft-studio, the university professor is part of a complex social institution. He is part of the intricate patterns of life that exist even at the smallest of campuses, and he is part of the whole higher education establishment.

The university professor spends his entire professional life in a galaxy of systems and supersystems. It is conceivable that he might be able to develop into a superior teacher with no knowledge of how these systems work. But if he is eager to improve himself as a teacher, it is likely that an understanding of the university as a social institution will contribute to that goal. He will probably become a better teacher if he sees the relationships between the roles he plays in the classroom and the degree system that is in operation on his campus, the university supersystem of which the degree system is a component, and the giant supersystems of which the university is itself a component. Decisions made in these systems and supersystems strongly affect what the professor does in his classroom.

The three chapters of Part Three are designed to give the reader, as simply as possible, this kind of knowledge. Chapter Seven analyzes the university as a supersystem and presents a preliminary definition of the degree system—the system within which the professor functions as a teacher. A dozen other systems that surround and support the degree system on every campus are also briefly described.

145

Chapter Eight moves from the university supersystem to the larger supersystems that lie beyond and around it: accrediting asociations, discipline organizations, academic consortia, government agencies, faculty organizations, textbook houses, testing agencies—to mention only a few. Each of these giant supersystems has goals which press upon the university and force it to modify its own intrinsic educational goals.

Chapter Nine returns to the degree system, to consider it in detail and to present a theoretical model of it. An analysis of the degree system demonstrates that its six "parts" cannot be separated; there are no static building blocks that can be pulled out and "reformed" and set back in place. Each part of the degree system is but an aspect of a single whole—a whole that includes both "curriculum" and "instruction," as we traditionally call them. Nothing in the degree system is static: all is in constant motion. In actuality, these parts are inseparable, but Chapter Nine distinguishes them analytically and shows how they are intertwined in amazingly complex ways when the system is running.

Part Three ends with a set of illustrations that suggest how the professor, within his own classroom, is both free to make decisions and is bound by the decisions already made in the total complex of systems in which he carries out his duties as a university professor. It is those decisions which the professor is himself free to make within his own classroom, even in the most conventional program, that enable him to develop —if he so desires—into an artist at teaching.

Chapter 7

The University as Supersystem

It is almost impossible for a person who is part of a social institution, who sees it only from the inside, to know how that institution really works. Consider the American university professor. He knows the university intimately; he has spent a lifetime in it, and he may even play a leadership role in it. But he has a *practitioner's*, not a scholar's, knowledge of the university. The typical university teacher, especially in the humanities, has little scientific knowledge about the workings of the university as an institution or about the teaching-learning process. The situation is understandable: even behavioral scientists cannot agree on a theoretical framework for describing how the university functions, and even specialists in learning theory admit that their knowledge is primitive.

But the problem extends beyond a simple lack of research-based knowledge. The real problem is that there is a profound difference between the way the typical university professor speculates about the nature of the university and how students learn, and the way the scholar in the field of higher education or of learning theory approaches the subject. It is a difference in the theoretical framework that governs the two approaches—in essence, the difference between the spirit that informs folklore and the spirit that characterizes science.

In this book, our attempt to analyze the nature of university teaching is based on the systems approach, a relatively new framework by which some scholars in the field are now analyzing various facets of higher education. Within this framework, we envision the university as a vast supersystem, including within itself several dozen major systems, but also representing only one component in other larger and more complex supersystems.

The systems which constitute the university are interdependent and interrelated in myriad ways. They do not—indeed, cannot—exist in isolation, even though we may isolate them artificially for purposes of analysis. Among the systems which make up the university, there is one over which the faculty body has almost complete control. This is the degree system. It consists of those processes—and the structures needed to carry them out—through which students in degree programs acquire certain kinds of knowledge and skills, predefined by university officials, and by means of which they obtain their degrees or other academic titles. Most professors believe that the degree system lies at the very center of the university supersystem. Let us pause here to ask whether there is any evidence to support this belief.

Place of Degree System

There are two general public misconceptions about the nature of higher education. First, whenever someone mentions educational institutions beyond the secondary level, most people assume that what is meant are colleges and universities. Yet those who have been in the business of higher education know that a vast number of postsecondary educational programs are not situated on college or university campuses and do not come under the aegis of the higher education establishment. There are, for example, the many training programs in business and industry that are not carried on under the auspices of degree-granting institutions, the schools that exist within the armed services, and the innumerable free-university-type courses offered in many cities around the United States. Postsecondary education, then, does not automatically mean college or university education.

Second, the general public assumes that the only function of a university is educational. And for almost everyone, the term *educational*, in this context, normally refers to the process in which professors teach students and students learn from professors, from each other, and from such objects as books. Yet, anyone who knows the American university at all knows that there are a vast number of important functions performed by universities that are not, in that sense, educational. On most campuses, many university offices and university officials function as consulting agencies for business, industry, and government. The university also functions as a center for hundreds of research projects that are not related to instructional programs. It functions as an employment agency for students. It often functions as a military orientation and preparation center. It serves as a convention center for visitors and, through its overseas programs, as a travel agency for students. It functions as an entertainment center for the community—an important service, but often no more educational than the entertainment supplied by commercial theaters. Many universities also function as data banks and as repositories for historical documents. The more prestigious universities run publishing houses, operate complete sets of hotels and restaurants called "conference centers" (quite apart from the set of hotels and restaurants called "residence halls"), and maintain sports and theater management bureaus. These services and functions are noneducational, in the usual conception of the term, but they are universally regarded by faculty and nonfaculty alike as legitimate for the university.

There are, as well, other noneducational services provided by universities. They keep many thousands of young people off the already crowded labor market, and they offer a place for young people of similar family background to meet and select future mates, friends, and business or professional associates. These services and others like them—sometimes called latent (as opposed to manifest) university functions—have been studied by sociologists, and their importance to our society is undeniable. Some scholars in higher education have even argued that they are reason enough for the existence of universities, aside from educational goals.

Postsecondary education, then, is not exclusively a university function in our society, and our universities provide many services in our society that are not educational. Since that is so, what is special about the university? The answer is simple: it is the only institution in our society authorized to award academic degrees.

Faculty members are justified, then, in their belief that the whole complex supersystem of university activity rests, in significant ways, on the degree system—and on the faculty body responsible for it. It is within this system that each department works out its degree patterns, that courses are offered, that classes are taught, that students are evaluated, that grades and credits are awarded. The degree system thus lies at the center of the professional life of every university teacher, and every other system in the complex supersystem which is the university has come into existence because, directly or indirectly, it supports the degree system.

Systems Surrounding the Degree System

The degree system, although central, is only one of a dozen major systems that constitute the university supersystem. All of these other systems have come into existence because the degree system could not properly function without them. The most important of these are the faculty reward system, the departmental system, and the academic advising system.

For the university faculty member, the *faculty reward system* is second in importance only to the degree system. It can be briefly defined as the process through which faculty members are hired, retained, promoted, given tenure, asked to leave the campus, and in other ways rewarded or penalized by their peers and superiors. The faculty reward system is an immensely complex system on every university campus, and many faculty members spend a lifetime trying to figure out how it works. It frequently has a strong influence on the roles played by faculty members in the degree system.

Although the *departmental system* can be simply described, it, too, is exceedingly complex. It is the process through which all of the people who work at the university—professors as well as nonteaching academicians and nonacademic employees—are grouped into working units. On most campuses, these units are labeled academic or nonacademic; and the academic units are further identified as schools or colleges, departments or institutes or centers. Ideally, each of these units is clearly differentiated from the others in function, and each is large enough to provide for efficient productivity while remaining small enough to prevent depersonalization. If the departmental system is working well in a university, there is little duplication of function. At the present time, there are complaints on almost every campus that the departmental system is not working well. On many campuses, the total departmental system has become so complex and so cumbersome, largely as a consequence of historical accretion, that its usefulness and necessity have come into question.

For university professors who teach in standard programs, the department is the center of their campus life; it controls just about everything that the teacher does on campus. Nonetheless, even his own department, in nine cases out of ten, allows the university teacher, within the domain of his own classroom, the freedom to make his own decisions about the most crucial aspects of his role in the degree system. For it is the individual teacher who is largely responsible for the week-to-week organization of his courses and for the way he teaches them.

Closely interrelated with the degree system is the academic *advising system,* which can be briefly defined as the process through which students seeking degrees are informed about the way the degree system works. The information given to students usually stresses alternative ways by which they may fulfill degree requirements. The objective of the advising system is to help each student understand the alternatives and select the ones that best fit his present needs and hopes for the future.

In the great majority of universities in the United States, the advising function lacks high status priority, and faculty members who perform it are not highly rewarded for the time they spend at it. The advising system, nevertheless, holds an extremely important place in the university supersystem. This importance is recognized by the administrators of most experimental colleges and other innovative programs, and some of them have been able to devise advising systems that are highly effective. In more conventional academic settings, however, academic advising is done in casual and routine ways by professors, leaving students with the necessity for supplementing their knowledge about the way the degree system works through informal assistance from other students.

There are two other systems which are closely interrelated with the degree system, and they affect the professional lives of faculty members differently on different campuses. They are more likely to have a direct effect on professors at small schools or on graduate faculties than on professors at large public institutions devoted primarily to undergraduate instruction. These are the student admissions system and the extracurricular system. The *admissions system* is the process through which certain prospective students, considered desirable for the degree system according to one criterion or another, are recruited for academic programs and then admitted into them. The *extracurricular system* is the process through which activities and experiences of various kinds (many of them obviously educational) are planned for students by students and faculty. In standard programs, these activities exist outside the degree system; they are not taken into consideration when credits are counted for a student's degree or when a faculty member's workload is calculated.

These five systems, taken together, constitute for the university teacher the central systems of the supersystem. But there are also other important systems in the university that surround and support the degree system and in various ways influence and affect the university professor. Some of these systems are the housing and health system; the plant, equipment, and supplies system; the security system; the legal system; and the public relations system.

The *housing and health system* is concerned with the physical needs of members of the campus community and provides, for certain segments of it, food services, housing, transportation, and medical attention. How this system affects faculty members depends in part on whether a campus is public or private, urban or rural. At a public urban campus, for instance, it is unlikely that any of these services would be provided for faculty members unless they were *directly* required by instructional duties—transportation to a community elementary school, for example, to supervise a student-teacher.

The *plant, equipment, and supplies system* is the process by which the university acquires and maintains buildings, furniture, books, supplies, and the tools that are needed for instruction, research, and the other functions of the university. It daily provides all of the university teacher's professional physical needs, supplying him in particular with the physical tools of his trade.

Two of the university's systems have taken on visibility in recent years. If the *security system* functions adequately, members of the campus community and their property, as well as the total holdings of the university itself, are protected against damage, injury, and loss. The security system is related in purpose to the *legal system,* the process by which the university creates, interprets, and administers its regulations. The legal system includes all aspects of justice on the campus: law enforcement, trials and other legal proceedings, correctional measures, and grievance procedures.

Also more visible at certain universities in recent years is the *public relations system,* which attempts to create attractive images of the university for prospective students, faculty, and staff, for prospective employers of students, and for private donors and foundation officials and government grantors and contractors, as well as the general public.

The most significant system not yet mentioned is the *governance system,* which determines how the other systems are to be controlled and changed, who decides what changes are to be made, and who is to be responsible for effecting the changes. The individuals and groups involved in governance include not only members of the university but also members of the supersystems in which the university participates. The governance system pervades every aspect of university life. Many professors are deeply involved in it, either through administrative assignment or through membership in the academic senate or council; and campus politicians among the faculty body often use the governance system to further their own professional goals.

This is the complex setting, then, within which the university teacher performs his tasks. To understand that setting adequately, we must look more closely at the university's relationships to the national and international networks that play such an influential role in the higher education establishment; we shall examine these giant supersystems in Chapter Eight. We must also look more closely at the degree system which, as we have affirmed, lies at the center of the life of the university; Chapter Nine is devoted to that analysis. Now, however, we must examine the methodological premises that are basic to the analyses which follow. Let us turn immediately, then, to the definition of two crucial terms that must be included in any discussion of educational models.

Theoretical and Blueprint Models

The systems approach, as we have said, is a relatively new way of thinking about the university, especially about the entities we traditionally call curriculum and instruction. It is perhaps not too difficult to accept the idea of a university as a supersystem, but the idea of the degree-granting process as a system may be harder to grasp. We are accustomed to taking a different kind of approach when we think about the matter of granting degrees, and the problem has something to do with the conventional concepts of curriculum and instruction.

Most professionals in higher education have traditionally looked at the curricular-instructional process with the aid of a metaphor that presents us with a picture of a structure: an edifice consisting of building blocks that are in fairly static relationship to each other and that can easily be moved in and out. In this conception, a change in the curriculum or a change in the instructional pattern—the professor's teaching style—is seen as the substitution of a new building block for an old one. The metaphor suggests that the process is architectonic in nature. Under the influence of this architectonic mode of thinking, administrators and faculty members accept the notion that once a committee reaches agreement about a desirable change in the structure—that is, once there is an agreement as to which of the old building blocks must be removed and which new ones must be inserted—the change ought to be simple to make. It is consequently a constant source of astonishment that any basic curricular-instructional reform—a change that is not merely superficial—generally proves impossible to effect. Or, if it seems effective at first, the effectiveness rarely lasts beyond a few years. The failure of these reforms is a source of perpetual frustration to faculty members. And analysis of such failures leaves us no farther ahead, because the model we typically use as the basis for our analysis—the architectonic model of the curricular-instructional process—by its nature gives us no insight into the reasons for the failure. The systems model, on the other hand, represents far more accurately how curricular-instructional processes actually work. It also demonstrates why the usual sorts of innovation must, sooner or later, fail—and it suggests the kinds of innovation that have a chance to succeed.

If we follow the systems model, it is not possible for us to think of separate "parts" in the degree system. There are no static building blocks. Each part is but an aspect of the whole, and nothing is static—all is in constant motion. Although the component parts of the degree system are not separable in actuality, Chapter Nine differentiates six component parts which, when the system is running, are intertwined in a complex and intricate pattern. We call these parts the *dimensions* of the degree system. The relationships between these dimensions work in complicated ways. An innovative faculty, for example, may create a change in one dimension of the program because it has decided that such a change will make it possible to implement one of their objectives more easily; but that change can trigger changes in some of the other dimensions that may not be at all desirable. If the innovative faculty has not considered the possibility of these other changes, insoluble problems may arise. Faculty members and administartors must therefore understand what conditions in which dimensions of the system are likely to be affected by specific changes in other dimensions. In short, we must understand thoroughly how the total system actually works and how the dimensions that constitute the system interrelate before we set out to induce any changes at all. We should also understand how the total degree system is interrelated with each of the other systems that surround it and support it. To effect such understanding, then, even practitioners working at the most concrete level need to have before them an accurate theoretical model of the system.

One of the assumptions basic to the argument of this book is that the systems approach leads to more useful theoretical models of both the university and the curricular-instructional process than do traditional conceptions of either of these entities. A faculty member who wants to examine his role as a teacher—and in particular, a professor who wants the become an artist at teaching—must have some realistic notion of how the university supersystem and the degree system operate.

The theoretical model of the degree system must be able to encompass unconventional degree programs as well as conventional ones, if the needs of planners, researchers, and reformers are to be met: the planner needs an accurate view of the essential parts of the system and how they interrelate; the researcher needs a model adequate enough to help him in his contrastive studies of concrete programs, whether or not they conform to the standard model; and the educational reformer needs such a model as a guide for constructing viable programs that depart from the standard pattern.

Basic to the systems approach is the concept of the interrelationship of "parts." The concept may be illustrated by considering the ordinary table. There are many kinds of tables—dining tables, card tables, drafting tables, coffee tables, conference tables—but it is possible to envision a single model that represents them all. This general model would consist of two parts: (a) a flat but not necessarily horizontal top, supported by (b) some structure, such as a set of legs, that will keep it fixed at a height appropriate to its function. This, then, is the theoretical model of table. Such a model identifies only the parts that are essential and defines them not structurally but functionally.

What is the purpose of a theoretical model? It analyzes and describes how the object or process under scrutiny works—whether it is a relatively simple and static entity like table or a complex supersystem like university. The purpose of a theoretical model is to explain. A blueprint model, on the other hand, provides a pattern for building a new structure or creating a new process—such as a program to retrain foreign language teachers for "second careers" in the educational world.

When we wish to judge the success of a theoretical model, we observe how well it explains the segment of the world it purports to analyze. When we wish to judge the success of a blueprint model, we observe how efficiently the structure or process that it brings into being (or that it reforms) actually functions. Since the theoretical model must describe all of the parts that are essential to the life of the system, it is possible to determine whether a particular blueprint model is complete by checking it against the theoretical model—thus ascertaining whether every part that is described in the theoretical model has been translated, at an appropriately concrete level, into mechanisms or structures that carry out the functions pertaining to that particular part.

At the most concrete blueprint-model level, a curriculum model is identical with a model curriculum, and a teacher model is equivalent to a model teacher. They are concrete examples of a curriculum design and a teacher in action that are worthy of emulation. At its highest level of abstraction, a model is pure theory. It is a framework that postulates what the essential parts of an entity are and how those parts interrelate.

It is possible, of course, that there may exist simultaneously several different concepts about the nature of a system and its parts and how the parts interrelate. As we examine the literature in any given field—either in the past or at present—we can find several models at the highest level of abstraction, each of them competing for acceptance. In the field of astronomy, the geocentric and heliocentric models were at one time competitors for prominence as views of the solar system. In the field of biology, the Darwinian model of "creation" came into conflict with the Genesis model. In other fields: Marx's model competed with Adam Smith's, Harvey's model competed with those created by medical practitioners of the ancient and medieval worlds, Einstein's model competed with Newton's. So, too, in curricular-instructional theory, the systems model is in competition with the more common architectonic model. In our view, the systems model is the more useful one, and when it replaces the architectonic model in the minds and imaginations of university professors and administrators, we will be one step closer to building more effective educational programs in our universities.

Chapter 8

%%%%%%%%%%%%%%%%%%%%%%%%%%%%%%%%%%%%%

University Goals and the
Educational Establishment

In the last chapter, we looked at the university supersystem from within and described some of the systems of which it is constituted. We saw that at its center lies the degree system—the one system whose operation faculty members control—and that the degree system interrelates in complex ways with a dozen major systems that surround it. We are now ready to look at the giant supersystems in which the university itself is but a component—for these have a greater impact than most professors realize on the shape of the degree system and the faculty member's roles in it.

As we examine this aspect of the labyrinth in which most professors are caught, we shall not find the picture a happy one. However the university defines its own goals, they are inevitably distorted by the larger supersystems of which the university is a part. These supersystems have *their* goals—and these differ, often greatly, from the goals of the university. The distortion of the university's goals is explained by a fundamental principle in systems theory: Every system imposes specific pressures and requirements on the various smaller systems of which it is constituted—even while, at the same time, allowing each of these systems a degree of autonomy. Thus, the university is autonomous in certain ways; and in the most popular image of itself that it paints for its various publics (of which its own faculty body is one), it highlights its autonomous functions. But it is affected in innumerable and decisive ways by the larger supersystems of which it is a component. In turn, it translates these influences into demands that it makes upon the systems that exist within it. And all of these influences, at all levels, operate simultaneously.

Let us see how this fundamental principle of systems theory works when we apply it to the goals of undergraduate degree programs. Undergraduate colleges in the United States—whether they are parts of large institutions or exist as separate institutions—have traditionally been expected to work toward two goals for their students: socialization and certification. These goals have been set largely by the giant supersystems. The goal of socialization requires the faculty at a college to find effective means by which a high school graduate coming to the institution can be brought into the adult fold by the time he is awarded his degree—that is, given status as a member of the adult community. The goal of certification requires the faculty to find effective means to prepare the student for earning a livelihood. This goal asks the faculty to train the student in some specialty and then, after evaluating his achievement in it, to certify that he has (or has not) a certain capability in a scholarly discipline or in a vocational or professional field.

To these two traditional goals, many colleges added a third goal during World War II: student self-actualization. During the quarter-century following World War II, many undergraduate colleges in the United States—and a fair number of community colleges, as well—accepted this third goal, claiming that their ideal was to provide far more than training to earn a livelihood. This third goal was sometimes described in rather grandiose language—for example, to provide a learning atmosphere for students in which the total human potential of every student would be realized to the highest degree possible. But at most of the large public campuses—those that give instruction to the great mass of college students today—this goal is now more or less neglected. Some of the larger colleges and universities are even disclaiming responsibility for any impact on their students beyond a rather narrowly defined range of academic achievement or vocational skill. American colleges and universities, especially those in large urban areas where most of the students commute, are thus shaping their educational goals in a way that makes them function more like the traditional Western European universities.

This appears to be the trend: university personnel—including almost all faculty members in conventional programs—are becoming less interested in what students do outside the classroom and beyond the control of examinations. (We are speaking, of course, of conventional institutions and not of experimental schools.) Even the faculty members at the residential colleges are becoming more indifferent to their students' behavior outside of class and beyond the campus. Most faculty members now believe, for example, that if students choose to break the laws of society at large, then the society's regular law-enforcement mechanisms should be called upon and campus authorities should not be involved. In all probability, only a certain kind of unconventional college will continue to take responsibility for the development of the "whole person," especially for those aspects of student development that are noncognitive and nonrational.

Along with this narrowing of educational goals, another trend is visible: the vocational and semiprofessional goals of undergraduate education are receiving increased emphasis. As this emphasis increases, most professors in humanistic subjects, at most four-year colleges and at all community colleges, will increasingly feel defensive about their own specialized fields.

The emphasis on vocational goals is reflected in the development of all sorts of new programs. But these programs, although new, are not experimental or innovative; they share the educational objectives of the traditional vocational programs and exist side-by-side with them. For example, there are programs attempting to reeducate individuals whose jobs have been eliminated by automation or have been greatly changed by new developments within their vocational fields. There are programs designed to launch older adults on second careers. There are programs claiming to meet the need for more middle-management personnel. And many campuses, following recommendations from the Carnegie Commission on Higher Education and other quarters, are beginning to introduce new programs to meet the overwhelming need for semiprofessionals in the health field.

All of these programs in vocational fields—the old as well as the new—run the risk of developing in students specific skills that will prove to be unmarketable. We appear to be entering another ring of the cycle that has characterized higher education production (to borrow a technical term from the economist) in this country for the last half century and more. Under pressure from this or that state or national supersystem, programs are designed to meet projections of job needs that turn out to be inaccurate. We have witnessed, for instance, alternate overproduction and underproduction of engineers. In the early years of the 1970s, a whole generation of young people and faculty members is feeling the impact of the university's poor judgment in yielding so readily to these pressures. And as the decade moves forward, our society will have to pay a high price for the current cutback in the production of Ph.D.'s, elementary and secondary school teachers, and many other college-trained personnel prepared to work at jobs in the public sector of our economy.

Wiser administrators, therefore, are now lending support to an antivocational countertrend. This stance is based on an old truth: Even if vocational goals are to be stressed, programs should nonetheless still develop the general interests and abilities of the student. They should strive to make students, upon completing their studies, employable in a more general way. Otherwise we will repeat one of the great failures of the past decade, the preparation of students for specific jobs that have ceased to exist by the time the training is completed. In programs training young people for middle-management posts, particularly, this countertrend manifests itself in the acceptance of the principle that development of a personally effective individual, with breadth of view and good communications skills, is a more important goal than training in specific techniques. The countertrend is based on a blurring of the distinction between vocational education and liberal education.

But this countertrend appears, at present, to be stronger at the verbal level than at the level of actual practice. The principle will likely gain support from administrators during the remaining years of the 1970s, and it will generally be agreed that an education for the future must emphasize problem-solving techniques, abilities that a person needs when he meets new situations, attitudes that are appropriate to change, and skills in observation, analysis, and communication. Yet the principle probably will not be translated into action at most campuses. It probably will not enter into the daily life of the teaching-learning process in most courses, especially in the natural sciences fields and in most departments in the social sciences. Most college teachers, a decade hence, will likely still teach toward the goals that dominate most courses now—mastery of certain bodies of cognitive knowledge and proficiency in specific practical skills. Even within this conventional framework, however, and even though many professors will fail as teachers, there will be some who will achieve excellence, either as teacher-craftsmen or as teacher-artists.

In recent years there have also been other pressures on the university to modify its goals. In the years after 1959, and especially in the years after 1964, an increasingly vocal segment of the student body in American higher education, joined by a liberal and radical faculty segment, has demanded that the university itself become an agent for social action in American society. Arguments against such goals for the university, presented by most conservative as well as many liberal faculty members, are now predominant on most campuses. The prevailing view asserts that the university must not compromise its primary intellectual responsibility, that it must not allow special interests to make it their pawn, and that it must not become subservient to political pressures. If the university associates itself intimately with the community and with pressing current problems, many academicians fear that it will fail in its more important intrinsic goals—the discovery of new knowledge, the synthesis of the new knowledge with the old, and the reinterpretation of the whole body of knowledge. While this view is now dominant in American higher education and most campuses are quiet (to those who lived through the 1960s on American campuses, this euphemism is full of significance), there are still large numbers of students and faculty members who assert that the scholar's duty is not to pursue the truth for its own sake but for society's sake. The scholar's work, they say, must be devoted not only to truth but to human needs, and the scholar's duty thereby becomes inevitably coupled to social issues. In response to the argument that the university must not become politicized, they declare that it has already become deeply politicized, because it reflects, on the whole, the ideology and the vested interests of those who hold political power.

Will these issues revolving around politicization affect the behavior of professors in the humanities disciplines? The likelihood is that, no matter how these issues affect out-of-class faculty behavior, they will not have significant impact on teaching styles or on student-instructor roles in the classroom.

Goals Unique to a University

During our interviews with professors, especially those that we held after 1970, we discovered that a large number of faculty members in humanistic studies desired a return to the goals that are intrinsic to the university. What are these goals? What are the unique goals of the American university, those for which no other institution in the society has responsibility? There are four of them, and they all revolve around knowledge—its discovery, its synthesis, its transmission, and its application.

Discovering new knowledge. This basic university goal is often spoken of as its research goal, and sometimes the terms *basic research* and *pure research* are used to distinguish this goal from the goal of applying new knowledge. (Discovering new knowledge is occasionally called "researchism" when it consists mainly of the discovery of insignificant bits of knowledge or the pseudo-discovery of significant bits.) The process is also called *scholarship.* Those people associated with the university who pursue this goal are usually called researchers or, less frequently, scholars.

Synthesizing knowledge. After knowledge is discovered, it must be assimilated into the already-existing body of knowledge. While new knowledge is in some sense added to old knowledge, this process is not additive. Indeed, if the new knowledge is significant, a reinterpretation of the total body of knowledge is required. Insofar as the work of the researcher or scholar is concerned, this second goal is crucial—it is at the very center of scholarly activity. Every researcher of high reputation in the academic world starts with the second goal, moving from it to the first and back again to the second. The second goal is distinctively different from the first, however, and it is the central goal. Yet we do not seem to have special terms by which we normally distinguish the two goals. There are a number of professors on every campus who concentrate on the second goal and depend on other colleagues in their fields to perform the first. They are generally regarded by their colleagues as bona fide scholars, even though they may not have national reputations if they do not publish. If their scholarly activity results in publication, it also is called research. However, the more typical kind of research upon which a professor's reputation as a scholar depends (and upon which his promotions are based in the university's reward system) stems primarily from activity directed toward the first goal. Nonetheless, when publication results from activity directed toward the second goal, the author often enjoys the highest prestige among scholars in the field. We are, of course, referring here to the important synthesizing works of scholarship in each of the disciplines, not to textbooks. The typical textbook never presents a new or original synthesis of knowledge in a field. The most widely used textbooks in any field usually lag behind current scholarship, because the framework they present must be old enough to have become generally accepted by most faculty members in the field. Textbook writing has low status among many scholars.

Transmitting knowledge. The third of the goals intrinsic to the university is the instructional goal, transmitting knowledge to students. During the past decade there has been much complaint about the neglect of this central function of higher education. The relationship between this goal and the second goal is obvious: a university faculty member must be an excellent scholar, as defined by the second goal, before he can be an excellent instructor. Again, as in the relationship between the first and second goals, the second lies at the crux.

Applying knowledge. The fourth institutional goal is the application of knowledge to problems that exist off-campus, and it includes the transmission of knowledge to the off-campus personnel who are engaged in working at those problems. This goal is usually referred to as "community services" or "applied research." In the field of agriculture, this goal has had a venerable tradition on the American university campus. And in recent years, many university departments, especially in the natural and social sciences, have rendered service to government and other agencies in our society to help solve difficult social and technological problems, such as the deterioration of our cities, the population explosion, and dysfunction in the biosphere. This goal also includes the training of personnel working on these problems.

Although these four goals are intrinsic to the American university, they have not been kept "pure." They have taken different shapes as each university has responded to pressures, from its own internal systems and from the external supersystems of which it is a component. Each of these other entities has its own goals, and many of these are at variance with the university's intrinsic goals. And as the four goals come to be implemented—that is, as they are translated into structures and functions at any particular campus—they are sifted through the other sets of goals maintained by the giant supersystems. Only after the institutional goals have gone through this sieve, and have been modified by it, are they then translated into structures and functions on the campus. For this reason, they may appear as different goals at different institutions. The force of various pressures—and therefore the various modifications—depends on the kinds of relationships that exist between a given university and the larger supersystems in the educational establishment.

Goals of Giant Supersystems

What are these other goals that so strongly affect the intrinsic goals of the university? There are, first of all, the broad social goals of our society—plans and hopes for the disadvantaged, for our cities, for hot wars and cold, for our senior citizens, for the health and welfare of the general populace, for the education of the young, and so on—which are formulated by public figures (including legislators and governors) and crystallized by the communications media and other agencies. Second, there are national goals expressed by organizations that have been given (or have taken) specific responsibility for educational affairs. Examples of these organizations are the governmental and semigovernmental agencies that are charged with funding educational programs; the associations of colleges and universities that represent the overall interests of higher education establishment (the American Council on Education, for instance); and the consortia, associations, or official groups of colleges and universities that represent certain segments of institutions in higher education. (These groupings are by type, as in associations of private colleges, medical colleges, junior colleges, or graduate schools; or by location, as in the Great Lakes Colleges Association; or by joint enterprise on the basis of other principles, as in the Union of Experimenting Colleges.) All of these organizations, along with others, constitute giant supersystems which influence university goals and have an impact on individual university members.

A third set of goals arises from a wide range of profit-making organizations in the world of commerce, which share, as American business enterprises traditionally have, in the responsibility for decisions about higher education. They exert pressure on the university, urging it to modify its goals in directions dictated by the profit motive. This influence is felt in three distinct ways: through direct pressure on university personnel; through pressure on the public and on public officials, thereby affecting political decisions about the financing of higher education; and through the general influence of American business as it helps to shape the values of our entire culture. These commercial organizations and agencies plan our campus buildings and build them. They manufacture and sell the equipment, furniture, and supplies that we use on our campuses. They write, produce, and sell the programs designed for various educational media—the computer, film and television, the products of the printing press. This giant supersystem, then, includes the vast publishing world, with its powerful influence over curricula and teaching styles, as well as the agencies responsible for writing, producing, and selling examinations and tests, the instruments that determine which students enter into and exit from universities.

A fourth set of goals is generated by the various populations within the academic world. These are the goals—the often *different* goals—of students, academic deans, personnel officers, business managers, and officials who may not be on the university payroll (especially at public institutions) but who are nonetheless important members of the academic community, such as campus ministers. The interests of a particular faculty member, for instance, may be represented by the American Association of University Professors, the American Association for Higher Education, and a half dozen organizations concerned with his academic specialty. Student interests are represented by the National Student Asociation and many other organizations, trustees are represented by the Association of Boards of Governors, and institutional researchers are represented by the Association for Institutional Research. The list is virtually endless.

It is not hard to see why there is often a tug-of-war between functions created to carry out the intrinsic goals of the university and functions created in response to pressures from the various elements in the giant supersystems. The result is a confusion of goals that makes it difficult for the university teacher to do his job effectively.

Goals and Educational Reform

An understanding of the intrinsic goals of the university and the goals of the supersystems that surround the university—along with the nature of the degree system (see Chapter Nine)—suggests why educational reform is so difficult to achieve. Many would-be reformers offer an easy solution to the problem: If what we suffer from is severe dysfunction, they argue, then there is no cure for it but the immediate replacement of the old organizational structures with new structures that will allow— indeed, require—more efficient modes of functioning. Their argument is unassailable; but the change does not take place, for a vast irony keeps us where we are: like a human body rejecting a new and healthy heart to replace an old one no longer adequately serving, the university super- system rejects a substantially new structure if it comes ready-made. And if an attempt is made to build up such a structure from within the system, another obstacle arises: the system simply refuses to accommodate the very processes by which new structures might be developed.

The pattern of the degree system in American higher education, desgined for another society and another century, stubbornly resists all of our efforts to modify it. In the past, changes in the pattern came about because forces outside the educational establishment swept through it, creating emergencies of national stature. For example, the most important single cause of educational change in America during the years since World War II was the launching of Sputnik. But almost all of the changes caused by Sputnik in the standard degree system in America have now disappeared. The web in which we are caught has been almost entirely respun.

The situation would appear hopeless, and many university ad- ministrators believe that it is. But for the professor whose life is largely devoted to teaching students, the situation is by no means hopeless. Within the various dimensions of the degree system, even in the most conventional programs, it is possible for the individual professor to discover exciting and effective ways of educating people. It is quite possi- ble, even in the most conventional department, for the university profes- sor, working quietly within the domain of his own classroom, to become an artist.

Chapter 9

Dimensions of the Degree System

The degree system has six essential parts, which we shall call dimensions. These six dimensions are always present in any degree program—no matter what the nature of the program is, no matter how it is described by the teachers and learners involved in it, and no matter how it is conceived by the administrators who operate it. In this chapter we shall present and illustrate a theoretical model of the university degree system. It will describe each dimension of the degree system functionally, but at a high level of abstraction, so that it will fit all conceivable degree systems at any type of postsecondary educational institution.

The six dimensions of every degree system fall into two categories— "structural" and "implemental." The three structural dimensions would appear in any blueprint model as those we ordinarily associate with the term *curriculum;* they are structures that are planned before the system goes into operation. They differ qualitatively from the other three dimensions, which we call the implemental dimensions.

Structural Dimensions

Program content. The first dimension consists of the organization or patterning of the program that the student follows to obtain a degree, diploma, or certificate. This dimension consists of the entire complex of topics, problems, texts, and study areas that are sampled or systematically covered in the student's program—all of the kinds of knowledge that are formally transmitted to students as they move from entrance to exit in the system. The term *knowledge,* in this context, includes facts and principles, skills and abilities, attitudes and values, everything that a student (in any given curriculum) is expected to acquire, master, or internalize in order to earn his degree.

If a researcher or an administrator wants to describe an existing program or change it, or if he wants to build a brand new program, there are specific questions he must be able to answer about this first dimension of the program. The questions fall into three groups: First, what kinds of knowledge does the program include? Is there any priority given to any aspects of this knowledge? For example, facts, principles, concepts, and theoretical frameworks; special skills and abilities; attitudes and values (such as scientific objectivity, open-mindedness, tolerance for ambiguity). What principles determine which of these kinds of knowledge are included in the program? What principles determine which specific pieces of knowledge of each kind are included?

Second, in what order is this knowledge to be acquired by students? On the basis of what principles is a long-range sequence determined? For instance, does the student move from concrete, "experiential" data to generalizations, or does he move from general principles to the analysis of specific problems? What levels of complexity are included? And what principles determine how a course at one level of complexity is to be distinguished from a course of similar content at another level of complexity? (How, for example, does a lower division course in Shakespeare differ from an upper division course in Shakespeare?)

Third, in what ways does the program manifest unity and also permit variety? That is, what *principles,* on the one hand, give unity to the curriculum and encourage variety and diversity? And what are the *mechanisms,* on the other hand, which determine that each student's formal education is similar in certain basic ways to that of every other student and yet is differentiated from that of every other student and "individualized"?

A blueprint model of any program should supply answers to these questions in the description it gives of the program's first dimension.

Scheduling system. The second dimension encompasses all of the arrangements by which groups of learners gather in certain specified locations, together with one or more college officers, to take part in the teaching-learning process. In the standard American degree system, the basic entities in the second dimension are the "class" and the "private conference." They always involve at least one college officer. In programs following the standard model, classes, no matter how large, are normally taught by only one professor, although in some situations the regular professor's lectures may be supplemented by guest lecturers or he may be aided by one or more assistants. In certain nonstandard curricular-instructional settings, however, groups of students may regularly meet together for some purposes without a faculty member in attendance; and in certain other settings a single learner may be scheduled to meet with several faculty members at one time.

In a description of any existing or proposed program, only one major question need be answered about the shape of the second dimension: In the teaching-learning sessions taking place within the program, which students and teachers get together with which other students and teachers, when, how often, where, and for how long? Implicit in this question is a second question: What principles determine why the scheduling design should take *its* particular shape rather than another shape?

The second dimension includes all arrangements regarding space, time, and logistics for class sessions and for all other activities that are an official part of the educational process leading to the degree, such as field work and other off-campus experience. The second dimension may take many different shapes, depending on which principles are adopted. It is seriously affected by the adoption, for example, of the block scheduling of classes, a 4-1-4 calendar, the division of the student body into "primary groups" (see Chapter Eleven), independent study as general rather than exceptional practice, "reading periods" in the middle of a term, a work-study plan, or freshman seminar requirements. And each of these structures, if adopted, would affect other dimensions as well. As we shall see, the relationship between the second dimension and the fourth (which involves teaching styles) is particularly intimate—it is impossible to make a change in one without seriously affecting the other.

Grading and credit system. The third dimension includes all of the arrangements by which students are (a) judged, periodically during their progress toward the degree, to be of better or worse "quality," and (b) certified, finally, as having fulfilled the requirements for the degree. Technically defined, the third dimension consists of the standards by which, and the means whereby, students are periodically evaluated and then certified to be in good standing in the program. In the conventional model, they are "graded" for quality as they move through the program and are finally approved or not approved to receive the degree. The basic entities that lie in the third dimension in the standard model are the "unit of credit" and the "grade point."

Some questions whose answers determine the concrete shape of the third dimension in any given program are: Who makes the judgments that are required? For a given student, is it the same college officer who also carries out the teaching function? Or is it an individual or agency external to the teaching process? If it is the latter, is it an on-campus or off-campus person or agency? And if it is an on-campus person or agency, is it the student himself, a group of his peers, a student-faculty committee, or a group of faculty members only? When and how often are these judgments made? On the basis of what procedures? Is it primarily the quality of a written "bluebook"? Is it the time, effort, and energy spent in a course of studies? Or is it a demonstration of ability through "performance" tests? On the basis of what principles is a particular set of procedures adopted for grading and certifying students rather than another set of procedures?

There is, at present, no accredited college or university in the United States that does not award a degree or a certificate of some kind at the successful conclusion of specific curricula. Although there has been some talk, particularly in certain experimental settings, of "abolishing" the degree (see Chapter Ten), such a possibility is not likely to occur during the present century within most varieties of both standard and nonstandard curricular-instructional models. And as long as the degree continues to exist, there must also be some procedure for determining who receives it and who does not. The policy governing that procedure, and the structures that are built to carry out that policy, constitute the third dimension.

Relationships between Structural and Implemental Dimensions

The first three dimensions remain static structures only—part of the world of paper reality—until the three implemental dimensions come into existence. Until then the structural dimensions are sets of potentials. Considered in their most *general* form—that is, even before they become part of a blueprint model—each of the structural dimensions has a virtually unlimited number of possibilties for realization. If one contemplates how many different specific frameworks are possible for selecting and ordering curricular content (the first dimension), for scheduling times and spaces and people (the second dimension), or for grading and certifying students (the third dimension), one must conclude that the number of concrete possibilities for each dimension is, for all practical purposes, without limit.

The number of possibilities is vastly reduced, however, as soon as one of the structural dimensions reaches the blueprint-model stage—that is, as soon as it is designed and described in a university bulletin or in a curriculum plan. Its nature is then determined, and its scope limited, by the answers given to the questions which we have raised in our descriptions of the structural dimensions. But even at this stage, the final shape is not really fixed; a relatively large number of possibilities remain. At this point it is the professor, when he enters the classroom and begins his teaching, who further reduces the possibilities. Indeed, when his class is formed all possibilities—save one—are eliminated. Thus, two identical curricula at two similar campuses, or even two sections of the same course within one particular curriculum, can prove thoroughly different in final realization. To put it another way, structural dimensions may be described in identical terms, but real differences emerge as soon as the implemental dimensions come alive.

Each of the three structural dimensions is formally planned by one or more university officials, usually a group of administrators and faculty members working together. When it exists only on paper, of course, a structural dimension is not yet an actual structure; it is only a *set of potentials*. The three implemental dimensions, by contrast, are not built in advance and do not have identifiable paper existence (except in certain unconventional degree systems which will be described later). Each of these implemental dimensions constitutes a *set of conditions* under which the structural dimensions take their concrete form.

As we have pointed out, it may be convenient to regard the three structural dimensions as the *curricular* side of the degree program. The three implemental dimensions can be regarded, then, as the *instructional* side. These terms arise from a different, though very common, conceptual framework and reflect a mode of analysis that is not completely compatible with the systems approach. (This different mode views curriculum and instruction as separate and separable entities.) Nonetheless, it might be helpful at this stage to keep both sets of terms in mind: to regard each of the first three dimensions of the degree system as a planned structure constituting a set of potentials (in ordinary language, covered by the term *curriculum*) and to regard the three implemental dimensions as processes constituting the conditions under which the structural dimensions enter the world of existential reality (covered, in ordinary language, by the term *instructional process.*)

To summarize: The structural dimensions, once they are given paper reality, constitute sets of potentials. The realization of these potentials is limited by the paper description set forth for each dimension, but despite such limitations many possibilities for realization still remain. The number of these possibilities is further reduced by the conditions under which the dimension comes to be realized. These conditions are set—and set precisely—by the three other dimensions which we call implemental. When all six dimensions come together, the total dynamic process that is the degree system comes alive; an attempt to carry on the teaching and learning process actually occurs.

Implemental Dimensions

We are now ready to consider definitions of the three implemental dimensions.

Professor and student roles in teaching-learning sessions. The fourth dimension encompasses the relationships between members of the teaching-learning group during class sessions or any other scheduled meetings where the teaching-learning process occurs. These relationships, viewed externally, are of three sorts: those existing between the faculty member (or perhaps several faculty members) and each student; those existing between each student in the group and every other student; and those existing between the teaching-learning group and each of its members.

Unfortunately, many university professors, including some who have developed the art of university lecturing to a high level, are grossly insensitive to these relationships. A teacher who is sensitive to them is a witness to a whole world of events occurring in the class. He is aware of the various "roles" that members of the group play at various times during the class session: teaching and learning roles, leader and follower roles, cohesive and disruptive roles, traffic-cop roles, father and mother roles, dominance and submission roles, and more. He is also sensitive to timing: he sees when such roles are played, and by whom, and whether the roles change within sessions and between sessions or whether they remain relatively constant. If the roles change, he is sensitive to the possible causes of change, and he observes the circumstances under which the change occurs.

In the standard model, the role expected of the instructor and the role expected of the student are fairly well defined. They are distinctly different, and in most university classes they do not vary to any large extent from the beginning to the end of a course. But even in conventional programs, experimentation with these roles can easily take place within the class session.

It should be noted that the activities which lie in the fourth dimension are specifically those activities carried on by members of the teaching-learning group during the times when the group—or any subgroup of the total group—is in session. The fourth dimension does not include learning activities or relationships entered into at other times by individual members of the group. Those activities and relationships are analytically separable, and they constitute the fifth dimension.

Student out-of-class learning. In the fifth dimension lie the experiences which each learner undergoes as he prepares for the class meetings and other sessions that are scheduled in accordance with the pattern operating in the second dimension. The fifth dimension consists of the network of activities that students must pursue outside of actual class meetings and related group sessions if they are to make satisfactory progress in the program. (Decisions about student progress are, of course, made in accordance with the evaluation pattern that operates in the third dimension.)

Examples of fifth dimension activities are: studying textbooks, reading other books, working at a job, taking a field trip, traveling abroad, relating to people, relating to objects other than books, undergoing nonverbal experiences of various sorts, doing laboratory exercises in a nongroup setting. In the standard degree system model, fifth dimension activities are usually limited to contacts with books and book-related objects, although some courses require the student to undergo certain experiences with objects other than books, usually within a setting (such as a laboratory) which exists on the campus.

The fifth dimension thus includes the student's relationships to the world that exists outside the teaching-learning groups of which he is formally a member. Because the universe under consideration here is the degree system, the fifth dimension does not include relationships which exist outside that system—for example, relationships formed in extracurricular activities or in residence hall life. What the fifth dimension does include, then, is every relationship (in the world outside his actual classes) into which the student is required to enter because of the expectations which have been set in his classes by his teachers and his classmates. These expectations are created by the particular shapes taken by all of the other dimensions—and above all, by the roles played by the professor in the fourth dimension.

An analysis of the fifth dimension can be made by posing a formal question: What relationships come into being between (a) the student and (b) symbols, objects, and people outside the teaching-learning group as a result of the demands of the degree system? Or more simply: What sorts of experiences does the student feel he is expected to undergo as he *prepares* for class sessions, tests or examinations, and other course assignments? For example: Does he feel he is expected to undergo only book-oriented experiences? What role is played by experiences with media other than books—film, television, the computer? What is the role of objects other than direct study materials? What is the role of experiences with human beings other than faculty members or other students? Does the community surrounding the campus play a part in these experiences? Do deviant cultures? Do foreign civilizations? What part do nonverbal and irrational phenomena have in the student's experiences—or is the student expected to work entirely within conceptual and rational frameworks?

Power syndrome in the teaching-learning process. In the sixth dimension of the degree system lies a complex network of freedoms and controls. These freedoms and controls are exercised, in both subtle and overt ways, *by* the learners (over themselves and over their teachers) and *over* the learners (by other learners and teachers) as they move forward toward the degree. In the standard degree system model, power over all decisions affecting the course of classroom life, as well as out-of-class

preparations for that life, lies entirely in the hands of the professor. The
professor may, occasionally or often, delegate a portion of his authority
to his students, but he does so at his own will. The professor, however,
does not possess absolute power; he is accountable to his superior (in the
standard model, the department chairman) in the event that he is
charged (by a student, for example) with an abuse of his power or (by
his colleagues, for example) with undue permissiveness and a lowering of
standards.

The shape that the sixth dimension takes in any given curricular-
instructional situation can be described by the answers given to these
questions: Who has—or is given—responsibility for making what decisions? On the basis of what principles? (In other words: *Who* decides
what, and what *determines* who decides what?) Who has—or takes, or
is given—power over which aspects of the process? And who rewards or
punishes whom, and for what?

Relationships between the Moving Parts

When we think of the six dimensions of the degree system as six
very complex parts and then imagine them all to be simultaneously in
motion, the metaphor most likely to guide our thinking likens the system
to a machine. We find it natural to speak of the system's "moving parts,"
and to say that the system has "broken down" or is "running smoothly."
There is, of course, no way we can avoid metaphor, unless we want to
stop using language altogether, and it can be useful to speak of a system
as a machine if we are careful not to take this imagery literally.

To analyze how any system works requires two separate tasks. First,
there must take place an inquiry into the nature of its parts. Second, an
exploration must be made of the relationships of the parts while the
machine is in operation—that is, when the parts are in motion. The first
of these two tasks was already undertaken, at least in a preliminary way,
earlier in this chapter. The second task, if it were to be done thoroughly
and successfully, would necessarily extend beyond the scope of this book.
It should therefore be understood that we shall not be examining in
detail the whole of the machine. Our goal is to focus on one part of
the machine—the fourth dimension (professor and student roles in class
sessions)—although we shall inevitably deal with relationships between
the fourth dimension and the other dimensions of the degree system. And
since we cannot now examine in detail all of its parts in their intricate
workings, we shall end this chapter by giving some general illustrations
to show how various dimensions of the degree system interact.

Program content and scheduling system. Our first three illustrations deal with influences between the first and second dimensions. On

one campus, the all-college General Studies Committee recommended some fundamental changes in the institution's general studies courses. Among other things, the committee recommended a shift in the content of the course that served to fulfill the "general studies in humanities" requirement. The course, for some time, had been concerned exclusively with the history of civilization; but now the committee suggested that the course shift its content in order to emphasize creative activity on the part of the students—in short, to revise the course so that students would have the experience of creating art works instead of simply reading or talking about them. The change, to mention only a few of its consequences, affected the time and length of class meetings in the course, the number of students who could be assigned to any teaching-learning group in the course, the choice of faculty members to teach various sections of the course, the need for workshop space, and the increased use of off-campus facilities. To change the shape of the first dimension—the content of the course—in the particular way recommended by the committee also made it necessary to change the shape of the second dimension—the scheduling system—in certain fundamental ways.

A second illustration: On another campus, a small women's college, a set of "experimental" courses were being designed for freshman students by a group of faculty committees. At the first meeting with the central administration, the members of the faculty committees were told by the president "not to hesitate to seek *entirely new* educational models," but they were also told—by the dean of the college—that they "must work *absolutely* within the time schedule and the general class-size pattern" for courses which already existed on the campus—that is, within the conventional shape of the second dimension. That directive, then, decidedly limited the possibilities the committees might consider regarding the first dimension—the content of courses to be planned. Not a very promising beginning for planning a set of "experimental" courses!

The third illustration is a case brought to the Danforth Workshop on Liberal Arts during a recent summer. One of the liberal arts teams participating in the workshop reported that their institution had run into difficulties in an attempt to reform the freshman composition course. A year earlier, the college had decided to replace its old plan for teaching freshman composition (Plan X) with a new plan (Plan Y). But Plan Y had not been successful during its first year of operation, and the workshop team set out to discover what had gone wrong. Analysis soon revealed that Plan X had one undeniable advantage over Plan Y: it fit perfectly into the standard scheduling system. Plan X, therefore, could be realized—and could even achieve a certain standard of excellence within its limited range—because it required fifty-minute, three-times-per-week periods. Plan Y, however, required for its realization a combination of different class periods, ranging from thirty-minute sessions for drill-type exercises to three-hour sessions for weekly panel discussions in which figures from the off-campus community participated.

But this was by no means the whole story. For its realization, Plan X required for space nothing more than regular classrooms on campus, and almost any available room would do. But Plan Y, for its sessions, required several kinds of space—fairly small rooms for small-group give-and-take, larger rooms for general discussion, and ocasionally still larger rooms for the sessions in which figures from off-campus participated. Moreover, while Plan X involved only the grouping of freshman students, Plan Y involved senior students as well, for it required that each senior pursuing a major in English, as part of the senior's own work, must meet with a group of freshmen in seminar. And, further, Plan X required only one faculty member for each student group, while Plan Y, for certain of its sessions, sometimes required several faculty members (for faculty panel sessions) and sometimes no faculty members at all (for the sessions with seniors).

Plan Y had captured the imagination of the English faculty, and it had been adopted with enthusiasm. Yet it lasted for only one year. The changes that Plan Y made in course content were easy enough to effect; but they necessitated changes in scheduling—in space, time, and logistics—which could not be accommodated at that particular college. This is often the case with plans of this sort: the limitations of one dimension in the degree system reduce the possibilities that are effectively open for another. A faculty that wishes to reform its curriculum and its teaching strategies must take into consideration all of the dimensions that are to be affected by the reform.

Program content and student out-of-class learning. The next illustration involves relationships between the first and fifth dimensions. It is obvious that the content of a course will determine the kinds of experiences that students are encouraged to undergo outside the class sessions. What is not so obvious is that the professor can reverse this causal relationship. If a teacher wants the student to undergo certain kinds of outside experiences, he can select course content that requires the student to go through those experiences. Let us consider, for instance, the typical course dealing with a foreign culture. Such a course is likely to be primarily concept-centered, asking the student to master a set of facts, principles, concepts, special vocabularies, and theoretical frameworks formulated by scholars in the field. These are presented to the student via the printed page or through such extensions of the printed page as formal lectures. In this kind of course, the experiences to which the student is likely to expose himself outside the classroom are: memorization, reasoning, perception of logical relationships, verbalization, inquiry, and problem solving.

But consider what would happen in such a course if certain kinds of direct experiences with the foreign culture were to become readily available. If physical accessibility to the foreign culture became easy to arrange, what is the likelihood that the course content would be altered to take advantage of this new condition? Would the course of study now actually require contact with the foreign culture outside the classroom?

The answer is not always self-evident. At a recent conference, the director of an overseas program for American students took pains to show how "academic" his program was. His program, he pointed out, required students to spend practically all of their time in libraries, museums, study sessions, and classrooms at the foreign universities, or else studying in their rooms. His audience was persuaded, by the time he had finished, that students in his program, if they followed the prescriptions set down for them, would have no time left for anything but their academic work. The director of this program suggested, in fact, that students in the program who spent time chatting with people in the foreign environment, participating in the social events of the foreign community, or exploring life in general in the foreign setting were specifically made to feel that they were wasting their time. They were warned that if they did not study hard enough, but spent their time "fraternizing" with the native population, academic credit would be denied them.

Surely his standards were topsy-turvy. This book-oriented program made such great academic demands on students that it prevented them from taking advantage of their physical location. Would it not have made better sense to modify the course content so that the students would be *required* to work directly in and with the foreign community, studying it systematically? Could not some of the students' time have been spent directly—through field experiences—studying some aspects of the demographic, legal, literary, historical, anthropological, political, and social characteristics of the foreign culture? This illustration shows how the first dimension can be shaped in such a way as to allow only one possible shape for the fifth dimension—in this case, a narrow and inappropriate one.

Case study: Frank, who pleaded in vain to be put on probation. The next illustration highlights certain relationships between the third and sixth dimensions—the grading and credit system and the power syndrome in the teaching-learning process. The following incident occurred some years ago when a student, whom we shall call Frank, was enrolled as a freshman at the College of the University of Chicago. At that time in the College, courses ran for three quarters and students typically completed four courses during one academic year. If students followed a normal time schedule, they took four final examinations (called the comprehensives), each six hours in length, at the close of the spring quarter. To aid students in preparing for the comprehensives, mid-term examinations (called quarterlies) were given in each course at the end of the autumn and winter quarters; these examinations were for advisory purposes only and were not officially required.

When the end of the autumn quarter came, Frank found himself unprepared and elected not to take the quarterlies. When he told his advisor at the close of the winter quarter that he again had no intention of taking the quarterlies, his advisor became concerned about whether Frank was learning to take responsibility for getting his own work done. At the beginning of the spring quarter, he told Frank that it might be well for him to be placed on probation, and Frank agreed that some such drastic means had to be taken in order to set him straight.

It was possible in the College of the University of Chicago for a student to prepare for the comprehensives by studying independently. Frank and his advisor consequently worked out, as the conditions of probation, an arrangement whereby Frank would take two of his four comprehensives in June and the remaining two in August, after a summer of independent study. Frank also agreed that if he failed to meet the conditions of the probation—if he did not take and pass the examinations as arranged—he would not continue his studies at the university. As it turned out, Frank was able to take the four difficult comprehensives according to the agreed-upon schedule, and he made high grades.

During Frank's sophomore year, the freshman-year pattern began to repeat itself. He did not feel prepared to take either the autumn or winter quarterlies, and at the opening of the spring quarter, he asked his advisor if he could be put on probation again. This time, however, the advisor refused. He tried to persuade Frank that a student ought not develop such a strong dependence upon external coercion, and he maintained that Frank should retain his freedom and be responsible for his own decisions. Moreover, he said, he did not want Frank to develop the habit of casting himself in the role of hero in life-or-death dramas.

Frank was dismayed. "But I'm *requesting* you to put me on probation," he said. "I'll never make it alone. I need that help."

"No, you don't," the advisor said, and he was adamant. So was Frank, who insisted on petitioning the Dean of Students to grant him probationary status. But the Dean of Students confirmed the advisor's recommendation, and Frank was not put on probation. He went through a period of anxiety (as did his advisor), but he took two of his sophomore comprehensives in June and the other two in August, as he had done the previous year, and again made high grades. He later entered a hospital internship after completing his medical studies with great distinction.

What this story tells us is that Frank's development as a student, and as a person, was forcibly helped by an unconventional solution to a problem that lay in the sixth dimension. This solution was possible in the relatively nonstandard degree system at Frank's college, but it would not have been within the realm of possibility in the standard degree system which operates at most campuses. This story illustrates not only the subtle relationships between the third and the sixth dimensions, but also the intimate relationships that exist between the various systems that, working together, constitute the supersystem that is a university. In this instance, two particular systems crisscrossed—the degree system and the advising system.

Case study: Richard, whose off-campus course project raised moral and academic questions. Our final illustration involves relationships between the third, fifth, and sixth dimensions—the grading and credit system, student out-of-class learning, and the power syndrome in the teaching-learning process—as well as several systems that lie outside the degree system. But before we present the concrete illustration, let us briefly pose some general questions about the supervision of off-campus projects. To what extent should the individual student in such programs carry responsibility for undertaking and carrying through his own off-campus project? How is he to be rewarded? How, for example, is a professor to grade members of subgroups within the teaching-learning group who share responsibility in a joint project—especially if unequally talented students are working together and their contributions are unequal? Furthermore, how is the problem of supervision of projects to be solved, especially if the project is not institutionalized in an off-campus agency? For example, how can control be exercised over a student who wishes to do a course project that will include some direct experiences with a nonconformist group in the off-campus world—let us say, a student commune in which group sex is a regular practice?

Many of these questions arose in the case of Richard's off-campus project in the Experimental Freshman Program at San Francisco State College, during its first year of existence. Richard presented a plan for an off-campus project in which he proposed "to study sex practices among employees on board a passenger ship." He had already made arrangements to work, during the several weeks scheduled for off-campus projects, on a passenger ship as a dishwasher. The project was to be based partly on direct experience and partly on scholarly research. Richard did, in fact, carry out extensive book research before he joined the crew of the ship; and once on board, he systematically gathered information by means of a modified interview technique. After he returned to campus, he wrote an extensive, analytic, well-documented paper on the subject.

When Richard first informally proposed the project, the program director said that he would not even consider the proposal unless Richard discussed the entire matter with his parents. Richard's father, it is interesting to note, is a well-known sociologist. Parental permission was given, and the program director received an excellently formulated proposal from Richard.

It is foolish to suppose that either Richard's parents or his professors could have exercised any real control over his behavior in this matter. In terms of the third and sixth dimensions, it was of course within the power of Richard's professors to deny academic credit for such a project as he proposed. But he was determined to undertake the project—with or without academic credit. Their denial of credit would probably have led to a confrontation; even if it had not, it certainly would not have kept Richard from carrying out the project on his own. Moreover, a confrontation on the issue of academic credit appeared pointless in the circumstances because, clearly, it would have served only to hide the larger moral issues involved. Richard's parents—whom the project director consulted by telephone—did not feel that the experience would be harmful for their son. In fact, they believed it would be helpful. Some of Richard's professors thought it would be helpful, too.

There still remained the problem of how academic credit could be given. Since Richard was physically removed from the area in which he could be observed, there was no practical way either to supervise his project or evaluate his experience—except on the basis of his own oral or written report. Fortunately, as we have said, Richard produced an excellent report, which satisfied those members of the faculty who had insisted that no amount of chatting with wine stewards about their sex lives on the ship, even if dignified by an "interview schedule," should earn academic credit. Other faculty members had insisted that the crucial part of this learning experience was the slice-of-life activity that Richard had planned and had actually lived through, not the ivory-tower activity of preparing an academic report. They were satisfied, too, because the faculty of the program had accepted the director's suggestion that they need not, in fact, decide whether academic credit was being given to Richard for his "experience" or for his report. As it happened, there was no need for them to settle the philosophic and moral issues brought up by the original proposal.

The foregoing illustrations suggest the complexity of the relationships between the moving "parts" of the degree system. They also show that the degree system, with its infinite capacity for assuming different shapes, is not an independent universe. As we have already seen, the degree system is part of a network of coordinate systems; it affects those other systems and is, in turn, affected by them. Every change we make—or try to make—in any one of the systems has repercussions, which are often unpredictable.

The most important feature of the supersystem that is a university is the constantly dynamic quality of the whole. This quality renders cause-and-effect relationships all but impossible to trace. Organizational charts notwithstanding, change does not take place linearly. To envisage how it does take place, let us solicit the aid of one more metaphor: a hydraulic system made up of many connected pipes filled with liquid. In a hydraulic system, any increase in pressure, anywhere in the system, increases the pressure on all of its parts, often forcing breaks in pipes in areas where breaking may be totally unexpected. The university's "pipes" respond to pressure in the same way. A new freshman curriculum, for example, may create sharp repercussions in the advising system or may result in a new demand for changes in tenure and promotion practices.

With this new metaphor in mind, we are ready to consider in some detail various aspects of educational change. The chapters of Part Four ask what structural changes in higher education—if any—will probably be taking place during the next decade and whether they will affect the professional lives of university teachers in the humanities.

April 16. *Away! Away!*

The spell of arms and voices: the white arms of roads,
their promise of close embraces and the black arms of tall
ships that stand against the moon, their tale of distant nations.
They are held out to say: We are alone—come. And the voices
say with them: We are your kinsmen. And the air is thick with
their company as they call to me, their kinsman, making
ready to go, shaking the wings of their exultant and terrible
youth.

April 26. *Mother is putting my new secondhand*
clothes in order. She prays now, she says, that I may learn in
my own life and away from home and friends what the heart
is and what it feels. Amen. So be it. Welcome, O life! I go to
encounter for the millionth time the reality of experience and
to forge in the smithy of my soul the uncreated conscience
of my race.

April 27. *Old father, old artificer, stand me now and*
ever in good stead.

James Joyce
A Portrait of the Artist as a Young Man

PART IV

The University Teacher
and Educational Reform

Planned changes in the curricular-instructional pattern are of two distinct kinds: those which can be made within the standard degree-system model, and those which cannot. Since the term *innovative*, as it is ordinarily used, refers to both of these two kinds of change, we shall make distinctions between them with the help of adjectives and various descriptive phrases before the word *innovative*. When we say that a program is "mildly innovative," we shall refer to the kind of moderate educational reform that has been made at many campuses since World War II—the kind of change that attempts to institutionalize improvement without in any significant way modifying the basic system. And when we speak of "radical innovation," we shall refer to the kind that makes necessary fundamental changes in one or more dimensions of the degree system and which therefore, in one way or another, changes the shape of all the dimensions. A synonym for this type of radically innovative program is *experimental*.

Generally speaking, at campuses that follow the standard degree-system model, whether or not mild innovation is introduced, professors are not encouraged, either by the shape of the structural dimensions or by the faculty reward system, to use any teaching modes but the con-

181

ventional ones. This is not to say that a professor cannot become an artist at teaching within the patterns of the conventional teaching styles—we have seen in Part One that he *can*—but the fact remains that a teacher's options for personally reforming the fourth dimension (his roles in the classroom) are fewer if the degree system pattern within which he is working is conventional.

There are more than 2500 universities in the United States—that is, accredited institutions of higher education. Of this number, how many have departed, in some fundamental way, from the conventional model of the degree system? Probably about 250, perhaps less—about one-tenth of the total number. When we compare the number of faculty members involved in such programs with the total number of American professors, we obtain an extremely meager proportion. To illustrate: California State University, San Francisco (CSUSF) is fairly typical of the large public institutions whose programs follow the standard degree system model. Many mild innovations have been introduced at CSUSF, but these have easily been accommodated within the conventional model. The faculty of CSUSF is about *fifty* times the size of the faculty of Justin Morrill College, which is one of the best known of the experimenting schools—schools that have departed from the standard curricular-instructional model. It is safe to say, therefore, that over 95 percent of faculty members now engaged in teaching humanistic subjects are working in programs that follow the conventional model.

In view of this fact, it might be well to review what we have said in Part Three about the major characteristics of the standard degree system model. Each of the following characteristics correlates with one of the six dimensions of the degree system:

1. In describing a conventional degree program, it is easiest and most natural to tell what *courses* (or what kinds of courses) the student must complete satisfactorily in order to earn his degree or diploma or title. There is usually a prescribed pattern to be followed, with a certain number of courses required in a single field (typically called a major) and a certain number of courses required in other fields according to some principle of the "distribution" of courses among fields.

2. Each of these courses, when actually offered, becomes a *class* (or sometimes several classes, as in the case of multisection courses). These classes are so scheduled that, with few exceptions, one faculty member is assigned to and is entirely responsible for each one. (In multisection courses, all of the instructors teaching the various sections may make some joint decisions, and there may even be some common activities, like weekly lectures, that their students all attend together.)

3. The work of each student in every class is officially evaluated by the professor who teaches the class—and by him alone. His task is to

assign each student a "grade" that symbolizes the quality of achievement. There are usually five categories of these grades, but there may be as few as three or as many as seven in some varieties of the standard grading system. There may also exist a supplementary system consisting of only two categories, in which instance, under certain limited conditions, students may opt for the simpler and less competitive system. If a student's work in a course is deemed satisfactory, he receives a specified number of points or units of *credit* toward the degree. When he has accumulated the required number of credit units in the proper pattern of distribution among fields, he receives his degree or diploma or title.

4. The student and faculty ethos defines a distinct role for the professor in the classroom as well as a distinct role for the student, and there are strong pressures for professors and students to limit themselves only to these conventional classroom *roles*.

5. The activity that students engage in, as they prepare for their classes and the course examinations, is expected to be of an *academic caliber*—that is, the student must reach a certain level of complexity in performing assigned activities that are conceptual, rational, analytic, and usually oriented almost exclusively to books and other printed materials. This expectation pervades even courses that stress performance skills, such as certain courses in music, drama, art, and dance.

6. Both the professoriate and the student body understand and accept, without much question, that the faculty member is in absolute control (or virtually so) in determining what he and the students do during the class hour, and in setting requirements for out-of-class activity for the student who wishes to earn credit. While the professor may delegate some of this *power,* allowing students to make some choices for themselves or to make some decisions affecting the class, all parties understand that it is within the professor's right not to do so if that is his preference.

These, then, are the six major aspects of the degree system as it manifests itself in the standard model in the American university. Of all faculty members now teaching in the humanistic disciplines, over 95 percent work in conventional programs—that is, programs that follow the standard model. The chapters of Part Four ask whether this situation is likely to change during the coming decade. Will campuses feel pressure to depart from the standard pattern to any greater extent than they have been willing to do during the past decade? The answer, we believe, is that such pressure will increase, but that what happens in university classrooms will not be affected. The major pressures for reform during the next ten or more years will not be directed to courses taught by professors in university classrooms. The pressures will be manifested most visibly in an increase of "nontraditional" study courses, where students will acquire a body of cognitive knowledge or a set of skills—and receive academic credit toward their degrees—without having to sit in a classroom at all.

If the pressures exerted in favor of institutionalizing nontraditional study are successful, there will be three probable consequences: (1) More students will pass through the degree system and will be served by a smaller number of faculty members. (2) Certain kinds of courses will eventually no longer be taught in the classroom setting—courses emphasizing elementary skills, for example, such as lower division language courses; or courses imparting purely informational knowledge, like the survey courses that cover the major names, works, and events of Western philosophy, music history, or the British novel. (3) All of the other types of university courses now taught by professors in the humanistic disciplines will be offered in the curricula of humanities programs; they will look very much as they do now—except, of course, for the updating of course content—and they will be taught in very much the same way.

The chapters of Part Four show us that, during the next decade, educational reforms of various kinds will take place on most campuses. But from the perspective of the humanities professor and his teaching responsibilities, the old French proverb will still apply: *Plus ça change, plus c'est la même chose.* The more it changes, the more it stays the same.

Chapter 10

Reform in the Grading System

Almost a decade has passed since the Free Speech Movement at the Berkeley campus of the University of California gained national attention. During this decade, attitudes toward the conventional grading system have undergone a whole cycle of change. In the 1960s, a large proportion of students and a powerful and highly verbal segment of faculty members strongly protested against the standard grading system. But now, on almost all campuses that follow the standard degree system model, the grading system is accepted once again.

The old system emerged from the 1960s almost totally intact. A minor change has been incorporated on most campuses—a supplementary grading system that is still basically competitive, which may be used under special circumstances—but this reform has had little effect on the shape of the third dimension (the grading and credit system) or the sixth dimension (the power syndrome). Except at the small number of colleges and universities which have had the courage to abandon it altogether, the conventional grading system, by allowing itself to undergo some minor changes, has everywhere survived every serious effort to reform it. The consequence is that it still has a powerful impact on the entire shape of American higher education.

In this chapter we shall explore some of the ways that the grading system (the third dimension) has come again—now, in the 1970s—to exert a subtle but unmistakable influence over the content of academic courses (the first dimension), over the styles in which courses are taught (the fourth dimension), and over the total reward-and-punishment system—that is, the power syndrome (the sixth dimension).

Erosion of Grading Reform

Within the last decade, the year in which protest against the grading system reached its highest point was 1968. In that year, Judson Jerome, the director of the "Inner College" program at Antioch College, wrote in *Life:* "If schools and colleges got out of the certification business, they might be able to educate more forcefully—leaving the testing to prospective employers and graduate schools."[1] Jerome raised an important and fundamental question: Should colleges grant degrees at all? If we stopped granting degrees and merely provided transcripts, he wondered, would it make any *practical* difference to graduate schools or employers? He argued that it would not. It would, however, make a great difference to the colleges, for the college degree, as Jerome pointed out, "is the keystone of the arch, and perhaps the one we ought to remove first if we plan any serious rebuilding. . . . If the degree is only a political agreement among faculty contending for a student's time, we have a moral obligation to undermine it."

Only a few months before Jerome's arguments appeared in *Life,* a student at the University of California in Berkeley, Brian McGuire, told 300 Phi Beta Kappa members attending an initiation banquet: "I have been informed that I have the highest grade point average of any graduating senior in the College of Letters and Science. The first thing I would like to say to you is that it was not worth it. My compulsive effort for a high grade point in my years at Berkeley contributed to an almost total alienation of myself from other people."[2] McGuire "electrified his audience," according to the *San Francisco Chronicle,* and he received a standing ovation at the close of his speech, after he had recommended that "grades should be totally abolished."

In view of some studies of grading practices that had just then been completed at McGuire's own campus, it came as no surprise that his statements were so well received. As we have said, distrust of the standard grading system had sharply increased during the years after the Free Speech Movement, the years between 1964 and 1968. A study involving more than 2500 Berkeley students, for example, showed that half of the respondents did not believe grades reflected even "fairly well" an indivi-

---

[1] Judson Jerome, "The System Really Isn't Working," *Life,* 5 (18), November 1, 1968, pp. 68–69.
[2] *San Francisco Chronicle,* May 17, 1968, p. 14.

dual's accomplishments in a course. Even the students most rewarded by the grading system—those with the highest grade point averages—did not think well of it. The Muscatine Report, *Education at Berkeley,* which appeared in 1966, voiced particular concern about the opinion of this honors group: "When two-fifths of an honors level student sample expressed such significant disbelief in the system which rewarded them, it is surely time to reconsider not only the grading system itself, but the increasing emphasis which we are pressed to place upon it."[3] And it was not only students who were dissatisfied with the grading system. Most faculty members who read the Muscatine Report, especially those in humanistic studies, must certainly have felt empathy with the professor who testified: "Grading is a nightmare."[4]

The poison of grading-system pressures seeped into student-student relationships as well. "Instead of encouraging me to form human bonds with my fellow students," honors student McGuire said, "the grade-oriented system of the University of California made it possible and sometimes comfortable for me to become caught up in the prison of my mind." The sense of personal loss felt by McGuire was so widely shared during those years by students at American educational institutions as to be almost universal. "I am anonymous—help me!" said a button that students wore in 1968.

But by 1972, the button had disappeared. So had most of the protest against the traditional grading system. And except on a handful of campuses, the grading system was not, to any practical extent, reformed. What happened?

On the basis of the principles set down in Part Three there is only one possible explanation: any program attempting to institute a fundamental grading system reform—attempting, that is, to reshape the third dimension—is doomed to failure, after the initial enthusiasm has waned, unless other dimensions in the system are also reshaped in ways that will support the new shape of the third dimension. The failure of grading system reform on American campuses can be explained only by the failure of the professoriate to change other dimensions in the degree system, especially the kinds of abilities and knowledge that students are expected to master (the first dimension), the way the professor behaves in the classroom or lecture hall (the fourth dimension), and the total power syndrome surrounding degree-system relationships (the sixth dimension). To see some of these multidimensional interrelationships at work, let us consider actual examples from our interview files. The first two examples

[3] University of California, Berkeley, Select Committee of the Academic Senate (Charles Muscatine, chairman), *Education at Berkeley* (Berkeley: University of California Press, 1966), p. 95.
[4] *Education at Berkeley,* p. 96.

illustrate relationships between the third dimension (the grading system) and the sixth dimension (the power syndrome).[5]

The Grading System and the Power Syndrome

Bliss Harrison, as we shall call him, is an eccentric English professor who is quite advanced in years, highly opinionated, and a considerable "power" in his department. He regards himself (and is generally regarded by his colleagues) as an excellent teacher. We visited his classes and also interviewed him several times.[6] In one of our interviews, he told us that he strongly believes in the conventional grading system. In the course of our conversation on the subject, he surprised us by saying that he was "proud" (his word) that he had given one of his best students, a young man named Powell, a C for a course grade, even though the level of Powell's performance in the course was equal to that of other students to whom he had given a grade of A. Professor Harrison's reason: "He hardly had to lift a finger to turn out that kind of performance. He did everything *effortlessly*." As our conversation continued and Professor Harrison described Powell's "casual attitude," he became angry, and he finally almost shouted at us: "No student of mine is going to get away with being a lazy slob if I can help it. I won't *let* him get away with that!"

It soon became clear to us that Professor Harrison, in his capacity as judge, paid less attention to a student's level of achievement at the close of a semester than to certain other criteria of an almost moral nature—specifically, to considerations of how hard the student worked, and the amount of time and energy he expended in studying for the course. We do not wish to oversimplify his view—for he is not a simple-minded person—but it can perhaps be summarized in this way: Professor Harrison believes that hard work is in itself good; that learning is hard work; that hard work is necessarily painful (although it may result in pleasure); and that hard work, like all other painful activities, is naturally avoided by everyone whenever possible—unless external pressures compel one to pursue it. Professor Harrison has a conception of the *polarity* of work and play that makes it impossible for him to believe that the two

[5] These two cases were first reported in J. Axelrod, "The Creative Student and the Grading System," in Paul Heist (Ed.), *The Creative College Student: An Unmet Challenge* (San Francisco: Jossey-Bass, 1969).

[6] In the technical language used in Part One of this book, Professor Harrison would probably be called a follower of the Principles-and-facts Prototype. However, project researchers who visited his classes concluded (to quote from their report) that "he followed the Prince-Prototype but illustrated a didactic approach in so many significant ways that we wondered whether he should be classified at all as an evocative teacher."

can merge in any life activity.[7] He is therefore suspicious of any kind of learning that a student has fun doing. He also often reminds students in his classes that there is a clear distinction to be made between a novel (or a play or a poem) that is an "artwork" and one that is an "entertainment." He does not object if a student spends a certain amount of time enjoying entertainments, but he believes that the pleasure yielded by them is sufficient reward in itself and that academic credit should not be given for such activity.

We soon understood why Professor Harrison could not have given Powell an A. He reserves the grade of A for students who suffer pain and make sacrifices while preparing their assignments. Powell had not suffered and was therefore not rewarded. This case illustrates what can happen when a certain ethical view, accompanied by a high sense of certainty, not to say pig-headedness, combines with absolute power. The instructor plays certain roles as judge—and for all practical purposes, final authority— which in turn affect his roles as teacher and as critic of students.

Not far from the college where Professor Harrison teaches, there is a large public university where we interviewed a professor of philosophy, William Kaye. Professor Kaye's views of the traditional grading system stand in sharp contrast to Professor Harrison's. These views emerged during conversations we had with Professor Kaye about his teaching assistant, a young man named Morton. When we met Morton, we were impressed by his general intelligence, and we were aware that Professor Kaye held him in high regard. Professor Kaye told us, in fact, that Morton was one of the most brilliant graduate students and one of the best assistants he had ever had. And we discovered that there was a story behind their relationship.

According to Professor Kaye, Morton had been, as an undergraduate, "a peculiar student"—He seemed capable of doing A work but consistently performed at the mid-B or low-B level. Professor Kaye became curious: he made some inquiries of his colleagues and discovered that they held similar views of Morton's ability but also gave him B grades. From our interview with Professor Kaye:

PROFESSOR KAYE: There was something there, but nobody tried to find out what it was. Everybody simply said that Morton wasn't working up to capacity. Such students, you know, are a dime a dozen around here, and nobody was particularly surprised about this one case, and nobody was particularly moved to do anything about it. In

[7] See David Riesman, Joseph Gusfield, and Zelda Gamson, *Academic Values and Mass Education* (New York: Doubleday, 1970), especially Chapter Seven, "Teaching Styles and the Polarity of Work and Play."

fact, what *needed* to be done? Morton didn't present a *problem* to anyone. Why should anyone on the faculty worry about him? We had enough on our hands with student discontent and everything else.

INTERVIEWER: But *you* did something.

K: Yes. I had a whole series of conferences with Morton, and I could see that there was some kind of hang-up. He had such great flashes of insight sometimes, and they were exciting when they happened. I came to the conclusion that the level of his work was being kept down by some sort of unreal view he had of himself. He thought of himself as just a B-minus student. It had never occurred to him that he might be capable of getting an A.

I: He had a distorted view of his own potential. And he got it from his teachers in the first place, too, I'll bet.

K: More than likely. But I was feeling experimental that semester, and I thought, "Oh, what the hell—it won't do any harm," and I gave him an A in the course he was taking with me. Even though he didn't deserve it. I thought maybe if I gave him an A, it would help him to see himself as capable of A work.

I: You mean you gave him an A even though he hadn't done A work in the course?

K: Yes. He didn't deserve it, but I gave him an A, anyway.

I: And it worked!

K: Well, who is to say what works? Something did. In any case, he was eventually admitted to graduate school, and he is now one of the brightest students around here.

I: But let's speculate for a minute. What if your plan hadn't worked? If the A hadn't given Morton the impetus he needed, would you have felt guilty?

K: Guilty? About what?

I: About compromising the standards of the grading system. About having lowered the standards of the university.

K: Alfred North Whitehead had the answer to that. This is from the *Dialogues.* [Reading.] "I am profoundly suspicious of the 'A'-man. He can say back what you want to hear in an examination, and . . . you must give him his A if he says it back; but the ability, not to say the willingness, to give you back what is expected of him argues a certain shallowness and superficiality. Your 'B'-man may be a bit muddle-headed, but muddle-headedness is a condition precedent to independent creative thought in the first stage. Of course it may get no farther than muddle-headedness. But when my colleagues chaff me for giving more A's than they are willing to do and tax me with tenderheartedness, I reflect that I would rather not have it on my head that I was the one who discouraged an incipient talent."[8]

The cases of Professor Harrison and Professor Kaye illustrate interesting and complex relationships between the power syndrome within the degree system (the sixth dimension) and the grading practices of these particular professors (the third dimension). Powell deserved an A but was not given one by Professor Harrison, while Morton did not deserve an A but was given one by Professor Kaye. Both professors exercised virtually absolute power in grading and used that power in the service of entirely different principles. Powell was not given an A because Professor Harrison believed that college study should be hard work and that Powell had not worked hard. Morton received an A because Professor Kaye was convinced that a professor could (and occasionally should), with conscious intent, use grades not to symbolize the quality of the student's past accomplishment but to encourage the student in his future efforts. In both cases, the professors gave grades on the basis of these widely differing criteria without asking anyone's approval and without questioning their supreme right to act exactly as they saw fit.

The absolute power of the faculty member, even in that most sacred of all academic realms, course grades, has of course been called into question during the past ten years. The absolute power of the professor—the encouragement the academic tradition gave him, for example, to adopt the "student-as-nigger" attitude in his relationships with his students—was first challenged by organized student protest in the years immediately following the Free Speech Movement. And now that student protest has abated, the absolute power of the professor over certain aspects of the degree system is again being challenged, quietly but seriously, from other quarters. Our next illustration deals with the pressures university administrators exert on the professor to conform to their views on the subject of grading.

Combating "Lax" Standards

According to *The Chronicle of Higher Education,* the campuses of the University of California now prepare annual reports to show the grade distribution in every department, indicating the percentage of each letter grade awarded to students enrolled in each department's courses. The Los Angeles campus (UCLA), the *Chronicle* article states, has gone even further: until last year, it placed reports on the undergraduate grade distribution given by each faculty member in the teacher's personal

---

[8] Lucien Price (Ed.), *Dialogues of Alfred North Whitehead* (Boston: Little, Brown, 1954), p. 46.

dossier.[9] This practice was attacked by the American Federation of Teachers (AFT) and other faculty groups on the campus, and the president of the local AFT charged that an attempt to regulate the grade distribution for any professor "violates academic freedom and intrudes improperly into the professional activities of teaching faculty."[10]

California's other university system is equally concerned with grading standards. The Chancellor of the California State University and Colleges has condemned the "drift toward lax grading," the *Chronicle* report says, and the system's trustees have initiated a study to determine the seriousness of the Chancellor's claim. The chairman of the board of trustees for the system stated in an interview: "What we need is uniform and meaningful grading on all the campuses. If it's going to be meaningful, it should follow some kind of standard curve."[11]

Faculty members at the individual campuses of the California State University and Colleges system have been feeling the pressure. At California State University, San Francisco (CSUSF), for example, a computer printout is sent each semester to every department chairman showing the grade distribution for the previous semester in every course. Lists are also circulated to the departments that show the grade point "average" for each department and each school at the university. Statistics of this sort are usually difficult to interpret, but in this case there are special problems of interpretation. One of the reasons is that there are two grading systems actually in use at CSUSF: regular letter grades, A to F, and an alternate system that consists of only two grades, CR (credit) and NCR (no credit). The use of the alternate system is completely at the discretion of the department and the individual instructor. Students are not permitted to count more than a limited number of CR units toward the degree, and many faculty members discourage students from asking to be graded under the CR-NCR system.

A survey of Fall 1971 grades at CSUSF showed that, if one counted A to F grades only, the faculty of the School of Humanities gave higher grades to more students than any other school on campus (except the School of Education, which offers courses almost completely on the graduate level). In April 1972 the dean of the School of Humanities wrote a memo to all faculty members in his school to suggest that "something is amiss." He did not say that faculty members within his school should conform to official university grading policy by employing the "normal" distribution curve, but the message was clear: in all probability grading standards within the School of Humanities were too lax. Shortly

[9] William A. Sievert, "Lax Grading Charged at California Colleges," *The Chronicle of Higher Education,* 7 (10), November 27, 1972, p. 3.
[10] *Ibid.*
[11] *Ibid.*

thereafter, some department chairmen, concerned about grades within their own departments, distributed copies of an earlier memo on grading that had been written by the vice-president of the university. That memo stated: "It is the obligation of the instructor to establish grading standards which can adequately distinguish five potential grades of student achievement (A, B, C, D, and F) which he must be prepared generally to find in every class."[12] The vice-president made clear, however, that there is no reason to suppose that C must always be the modal grade and that, in advanced classes, "where greater student selectivity usually exists, the mode may vary from time to time, and might be above C. However, it is desirable that the instructor continually reappraise his standards and grading practices in order not to depart too far from the expected mode." In lower-division courses, "the modal grade generally should be C," faculty members were told. No warnings were issued; no threats were made. The advice was given gently: "Over a period of several semesters, a mode other than C would indicate a need for the instructor to reappraise his standards."

Many faculty members in the School of Humanities disregarded the Fall 1971 grade survey, but others took it seriously. What do the figures mean? they asked one another. Why should the courses given in the School of Humanities show a higher grade average than courses given elsewhere on campus? There arose at once three schools of thought. One group of professors stated: "The cause is clear. Some of our departments have high prestige regionally and nationally. They attract a higher-caliber student than other schools on campus. And the high caliber of our students is reflected in the high grade average of the School of Humanities courses." A second group of professors said: "Everyone knows that humanists are an especially conscientious faculty group. We practice a teaching style that is humanistic in mode as well as in substance. It happens to be successful in motivating students; and highly motivated students, other things being equal, make higher grades." A third group of professors, made up of older men and women who were conservative on educational questions and who were out of sympathy with the new permissiveness, laughed at the explanations offered by their colleagues and said: "Don't be simplistic. There is only one explanation. Grading standards simply *are* lower in the School of Humanities than in other schools on this campus. Let's face facts."

The "facts" were faced by the School of Humanities Council, at whose meeting there was much discussion about the whole concept of the normal distribution curve. There were also questions about the "com-

[12] Memorandum to Faculty from the Vice-President, Academic Affairs, California State University, San Francisco (San Francisco State College), on the subject "Grading Policies and Procedures," August 31, 1970.

parability" of one grade-point-average figure with another. One member of the Council, who had interviewed several statisticians, prepared a report that caused some excitement. It declared that in order to "compare" grade-point-average figures from one department to another, or from one school to another, and above all from one faculty member to another —especially if they were both up for promotion or tenure consideration— the figures must be established as "comparable." This meant that other factors which *might* affect the grade-point-average figure would have to be proved to have only negligible influence.

These examples were offered: (1) Female students invariably make higher grades than male students. If one department has predominantly male enrollments, and another has predominantly female enrollments, then this factor may impair comparability of raw figures. (2) Older students make better grades than younger students in the same course. If one department has a considerable number of older students, the comparability of its grade-point-average figure with that of other departments may be lessened. (3) In some departments, the skills requisite for excellent performance are entirely verbal, while in others they may be, to a large extent, quantitative. If the student population on a given campus is to an unusual extent nonverbal or to an unusual extent verbal, then grade-point-average comparability between certain departments is endangered.

As the investigation continued, researchers suggested other factors that might conceivably have bearing. One was the number of required courses in given departments versus a free-elective policy in others. The expectation is that students will be more highly motivated in working at subjects in which they have relatively high interest, background, curiosity, skill, previous record of success, recommendations from friends, and so forth. A second factor to which researchers pointed was the elimination of mediocre students as courses move to more advanced levels. The department that most thoroughly discourages its mediocre students from taking more advanced courses will show a higher grade point average, other things being equal, than the department which encourages C and C+ students to continue.

As a result of its investigation, the School of Humanities Council became convinced that raw grade-point-average figures for a faculty member, a department, or a whole school on the campus were woefully inadequate. Unless they were accompanied by other data, the figures could not validly be interpreted.

Professor Theodore Howe, Gamesman

Aside from the campuswide distribution of departmental grade-point-average figures, there is another practice university officials have found effective with younger faculty members. They set the faculty member's grade distribution as one of the criteria for judging teaching effectiveness. They ask: "How close do the grades of this faculty member come to approaching the normal distribution curve?" Consider the case of Professor Theodore Howe, a young assistant professor at California State University, San Francisco, who knew that the grades he gave in each of his courses would be examined as part of his evaluation for tenure (which would begin the following year, if granted). By a series of stratagems, he was able to place his grade average close to C.

How did Professor Howe manage to do this? One stratagem he employed was to discourage his students, especially those at the low-pass level, from requesting a grade under the CR-NCR system. He reasoned that if a low-pass student receives the grade of CR, it does not help to lower the instructor's grade point average, whereas if such a student receives a D, it does. A second stratagem he employed was to deny, whenever possible, petitions for the grade of W (withdrawal). At CSUSF, a student who must withdraw from a course after the fourth week of the semester may petition for the grade of W; if he can persuade his instructor that circumstances beyond his control have forced the withdrawal, the instructor is expected to recommend that the request be granted. A grade of W carries no academic credit, but it does not penalize the student. On the other hand, if Professor Howe were faced with such a request, and if he refused to recommend that the request be granted, the student would not be permitted to withdraw officially from the course; if the student then dropped the course, he would receive the grade of F. Every F grade Professor Howe gives serves to balance every A that he gives. So Professor Howe developed the following stratagem: he created class conditions that encouraged poor students to give up trying to master the materials of his course; when they petitioned him to allow them to withdraw from the course, he refused to recommend that their withdrawal requests be granted.

Professor Howe used this stratagem subtly, and it was unusually effective. It left his reputation among his colleagues not only unblemished, but enhanced, for it showed that he was upholding high standards; it allowed him to devote his time and energies only to his better students and justified giving only routine and ceremonial attention to the students he wished to discourage; and by contributing to a lowered grade average in his courses, it gave the administration and the Faculty Committee on Tenure a piece of hard evidence that he had been an "effective teacher."

But there remained something of a moral dilemma for Professor Howe to resolve. Had the students who had been encouraged by him to give up, he wondered, really been fairly treated? If he had really been an "effective teacher," would he not have encouraged them to continue, and even tried to help them succeed? Or if he had not had enough time for them—for low-ability students often require more time than professors are able to give—then should he not have permitted them to withdraw, even though it was after the fourth week of the semester?

Fortunately, the Council of Academic Deans at CSUSF offered Professor Howe an easy way out of his dilemma. In March 1972 the Council adopted the following guideline for granting the grade of W: "Allowing withdrawal at the time of finals or, in fact, any time after the fourth week seems to ignore completely the college resource potential. The student entering a class contracts for the time of the instructor, the class space, the operational money, and any related resources. By entering the class he deprives another of an opportunity to contract for the class. The consideration is clear. He pays his fees and in return he receives the commitment as outlined. In equity he should be allowed relief for verified illness, sudden and unplanned changes in job, and any serious matter beyond his control. No other reason should suffice after a properly allowed time for class contact and adjustment."[13]

The resolution of Professor Howe's dilemma rests on an impersonal, legal base, the concept of the contract. The guideline argues that the student in fact enters into a contract with the university, and when he does not carry out his part of the bargain, he not only deserves to have academic credit withheld but he must also be penalized. Professor Howe is thus vindicated.[14]

Two Incompatible Roles: Teacher-Critic and Judge

Behind the moral problem posed by the case of Professor Howe, there lies an even larger educational question: Is the "normal" distribution curve the appropriate means for grading students in university classes? "We have for so long used the normal curve in grading students we have come to believe in it," Benjamin S. Bloom points out.[15] And he goes on

---

[13] Adopted as "a statement-of-advice to the deans and department chairmen, and for recommendation to the faculty, as a guideline for the assignment and approval of the W grade." From the minutes of the meeting of the Council of Academic Deans, California State University, San Francisco, March 14, 1972.

[14] This is not the place to inquire into such a complex topic as the validity of the concept of contract when it is applied to such cases, but it might be well to remind the reader of the observation made in the White Paper issued by the American Association of State Colleges and Universities in 1970. The contract concept, the White Paper states, is "the most common refuge of persons describing the relationship between student and institution," but "despite its popularity, it is woefully inadequate." Thomas C. Fischer, *The Student-Institutional Relationship* (Washington, D.C.: American Association of State Colleges and Universities, 1970), p. 4.

[15] Benjamin S. Bloom, "Learning for Mastery," *Evaluation Comment,* 1 (2), May 1968, p. 3. The magazine is published by the Center for the Study of Evaluation of Instructional Programs, University of California at Los Angeles.

to say that there is nothing sacred about the normal curve, that it is simply the distribution most appropriate to chance and random activity. But education is a *purposeful* activity, and it is logical to conclude, as Bloom does, that "our educational efforts have been unsuccessful to the extent to which our distribution of achievement approximates the normal distribution." Most academicians, instead of taking it as a possible sign of success when a professor's grades show a preponderance of A's and B's in an undergraduate course, jump to the conclusion that the professor is soft in his grading practices, that he is too lenient. And an increasing number of campuses have now established a policy similar to that illustrated in the preceding paragraphs; such a professor would either be politely called to order by a Committee on Academic Standards, consisting of his peers, or he would be spoken to by his department chairman or a central administration official.

The crux of the problem is this: In his relationship to students, the professor in almost any conventional program is expected to fulfill two very different functions. He is, first of all, a teacher and critic. But the grading system also requires him to serve as a judge—and sometimes as an executioner, as well. The professor's teacher-critic role (especially if he is following any of the evocative teacher prototypes described in Part One) presses him toward a personal relationship with his students. But his role as judge—rewarding and punishing his students—pushes him in the opposite direction. One may be able to teach a friend (indeed, many professors who follow the student-centered teacher prototypes presented in Part One believe it is not possible to teach anyone unless he is a friend), but one cannot comfortably give an F to a friend—and certainly not when one is caught in a system where an F in a single course may have repercussions in a student's future that are far out of proportion to the grade's actual significance.

Many college teachers, having experienced the discomfort of this conflict in their first years of teaching, have grown wary of showing or encouraging any sign of friendship—or even friendliness—with students. They may believe in such friendships with other professors' students, but not with their own. And the facts are plain: it *is* easier and no doubt fairer to everyone, when grading time comes around, if the instructor has been impersonal with *all* of his students. The grading relationship, as David Riesman states it, tends to "contaminate" the teaching relationship.[16] The reverse is also true: a professor who plays a certain kind of role as teacher will lose his capability of conforming to the grading rules and procedures that characterize standard programs. Such a professor

---

[16] David Riesman, in a Foreword to Roy Heath, *The Reasonable Adventurer: A Study of the Development of Thirty-Six Undergraduates at Princeton* (University of Pittsburgh Press, 1964), p. xvi.

may find himself in an impossible situation. In the past, he might have attempted to establish procedures whereby his students would grade themselves or each other, but such practices are now frowned upon at many campuses, and the professor who persists in them will be warned that they constitute dereliction of duty—and the practice may even be used as grounds for dismissal.

The point is no longer even debated in campus discussions in any serious way, and faculty members accused of being "soft" in grading are no longer as outspoken as they were in the 1960s. When evidence was being collected on the University of California, Berkeley, campus about the uses and abuses of the grading system in the mid-sixties, there were eloquent spokesmen representing both the "hard" and "soft" graders; fortunately, the high points of that debate have been preserved in the Muscatine Report. In that debate, the view against "permissiveness" was well stated by a faculty member: "It would be deplorable if the rather harsh, critical environment appropriate to an educational institution gave way to a congenial, unevaluative one, in which scholars went about their business and students were simply welcome to pick up what they liked. . . . The most effective way of inculcating habits of self-criticism in one's students is as a critic, and only secondarily as an example. . . . But unless one is forced to do this, one will tend to avoid it. . . . And this is my main argument for grading: it forces teachers to evaluate their students' work and to justify those evaluations in detail—activities which neither party particularly enjoys."[17]

Clearly, for this professor, criticism and evaluation of student work do not take place in the course of the *teaching* process itself, as he conceives it. For him, these elements would be largely—or perhaps entirely—absent if the grading system did not (to use his words) force teachers to include them.

But let us look more closely at how this professor puts his words together. He speaks of a "rather harsh, critical environment" which he finds appropriate to the teaching-learning process. Opposed to this environment, in his view, is a "congenial, unevaluative one." Must "critical" go with "harsh"? And must "unevaluative" go with "congenial"? Are there not some groups which can be characterized as not harsh but *congenial* and not unevaluative but *critical*? An atmosphere that is both congenial and critical is to be found, for example, in certain family groups. Is such an environment possible also in the educational world? Professors who follow the student-centered teaching prototypes (described in Part One) base their whole philosophies on an affirmative answer to this question. But for the faculty member just quoted, the answer is

[17] *Education at Berkeley,* pp. 95–96.

apparently in the negative. He finds that it is precisely the conventional grading system—with its judgmental atmosphere and its often irrevocable rewards and punishments—that forces the teacher to perform his role of critic. Student-centered professors maintain that it is not only the role of critic that the grading system forces the teacher to play, however—it also forces him to play the role of judge. And the relationship he must establish with his students as he plays the role of judge, if he is to play the role well, necessarily reduces his effectiveness as both teacher and critic.

For this reason, many experimental colleges have sought to change radically the shape of the third dimension. Their planners believe that the professor can be encouraged to play his role as teacher and critic better if his role as judge is entirely eliminated. On some campuses—Johnston College, University of Redlands, and Justin Morrill College, Michigan State University, to name only two—grades have been eliminated altogether, and a complex but highly effective system of student evaluation has been substituted for the conventional grading practices of their parent institutions.

But in these experimental settings, it is more than the grading system that has been changed. All of the other five dimensions have been altered, too. For the interrelationships among the six dimensions of the degree system are complex, and innovative programs must take them all into account. In the next chapter we shall look at two blueprint models of innovative institutions in some detail, and we shall be able to see how new approaches within the structural dimensions of the degree system actually work.

Chapter 11

Innovative Programs

Our theoretical model of the degree system, presented in Part Three, has emphasized the intimate relationships that exist between the structural dimensions (the first, second, and third) and the fourth dimension, which encompasses the behaviors of instructor and students in the classroom. In this chapter we shall illustrate these relationships by means of two blueprint models in which innovations have been introduced in the structural dimensions (especially the first and second).

The blueprint models describe an imaginary institution, the University of Z, which consists of two major divisions called Old College and Meiklejohn College.[1] Old College is a lively, mildly innovative school, while Meiklejohn College is highly experimental. The two blueprint

---

[1] The University of Z is here conceived as similar in structure to the University of Redlands, with its two divisions—the more conventional University College, devoted to both undergraduate and graduate programs, and the highly experimental Johnston College, which gives exclusive attention to undergraduates. The resemblance ends at this point, however. The blueprint for Old College of the University of Z is based on the original blueprint drawn up by a team of educators (of which the author was a member) for California State College, Palos Verdes (now called California State College, Dominguez Hills); the blueprint for Meiklejohn College is based on a plan originally drawn up by the author for an experimental "satellite" college at San Francisco State College (now California State University, San Francisco).

models—aside from showing how the three structural dimensions of the degree system can take vastly different concrete shapes, even on a single campus—illustrate how traditionally trained professors in the humanities can avoid the problems of dislocation brought on by certain kinds of structural reforms in the degree system.

Old College offers both undergraduate and graduate degrees, while Meiklejohn College awards only the undergraduate degree. On the undergraduate level, Old College has a strong emphasis on interdisciplinary programs. It also offers graduate programs in twenty-four fields and, except for two Doctorate in Arts programs that are designed for training community college teachers, these graduate programs are of the standard pattern.

Meiklejohn College, on the other hand, is innovative in every dimension. It has several basic purposes. First, it is an experimental school —or an *experimenting* school, in its own usage—that concentrates all of its energies on undergraduate education. Second, it is specifically charged by the University governing board with the responsibility for generating discussion, throughout the University of Z campus, about teaching styles, learning theory, and innovative course models. Third, it has been authorized to institute and conduct internship experiences for the graduate students in Old College's two Doctorate in Arts programs who intend to make their careers in college teaching. By encouraging the establishment of this internship program, the governing board intended that the faculty of Meiklejohn College would develop a working relationship with the departmental faculty at Old College responsible for graduate programs. Moreover, as a result of this arrangement, the board hoped that the faculty of Meiklejohn College, although recruited for excellence in undergraduate teaching, would acquire the prestige of working in an intimate relationship with graduate students and would play an important role in influencing the coming generation of community college teachers in the geographic area in which the University of Z is located.

The Undergraduate Program at Old College

The program for the bachelor's degree at Old College, like all conventional programs, is a four-year program divided into upper and lower divisions. For the lower division, all courses are designed to develop to sophisticated levels the skills of reading, writing, speaking, and listening. In the various courses, students practice these skills on materials taken from the fields of the humanities, the social sciences, and the natural sciences. The principle of subject matter flexibility has the highest priority, and each course deals with topics, during a given semester, that are of special interest to the particular faculty member offering it. The course topics—and the readings, too, of course—thus vary from semester to semester.

The goal of these lower-division courses is not to turn freshmen and sophomores into experts but, rather, to make them intelligent laymen in as many fields of knowledge as possible. The test of whether the lower-division program is successful consists of a single question: Can a student, after completing the lower-division courses, easily understand what is said and written by experts when they address themselves to any audience other than specialized scholars or professionals? The objective of the lower-division programs, then, is not the acquisition of current information on a subject; it is, instead, the ability (a) to participate in a fairly high-level discussion on the subject, both orally and in writing, (b) to understand the basic questions facing scholars and professionals in these fields today, and (c) above all, to anticipate what might be the basic questions a decade or a quarter-century hence. During his four lower-division semesters, each full-time student takes twelve courses (three per semester, five semester credits each). Two of these are from a humanities course list; two are from a social science list; two are from a natural science list; and the remaining six are from a list labeled "Interdisciplinary Courses."

During the upper-division semesters, each student at Old College concentrates in *two* fields. One of these is known as his "discipline field" and the other is called his "interdisciplinary field." The student must satisfy his advisor that his choices in these two fields show some relationship to each other in terms of the student's goals. The possibilities are not unlimited, for only two dozen disciplines are available as fields of concentration, and the interdisciplinary fields are limited to those which can adequately be handled by the faculty.

Three principles serve to organize the various interdisciplinary fields: geography, subject matter, and time. The fields organized around geography focus on particular world regions—America, Latin America, Eastern Europe and the Soviet Union, Africa, the Far East, South Asia, the Middle East. The fields organized around subject matter make a distinction between the terms *subject matter* and *discipline*. For curriculum planners at Old College, "discipline" is defined as a methodological framework; it includes the tools and the particular methods of investigation that scholars in the field use. The subject matter with which the scholar in a given discipline may deal is essentially irrelevant in this definition—or to be more precise, *any* subject matter is relevant as long as the tools and the methods of the given discipline are appropriate to the analysis or exploration of that subject matter. The term "discipline," then, as it is used at Old College, distinguishes methodologically between fields—philosophy, history, political science. The term "subject matter" emphasizes the substantive and not the methodological aspect—village organization, surrealism, the black man in the United States, the elementary school, nationalism, Islam. Thus, many subjects are appropriately contained within the traditional domain of a single discipline. But the study of some subjects (which is true for the six just listed) may be seriously distorted if they are treated exclusively from the perspective of a single discipline. At Old College, consequently, the principle of organization for a number of the interdisciplinary fields is subject matter per se.

The fields organized around the third principle, time, cover all important aspects of a particular era—the Renaissance, the Ancient World, the Age of Reason, or some other period in Western or other civilizations. Some of these interdisciplinary programs may even encompass two or three different epochs, attempting to abstract from them certain truths—for example, a study of several revolutionary periods in the history of man in order to discover what characteristics such epochs have in common.

Every faculty member at Old College is a member of a disciplinary *"staff"* (the term *department* is not used), and all faculty members on a particular staff have been trained in the same discipline. But each faculty member is also a member of one or more interdisciplinary staffs. In this way, the college attempts to attract new staff members whose sound disciplinary training is complemented by strong interdisciplinary interests. The college makes every effort to discourage faculty applicants who are not qualified to serve on any interdisciplinary staff or who have no interest in such activity. For the humanities faculty, this requirement creates no problem. almost every highly qualified faculty member in a humanities discipline has areas of interdisciplinary interest and training. Among faculty members recently recruited for posts at Old College, one of the historians is a medievalist and another historian has a special interest in South Asia; a scholar in French has recently published a study of the relationship between art and literature in Western Europe during the pre-World War I period; an American literature professor is also an expert in education who has written a dissertation on the way American writers describe teachers; and one of the art professors has received considerable training in biology.

Each student at Old College is required not only to have a double major but also to undertake an individual project—as work toward his bachelor's degree—that focuses on a topic located at the point where his disciplinary field and his interdisciplinary field meet. If his disciplinary program is in music and his interdisciplinary program is in South Asian studies, his project would deal, for example, with some aspect of the music of India.

Aside from these innovations—limited to the first dimension of its degree system—Old College is fairly conventional. Everything else about the school is standard: its scheduling of faculty, students, and classes; its grading system; its accommodation of the implemental dimensions. There is nothing radically innovative about Old College. Its curriculum plan may appear like a major reform when it is described, but it is, in fact, only mildly innovative. Let us recall the principle set forth in Chapter Seven: If a change is effected within a single dimension of the degree system without creating some dislocation within one or more of the other dimensions, then, in all likelihood, it is not a fundamental change. The innovations at Old College do not constitute a fundamental change, and they have not created dislocation.

Still, for some faculty members in the humanistic disciplines, even the mild reforms in the Old College curriculum are important. In the foreign languages, for example, especially with falling enrollments (due to the abolition of the blanket requirement in foreign languages for all undergraduates), faculty members are able to participate in other programs. They are qualified to devote more time to the interdisciplinary programs without additional formal training and without any schedule dislocation. As a morale booster for the foreign language faculty, this feature of Old College's curriculum cannot be overestimated.

Old College is an example of a college that generally follows the conventional model, but with a bit of a twist—a twist that makes a difference. Meiklejohn College, on the other hand, is far from conventional. It is innovative at many levels, and its plan is deservedly looked upon as *experimental*.

An Experimenting School

Meiklejohn College, nicknamed College M, was designed specifically for students who plan to be enrolled on a full-time basis. Due to the peculiar sequencing of the curriculum, the freshman and sophomore years each constitute an integral unit of study. For this reason, students may not enter or transfer into College M except at the beginning of the fall semester, even though a student may transfer from College M to Old College at the midyear break. If a student is attracted to College M and cannot attend on a full-time basis for at least one year, he is advised to apply for entrance to Old College and plan to transfer to College M later. If a student in College M finds, after he has attended school for a time, that he must drop out of full-time participation, he is able to transfer to Old College without penalty.

While the particular principles that shape the first dimension at College M—those that determine the content of the program for the bachelor's degree—are highly distinctive, the innovative features that will probably seem most striking to an observer are those concerned with the unusual shape of the second dimension—the way in which students and faculty are grouped together for their learning sessions. We will begin, then, with a description of the unique features of the second dimension, the scheduling system at College M.

Second dimension: A unique scheduling system. In College M's lower division, the basic learning group consists of seventy-five students and five full-time faculty members—four regular faculty members and a new type of staff member called a Faculty Aid. This student-faculty group is popularly called a Prime (short for primary group), and each Prime is identified by a distinctive name. This organizational structure applies for the lower division only; the upper division (as we shall see) is organized differently.

There are three basic features that differentiate the shape of the second dimension in College M from the scheduling system in the standard model. First, the members of the Prime "belong" to each other: in any given term, students in a given Prime normally receive instruction only from the faculty team which is part of that Prime, and the faculty members normally give instruction only to the members of their own Prime. It should be noted, however, that this general rule applies only to instruction given through courses; for certain subjects, instruction is given outside the Prime altogether at what is called the Learning Laboratory Center, a place where students find many programs on film, tape, and other media, and where they receive help from special instructional assistants. More information about this Center will be given presently.

Second, the student members of each Prime are divided into sub groups. For certain class sessions, there are three subgroups of twenty-five students each, while for other class sessions, the subgroups are even smaller. Subgrouping is completely flexible—it can change with ease from hour to hour and from day to day. One of the roles of the Faculty Aid is to keep track of the daily pattern of the subgroups.

Third, all seventy-five students within each Prime take all of their courses together for the entire semester. For any given semester, then, each student spends most of his time exclusively with the other members of his Prime. The students may not, however, remain together for more than one semester—unless they formally make a decision to continue together as a group for a full academic year. About a month before the end of Term I or Term III, the students are given the opportunity to make this decision. But at the end of Term II—that is, at the end of the freshman year—every Prime is reconstituted. If a Prime remains intact for a second semester, it retains its faculty members as well as its students, so that the unit remains essentially the same.

This arrangement complicates faculty and student schedules at

College M. For bookkeeping purposes, faculty members of each faculty team officially have twelve-hour teaching loads per week—four contact hours with each of the three twenty-five-student subgroups in the Prime. The *actual* scheduling of classes and other activities, however, varies week by week and day by day, depending upon assignments and other tasks. Each student is officially registered for four four-hour credit courses, yielding sixteen units per semester, but again, the student's *actual* class schedule varies with the daily and weekly plans of his Prime and his subgroup.

When a faculty member begins his assignment with College M, he joins a freshman-year staff team. In his second year, he serves on a sophomore-year staff team. In his third and fourth years, he serves groups of upper-division students. These four years constitute his probationary period, and at this time his work at College M is formally evaluated while he, in turn, evaluates the college. If both the faculty member and the college are satisfied with each other, the faculty member begins a new cycle which will last for five years. Tenure does not exist; faculty contracts are renewed at the end of each five-year cycle.

The first year of each five-year cycle is devoted to study, research, travel, and writing. It is called the Study Year, and the faculty member receives full pay. The Study Year is not, however, a sabbatical leave, even though it fulfills some of the same functions. Both College M and Old College have extremely inadequate sabbatical plans: because of budgetary problems, only a small percentage of faculty members are given sabbatical leaves, and the leaves go normally to the older faculty members with many years of service. Since most of the faculty members at College M are young men and women, the Study Year serves as substitute and compensation—but there are significant differences between a sabbatical plan and the Study Year, and the faculty members are made aware of these differences. The Study Year, which comes every fifth year, is a year of work done for the college. It is therefore not as free as a sabbatical leave would be, and the faculty member is not officially on leave at all. He is on a nonteaching assignment for the college, and this assignment may, in fact, require his presence on campus. In certain years, for instance, faculty members are asked to work on curricular planning or in other planning or research projects. Occasionally these projects may involve travel to other campuses in the United States or abroad.

After a Study Year, the faculty member returns to his teaching duties; he moves into a four-year teaching cycle, repeating the assignment pattern of freshman year, sophomore year, upper division. In the first two years of this cycle, as we have noted, the faculty member works as part of a staff team consisting of four faculty members and a Faculty Aid. Each of these faculty members comes from a different department in the college. As College M is organized, there are only four departments in the entire college: the "Hum" department, devoted to humanistic studies; the "Lang" department, devoted to the study of languages, including mathematics and computer language as well as natural languages; the "Nat" department, devoted to the study of the natural world; and the "Sosh" department (pronounced like the first three sounds in "social"), devoted to the study of human societies.

In the first two years of every four-year period, when the faculty member works with a staff team, he is involved mainly with the other three faculty members and the Faculty Aid on his team. He maintains, however, close contact with the members of his own department through office location, monthly departmental meetings, and the usual departmental business. In the third and fourth years of the cycle, he works with groups of upper-division students who are concentrating on studies within his own department. Thus he spends two years of every four teaching years primarily outside his own department, but the remaining two are spent within his department.

The Faculty Aid plays an important role in the Prime. Since this post was created by the planners of College M and does not exist on other campuses, perhaps it should be explained in some detail. The post is administrative rather than instructional. The Faculty Aid is the "legman" for the staff team; he is responsible for all administrative and record-keeping matters for the Prime to which he is assigned in a given term. One of his important functions is to serve as a trouble-shooter, facilitating communication between students and faculty in the Prime and serving as the group's liaison with student personnel services. He serves as the major clearinghouse for information regarding group movements— an exceedingly important function for all members of the group, faculty members as well as students. He is the morale builder, and he is the "father" and the "mother" to all members of the Prime.

More often than not, the Faculty Aid is mature in years and experience. Typically, he holds a college degree, is remarkably efficient, is at ease with organizational details, and has the kind of personality that helps alleviate the immediate problems of nervous students and anxious faculty members. The Faculty Aid post is a career in its own right, and the person occupying the position does not aspire to become a faculty member. The salary for the post lies somewhere between the salaries of a senior secretary and a young instructor. Educated women, whose lives have been devoted to homemaking, whose children are now in college and beyond, and who now wish to build careers for themselves, are attracted to this type of post and seem to make excellent Faculty Aids. No specialized training is needed, and office skills are not required because the Faculty Aid is not a clerk or a secretary.

First dimension and its four frameworks. College M offers no curricular options designed to train students for specific jobs or professional careers. The college therefore "fits"only those students who will be receiving training for careers elsewhere—either in postbaccalaureate or on-the-job programs.

The curriculum is organized through courses. In the lower division, they are set up in two-semester sequences, and each semester the student is registered for four of these courses—one with each faculty member on the staff team. (We shall describe these courses in detail in a moment.) In the upper division, the student also registers for the equivalent of four courses per semester. Not all of these courses are actual classes, however. The student also has some choices, in the upper division, about the method he uses in pursuing his studies: he may spend a semester in a work-study relationship, holding an actual job under the supervision of his department, or he may elect to spend a semester on another campus elsewhere in the United States or abroad. These choices are made on an individual basis by the student working with his advisor.

During the final semester, each student undertakes a comprehensive "examination" that uses, as evaluative instruments, seminar sessions and public discussions rather than written tests. As part of this examination, the student makes a presentation which is of interest to the college community: he may give one or more public lectures on topics of concern to the college; he may take part in performances of the arts; or he may exhibit his work in one of the arts or the sciences, depending upon his field of specialization.

During the freshman and sophomore years, each student is registered for four courses simultaneously, one course from each of the four departments. The program for each Prime has four aspects or frameworks (called *frames*). Two of these frameworks, called *first frame* and *second frame,* contribute to curricular unity; the other two, called *third frame* and *fourth frame,* contribute to curricular variety. The first and third frames are methodological, while the second and fourth frames deal with subject matter. The relationships of these frames are illustrated in Table 2.

First Frame: The overall methodological frame for the freshman and sophomore years may be stated as a question: What is knowledge and how may it serve mankind? The question can further be divided into three parts to demonstrate the way it serves the general framework for the entire program—that is, how it determines or colors the form of all inquiries made in every course: (1) What are the "tools" by means of which new facts, principles, concepts, systems, and so forth are discovered —and what does it mean to "discover" new knowledge? (2) What are the "tools" by means of which this new knowledge is assimilated with the old knowledge—that is, how is the total body of knowledge reshaped to

Table 2

FORM-CONTENT AND UNITY-VARIETY RELATIONSHIPS IN THE
LOWER-DIVISION COURSES AT MEIKLEJOHN COLLEGE

	METHOD *Form of the Inquiry*	SUBJECT MATTER *Content of the Inquiry*
UNITY The common frames	*First Frame* THE OVERALL METHODOLOGICAL THEME: KNOWLEDGE How is new knowledge discovered and assimilated?	*Second Frame* THE OVERALL SUBJECT-MATTER THEME: COMMUNITY City, nation, and international community
VARIETY The differentiating frames	*Third Frame* MULTIDISCIPLINARY APPROACH Four members of each faculty team represent four major disciplines	*Fourth Frame* "THE IMMEDIATE TOPIC" Each Primary Group sets a different topic

accommodate these new "discoveries"? (3) How are the preceding two questions relevant to the individual student, to the subcultures of which he is a member, and to mankind in general?

These questions, when expressed in appropriate logical, pedagogical, and psychological terms, constitute the overall methodological frame for all studies carried on by all of the Primes during the freshman and middle years of study. Every educational activity planned for any of the Primes is thus governed, directly or indirectly, by the framework. It is of absolutely central significance, and it points to the relationships that are most significant in the College M blueprint model between the first and fourth dimensions. The basic goal is for students to learn how to learn. The teacher's most effective role in any inquiry is as a model learner.

Second Frame: The second framework contributing to unity in

the total program concerns not method—that is, the form of the inquiry—but content. A single subject-matter theme is set for all Primes. In the freshman year, the theme is "The City in History and in the Future." In the sophomore year, it is "America, the West, and the World." Studies thus begin by focusing, during both years, on the United States. The first year's focus moves inward to its cities (although non-American cities are also studied), and the second year's focus moves outward to the world community of nations. The approach each year is multidisciplinary, for each member of each faculty team represents a different discipline. As a consequence, the city can be viewed not merely in its economic or political aspects, or as primarily a sociological entity (the characteristic bias of most urban studies programs), but in other important ways as well to include aspects that are medical, cultural, legal, educational, military, technological, criminal, aesthetic, transportational, linguistic, marital, and so forth. In a similar way, the work of the second year is not confined to an examination of nations as political entities (the characteristic bias of most international relations programs), but focuses on intercultural studies in the widest sense.

Third and Fourth Frames: While the first and second frames are unifying frameworks in the curriculum, the third and fourth frames introduce differentiation. In the third frame, every course a student takes in a given term is differentiated from every other course because each has its own disciplinary orientation. The fourth frame individualizes the work of every Prime: no two Primes deal with precisely the same topic in any given term. To distinguish the immediate topic of study from the overall subject-matter framework (second frame), the fourth frame is labeled "The Immediate Topic."

The Immediate Topic for study in any given semester is decided in advance by each faculty team; as a rule, it is announced before the choice of Prime is made by students. The topics may differ considerably in their very nature: some constitute fields for systematic investigation; others are simply points of departure for an exploration that often ends up somewhere else in a quite unanticipated way. For example, one Prime in the third semester may systematically explore several crises in Western civilization, while another Prime may take as a point of departure the question: What exactly is a developed nation and how does an undeveloped nation become developed? But the point of departure can lead in one direction in one year and in another direction in another year. Such a topic as "The Contemporary Roles of Religious Institutions" may lead a freshman group to explore the contributions of religious leaders in civil rights movements in their own city, while it may lead a sophomore group to explore the ecumenical movement as part of a larger study of multinational or intercultural institutions. In any event, and by every possible means—field experiences, reading materials, nonacademic-guest discussion participants, student projects, and so forth—the group tries to tie the Immediate Topic into the larger subject matter framework set for the whole year.

The principle of flexibility in these structures is basic to the implementation of this model. Because there is no single "best" way of organizing a group of learning experiences, the faculty teams do not feel that their procedures must necessarily be consistent with previous procedures they or other teams may have used. In some teams, for instance, the members may decide to use a common group of readings, projects, and other activities, with each faculty member then taking responsibility for exploring a different aspect of these common materials. In other teams, the readings and activities suggested for each course may be quite different, even though all instructors address themselves to the same Immediate Topic. In a third instance, the Immediate Topic treated in each course, while related to a common problem, may be in fact quite a different topic. What actually happens is that the members of the Prime—the faculty team and the students, working together, organize the inquiry according to the whole group's needs and preferences.

A word should be said about the Immediate Topic and its relationship to the "problems approach." It would be an error to say that College M's curriculum adopts a problems approach. As this term is generally understood, a course taking the problems approach focuses on some societal ill—such as unemployment, poverty, overpopulation, vice, juvenile delinquency, drug use, substandard housing—and attempts to analyze the nature of the problem and seek directions for possible solution. The weakness of this approach, from College M's point of view, is that the "problem" is already formulated before the course begins. College M's curricular plan attempts to help the student free his mind of the middle-class biases that determine, more often than not, how a societal problem is perceived and formulated. Thus, at College M, while a problem such as drug use among young people in this country might possibly serve as an Immediate Topic for a freshman or sophomore group, a faculty team would probably want to utilize the topic primarily as a point of departure for an analysis of larger aspects of the counterculture in urban America, or for an inquiry into generational differences in general; and the topic would be illustrated by the study of several cultures and historical periods.

The movement from freshman to senior begins with a study of particulars in which there is a strong experiential element without systematic attempts at generalization. This study moves gradually to a knowledge of first principles in some selected field, and as it moves it emphasizes such processes as generalization, analysis of evidence, validation, and prediction, where they are relevant. At Old College, by contrast, as a student moves through his studies, there is no progression at all—or if there is a progression, it is of a different sort: a student begins his first course with a study of principles and ends his courses by taking a problems approach. In College M, the student stays with rather limited Immediate Topics for two years, and he does not attempt, in any systematic way, to generate abstract principles until he moves into a single discipline during his last two years. For the senior year, new Primes are formed as students choose their work with faculty teams made up entirely from within a single department. The organization of studies is then much looser than it is during the freshman and middle years, for students have been prepared to work independently.

The Place of Teaching at College M

One of the most crucial distinctions in the blueprint plan for College M is between the kind of learning that can be promoted only by university teacher-artists and the kind that can be carried out by instructional technicians with the aid of mechanical instruments. Class sessions taught by faculty members are reserved, at College M, primarily for learning of the kind characterized by inquiry and discovery, where the professor must be an artist at teaching. College M therefore makes exactly the distinction drawn in Chapter One between didactic modes of teaching, carried on by teacher-craftsmen, and evocative modes of teaching, carried on by teacher-artists. The blueprint plan for College M specifies that the transmission of knowledge for which didactic modes of teaching are appropriate is the responsibility of the technical staff at the Learning Laboratory Center set up by the College. The responsibility of faculty members, on the other hand, is exclusively for the transmission of that kind of knowledge for which evocative modes of teaching are appropriate.

There are therefore no courses offered at College M devoted exclusively to the acquisition of relatively elementary skills—such courses, for example, as those where a student learns to type, to speak Russian at an elementary level, to solve certain problems in statistics, to acquire elementary piano skill. Yet these skills are of course needed by students and faculty. In conjunction with some of the work in linguistics or intercultural work, for instance, students and faculty at College M often wish to acquire or improve skills in foreign languages. (It should be noted that we are not speaking here about knowledge of the way language systems in general work, or about inquiries into contrasting cultural phenomena exhibited by speakers of these languages; these kinds of knowledge are available through the regular course offerings of the Lang and Hum departments.)

For the acquisition of skills which do not involve inquiry, College M students and faculty use the Learning Laboratory Center (called the Lab Center), which is staffed by technician experts and instructional assistants. At the Lab Center, such knowledge is systematically and efficiently acquired whenever the need arises, and the student or faculty member may study at his own pace. The Lab Center contains the very latest electronic equipment designed for the acquisition of language skills in English and many foreign languages, and it also has programmed materials covering informational knowledge in a large number of subject-matter areas.

The Lab Center, however, cannot fulfill its function unless communication between its staff and the faculty at College M is active. Mechanisms have been developed to keep information flowing back and forth because both sides strongly believe that full communication is crucial to the work of the college. Faculty members know that they cannot perform well as teacher-artists unless they use these mechanisms, and they are aware that such mechanisms frequently go unused in conventional programs, including the programs of Old College. (The one obvious exception at Old College is the work in foreign language skills.) For faculty members in the Hum and Lang departments, especially, the presence of the Lab Center on campus makes an enormous difference.

The Lab Center, using methods that are modern and effective, takes responsibility for instruction in certain areas, supplying the basic information and the elementary skills that students in humanistic studies need before they can undertake real inquiry into problems in literature or the history of civilization, in linguistics or philosophy or the arts. The Lab Center frees the faculty member so that he can spend his class time performing teaching tasks that no machine can do: probing and learning, inquiring and discovering, *together* with his students. At the same time, the Lab Center makes it virtually unnecessary for a faculty member to devote any of his valuable classroom time to dispensing basic information or to drilling students in elementary skills or factual knowledge. The Lab Center thus contributes to the central aim of the whole curricular plan at College M—it literally forces the faculty member to practice the art of teaching.

College M and Old College adopted a number of innovative features in the structural dimensions of their degree systems and, as we have seen, these innovations affect the fourth dimension as well. Consequently, they have an impact on the instructional strategies and on the teaching styles of faculty members at both institutions. At both colleges—and especially at College M—there are strong forces motivating the faculty member to become an artist at teaching.

At the vast majority of American colleges and universities, however, such forces—if they exist at all—are overwhelmed by other forces pushing in the opposite direction. We shall look at some of these other forces in the next chapter.

Chapter 12

Educational Change
and the University Teacher

Are there likely to be any changes in American higher education, between now and 1985, that will in any fundamental way affect what professors in the humanistic disciplines actually do in their classrooms? For more than 95 percent of the humanists now teaching on American campuses, the answer is no.[1]

This is not to say that there will not be important changes in American higher education during the next dozen or so years. Important evolutionary changes began to occur during the years immediately following World War II, and this pattern of change will continue into the 1980s. Changes already made, however, have not to any appreciable extent affected the classroom practices of university professors—and it is not likely that the changes yet to come will affect those practices, either.

Just as classrooms and lecture halls—and what goes on in them—will look, a decade from now, much as they do at present, so will the institutional types of American colleges and universities. A faculty member who is now teaching in an American college or university, and who will still be engaged in higher education in the 1980s, can expect that he will be employed by one of nine types of educational institutions.

[1] The analysis that follows is based on data collected by the author for an OECD report, *The Future of American Postsecondary Education* (Paris: Office of Economic Cooperation and Development, 1971.)

215

Sociotechnological Institutes. These high prestige institutions (Type 1) will continue to follow the models of RAND Corporation, the Oak Ridge National Laboratory, and other "think tanks." A national network of these institutes will probably become visible by the end of the 1970s. Included in Type 1, as well, are the research and development centers established by various agencies of the federal government when these are not affiliated with the research universities of Type 2, or when they are only loosely affiliated with those universities and are not physically situated on their campuses. The institutions of Type 1 will continue to be noninstructional in nature. They will become an increasingly important part of the higher education establishment, but they will carry no responsibility for contributing to the teaching function of the American university, except for highly specialized work offered to a limited number of research-oriented postdoctoral trainees.

It is unlikely that humanistically trained personnel will be much involved with these research institutes and centers; but a number of humanities professors, moving into second careers in the behavioral sciences, will be working at these institutions. What is significant about the Type 1 institutions—from the point of view of university teaching—is that the distance, already considerable, between them and undergraduate programs will increase during the decade to come. Aside from their quite important contribution to new knowledge—which clearly will affect the undergraduate curriculum, although the impact will be felt only indirectly—the work of the sociotechnological institutes is not at all likely to influence the course of undergraduate education or of university instruction in any way.

Major research universities. Half of the federal funds thus far allocated for higher education in the United States have been funneled into only two percent of the nation's colleges and universities—that is, into the major research universities.[2] This institutional type (Type 2), which includes both public and private universities, will increasingly focus on its traditional primary concerns: research and training on the graduate, professional, and postdoctoral levels. The undergraduate student bodies at these national universities will become even more highly selective and even smaller than at present. At the same time, the structure of undergraduate instruction at these institutions—and this includes *all* six dimensions of the degree system—will change very little in the decade ahead, except of course for the updating of subject matter.

Hence, for a professor now teaching at a university that is, or

---

[2] The reader is reminded that the word *university* is used here, as throughout this book, in a generic sense to include all institutions of higher education, whether their official names carry the term "university," "institute of technology" (or simply "institute"), "college," or "school."

is likely to become, a Type 2 institution, any basic change in teaching style will depend entirely on his own personal initiative. Conditions for developing into a teacher-artist will continue to remain very far from ideal. But these conditions do not now—nor will they in the 1980s—make such development impossible, if a faculty member is determined to learn and practice the art of teaching.

Regional public universities and comprehensive state colleges. Of the more than 2500 nonprofit institutions of higher education in the United States, perhaps as many as 300 can be classified as Types 3 and 4. These schools constitute a very fast-growing segment of higher education, and by the end of the decade they may be enrolling as many as a third of all students in higher education in the nation.

In many states, the colleges and universities of Types 3 and 4 have, in recent years, limited their entrance requirements so that only the upper half or upper third of high school graduates will qualify for entrance. (The community college, Type 8, is expected to provide greater access to the lower half or lower two-thirds of secondary school graduates.) What has been the effect of this change in entrance standards? Mainly, the effect has been to encourage Type 3 and Type 4 institutions to become more like the universities of Type 2. Type 2 universities (Harvard, Chicago, Berkeley) have long represented the condition to which all Type 3 and Type 4 schools aspire (which is also true for Type 6, regional private universities); and the Type 2 universities will continue, during the decade ahead, to provide the image that these schools seek to imitate. But of course, Type 4 institutions do not now—and will not, in the foreseeable future—offer programs in the older established professions, such as law, medicine, pharmacy, or dentistry; training for these professions is given comprehensively at the major national universities (Type 2) and more selectively at the regional universities (Types 3 and 6).

The order of prestige among these institutional types—that is, Types 2, 3, 4, and 6—is very clear: Type 2 schools have the highest status; Types 3 and 6 are next in status, emulating Type 2 schools as much as possible; and Type 4 schools follow, attempting to be taken for Type 3 schools and even undergoing name changes to help create the illusion. For all of these types—Type 3, Type 4, and Type 6—Type 2 remains the coveted though unrealizable ideal. And in view of this tendency, which is more likely to grow than to recede in the years ahead, faculty members at the Type 3, Type 4, and Type 6 schools who are determined to develop into teacher-artists can expect to encounter great obstacles. Fortunately, for reasons that are given in Part One, these obstacles need not be insurmountable.

The regional public university, although it emulates the Type 2 institution, can be distinguished from it in several ways: it receives relatively small federal support; it places a greater emphasis on applied research; and it is oriented toward the immediate problems and concerns of its region, having instructional programs that emphasize public service and that prepare students for the professions which are strong in the geographic area it serves. Several regional universities, however, have resources equal to those of the national universities—and within the next decade, some of them will move from Type 3 to Type 2. It will not be easy for this to happen, because the Type 2 institutions have built strong fences to keep interlopers out; but some Type 3 universities will nonetheless succeed. And when this happens, faculty members on those campuses who are interested primarily in university teaching will find themselves being subtly encouraged to move elsewhere. At these universities, untenured professors who are working at becoming teacher-artists would do well to keep this knowledge from their superiors until they have attained full professorships.

The comprehensive state college is an institution that is oriented to instruction rather than to research, that offers a wide variety of curricula at the bachelor's level and, usually, at the master's level as well. Teacher education and preparation for the helping-service professions have been major functions at these institutions. A new development of institutional type within Type 4 is the "upper-division college," which accepts as entering students only those who are ready for their third year of undergraduate studies. These colleges are currently being developed to accommodate the large number of students who complete the work of the junior colleges and are qualified to continue baccalaureate studies. Since these upper-division institutions are designed to "articulate" with the community colleges (Type 8) which supply them with students, and with the graduate schools to which they send their graduates, they are trapped, on all sides, by the standard degree system. It is therefore almost certain that in the years directly ahead, innovations of only the mildest sort will take place on the vast majority of such campuses—except within the private domain of some faculty members' classrooms.[3]

In general, all varieties of the comprehensive public college will be responding to the increasing emphasis on the need for semiprofessional and professional training. But some of these schools will also respond—depending on the stance taken by officers in their administrations—to the countertrend that stresses the important role of liberal studies in vocational and professional programs.

[3] As an example of a blueprint plan of an upper-division college for which this statement is not true, see David Sweet, "A Model for an Upper-Division Urban College," in Dyckman Vermilye (Ed.), *The Expanded Campus: Current Issues in Higher Education 1972* (San Francisco: Jossey-Bass, 1972), pp. 211–224.

Single-purpose, specialized colleges. The trend toward greater vocational and professional training on the undergraduate level, visible at the public colleges of Type 4 and Type 8, will also increase at Type 5, the single-purpose, specialized colleges—both public and private—which include teachers colleges and specialized institutions in other professional fields, such as business, art, music, and foreign languages and cultures. (Such institutions sometimes carry the word "institute" as part of their official names.) At the present time, there are between thirty-five and forty teachers colleges in the United States, but the name, as such, has all but disappeared. The teachers college itself, as an institutional type, will in all probability disappear completely by 1985. But other Type 5 colleges will survive, with their courses and their instruction probably moving toward even more intensive specialization.

Regional private universities. The regional private university (Type 6) is the private counterpart of the regional state university (Type 3), with about the same relationship to the federal government, with emphasis on applied research, and with programs in public service and business preparation designed to serve the needs of the area in which the school is located. Many Type 6 institutions are located in urban areas, and they frequently offer professional programs for commuters in such fields as law, pharmacy, dentistry, and—if church-related—theology. In general, the regional private university, even more than its public counterpart, will increasingly, in the decade ahead, stress semiprofessional and professional programs, and their liberal arts courses will come to be regarded as routine "service courses" by most administrative and teaching personnel.

Most of the observations made earlier about the expected development of the regional public university (Type 3) also apply to Type 6 universities. But the faculty on these campuses—partly because of the magic of the label "private"—will encourage a large number of humanities and social science professors to experiment, within the private domain of their own classrooms, with new instructional strategies in the fourth and fifth dimensions.

It is predicted by some observers of the national scene that by the 1980s most Type 6 universities (following the examples of Howard University and New York University) will become almost completely supported by the federal government.

Private liberal arts colleges. The Type 7 college is typically a residential campus, strongly oriented toward undergraduate instruction, with much emphasis on personal relationships between individual students and between faculty members and students. This type of college is usually heavily value-oriented, as well, although the value framework varies widely from one campus to the next. Some of these schools, for example, strongly stress traditional religious values, while others prize a nonreligious attitude toward education and life that is centered on a high sense of social and individual responsibility. Some assert the values of classical education, stressing also moderation and restraint in personal behavior, while others encourage a high level of impulse expression. All varieties of Type 7 colleges will continue to flourish in the decade ahead, in spite of the financial problems they have suffered along with all public-service enterprises in our society during the inflationary spiral of the 1960s and 1970s.

As we draw this portrait of institutional types in the 1980s, it might be desirable to classify the various kinds of liberal arts colleges by category. The difficulty with such classification is that there are many possible ways to do it—various contexts demand different descriptive distinctions. In one context, for example, it might be worthwhile to distinguish between the private sectarian and private nonsectarian colleges. In another context, it might be worthwhile to distinguish the coeducational from the men's and women's colleges. And in a third context, it might be worthwhile to distinguish between the elite private colleges and the colleges which are not usually so designated. But these categories crisscross, because each of these distinctions is not correlative with the others. Nonetheless, a word about some of these categories may be appropriate.

The *sectarian college* is a private liberal arts college distinguished from other Type 7 institutions by its affiliation with a religious denominaton. More than 800 colleges in the United States are church-related. The majority of these are four-year colleges, but the category includes many junior colleges—perhaps 150. About 250 of these church-related institutions are located in the southern states, and of these about 60 are predominantly black colleges.

In all, there are over a hundred predominantly *black colleges and universities* in the United States, about half of them public institutions. A number of these schools offer academic work that is generally considered marginal in quality. At some of the schools, the average achievement of the black student entering as a freshman is approximately at the ninth- or tenth-grade level. At the present time, the economic condition of the black college is very poor; many of the best faculty members and students leave, attracted by recruiters from northern colleges and universities. Although the situation is expected to improve during the next decade, it is clear that the black schools will have an uphill struggle.

The *men's* or *women's college* has been looked upon, for some years now, as an anachronism in contemporary society. Actually, there has been a rapid decrease in the number of these colleges since the end of World War II, and this trend will surely continue during the coming decade. Several of the most prestigious institutions in this category have now admitted students of the opposite sex, and it is probably only a matter of time until the remaining schools of this type also become coeducational.

Public community colleges and private junior colleges. There are now more than 1000 two-year institutions of higher education in the United States. The number of public community colleges (Type 8) has doubled in the last decade, and these schools now enroll about a quarter of the total number of students in higher education in the country. (Half of all students in higher education attend institutions of Types 3, 4, and 8.) There are about 250 private junior colleges (Type 9).

The community college is the principal educational agent beyond high school that is designed to equalize opportunities and to serve both the lower socioeconomic strata and the lower-ability youth. While there has been an increase in programs for students of lower ability, particularly for the educationally disadvantaged, very few community colleges—during the 1960s and early 1970s—came to grips with this problem. It is not likely that they will succeed in doing so during the decade ahead, either. One of the reasons for this failure is that many community college faculty members like to think of their institutions as truncated four-year colleges—that is, schools that match in nature and function, and in the quality of instruction, the lower-division programs found in neighboring institutions of Type 3 or Type 4. This deliberate masking of the uniqueness of the community college by its own faculty is another symptom of the malady that takes the Type 2 institutions as the model for all "respectable" postsecondary education. Under the burden of this misconception, community college faculty cannot meet the educational needs of young people whom standard test instruments classify as "lower-ability" youth. It is therefore said of the community college in recent years that it has welcomed these young people not with an open door but with a revolving door. There is "equal" opportunity for entrance, but many of these students encounter teaching styles and conceptions of education which encourage them to exit as quickly as they have entered.

For the faculty member who is oriented to teaching, the community college provides a great challenge and offers a splendid opportunity for development as a teacher-craftsman or teacher-artist. But the obstacles he must overcome if he wants to develop and practice his art are just as great—although different in some ways—as those that beset the teaching-oriented professor at more prestigious schools. These obstacles are not likely to decrease during the next decade.

In addition to training students for their first jobs, community colleges will, in the future, feel an even greater responsibility for vocational upgrading and retraining. It is probable that upgrading and retraining will be needed in all fields, including what are often called middle-level managerial jobs. But it is unikely that the community college will attack the matter of vocational education imaginatively during the foreseeable future. In this field, too, a large part of the problem resides with the community college faculty members and the kind of image they would like the two-year college to acquire. But it should be noted that community college leadership, both at faculty and administrative levels, has worked toward the implementation of a different identity concept for the future—an attempt to identify the community college as a learning center specifically designed for the needs of the community. Hence, the name *community* college.

If this concept should become legitimized, then the coming decade will see more and more faculty members becoming community-oriented. They will be not only eager to serve the needs of the community but also trained to translate the intention into effective action. Progress toward this new concept has been painfully slow, however. It is obvious that the higher education establishment is still elitist in its deepest feelings about higher education. Nonetheless, even on the most traditional community college campuses, pockets of innovation can be found, and there are many classrooms where, invisibly and quietly, experimentation in the fourth and fifth dimensions is being practiced by young faculty members who have become impatient while waiting for the system itself to change. These faculty members have concluded that the system will not change, but that in the privacy of their own classrooms *they* can change.

Other institutional types. In addition to the institutions already described, American higher education includes a number of other institutional types—although most faculty members working in degree-granting programs will have little involvement with them. Examples of these institutional types are: technical institutes, vocational schools, adult education centers, university extension centers, and centers for "group interaction," such as the Esalen Institute and other "free university" types of informal educational programs.[4] The university extension centers, in most instances, are not comprehensive in nature and are not likely to become so, although many officials now connected with extension programs hope they may play a major role in the development of external-degree and off-campus programs like those in England's Open University. Such developments will certainly take place within the next decade, but they will probably not be connected to the standard extension programs and they will have little impact on degree-system patterns in regular campus programs.

[4] A directory of free universities is available; see Jane Lichtman, *Free University Directory* (Washington, D.C.: American Association for Higher Education, 1972), as well as an essay by the same author, "Free Universities," in Dyckman Vermilye (Ed.), *The Expanded Campus: Current Issues in Higher Education 1972* (San Francisco: Jossey-Bass, 1972), pp. 149–59.

There also exist postsecondary proprietary institutions, particularly in the urban centers of the nation, but they are outside the area generally inhabited by college and university professors. These schools offer courses by correspondence ("home-study" institutes) or courses that last for three or six or nine months (or longer) in a variety of semiskilled curricula—such as engineering, technology, television repair, business, computer programming, secretarial services, and cosmetology. Such schools will probably diminish in importance in those areas where community colleges develop and expand.

A number of large corporations have, with the assistance of federal grants, established their own schools, where they combine general education skill courses with on-the-job training. Several large firms in the communications field actually own sizable groups of proprietary institutions. It is predicted by many educators that during the next decade, a startling breakthrough will take place in this new area. Firms involved in the communications industry and in new educational technologies will probably try to establish, or work together with, proprietary institutions for the purpose of developing packaged educational programs that will be taught to students on some kind of contract basis. Although these packaged, "standardized" courses are not likely to affect regular campus degree programs, they will probably play a major role in external-degree programs and other types of off-campus curricula that have already begun to develop. A movement in this direction is strongly supported, as might be expected, by testing agencies and other interests in the education industry which have relevant products to sell.

Trends Involving Types of Institutions

The private colleges and universities—the private institutions of Type 2 and all of the institutions of Type 6, Type 7, and Type 9—enroll about 30 percent of the student population in higher education in the United States. This represents a decline from about 50 percent in 1950, and the percentage will probably decline even further during the next decade. This trend should be read, however, within the context of other developments. The clear distinction that historically existed between public and private educational institutions has steadily blurred since the end of World War II, and this trend will continue. In at least a dozen states, studies have been made, or are being made, to determine future policy concerning state financial aid to private colleges and universities. While there is general consensus that funds from individual states should be made available to private institutions, it is likely that the pressure to allot these funds wil decrease as federal funds for such purposes become more readily available. As we have already pointed out in regard to Type 6 institutions, the federal government is increasingly supporting and controlling private educational institutions.

The range of institutional types that we have described is the product of a long American tradition of diversity in higher education. That tradition is still strong, but it is clearly being overwhelmed by the trend toward greater centralism and greater uniformity. Administrators and faculty members at public institutions, for example, are finding—and will continue to find—that they can no longer make final decisions on many policies where standardized formulas have been adopted, particularly in such matters as institutional size, cost of construction, standards for space utilized, average class size, student-faculty ratio, and faculty work load.

Attempts to create new types of institutions to meet newly recognized social needs have been regarded, in general, with suspicion, and they have been strenuously opposed by most high-level administrative officers at existing colleges and universities. It is likely that during the next decade and beyond, the majority of these decision makers will continue to oppose the establishment of new types of institutions. The majority of them are opposed with equal vigor to the establishment of experimental colleges on their own campuses. In the view of these administrators, experimental colleges attract both publicity and trouble; their faculties frequently exert increasingly strong demands for autonomy, and their students often engage in unorthodox behavior. It is true: cluster colleges attract, to otherwise conventional campuses, students and faculty members who are eager for academic innovation.

During the 1960s, approximately fifty cluster colleges were established on more than twenty-five college or university campuses. Although the movement is still relatively small, it may be significant, because these colleges are attempting to meet some of the most serious problems facing undergraduate education: the impersonality of large institutions, the irrelevance of conventional academic programs, the financial problems confronting small schools. And there is little doubt that cluster colleges foster a greater sense of community and closer student-faculty relationships than do other administrative units on the same campuses. Nonetheless, all of the cluster colleges, taken together, *directly* affect the lives of only a small percentage of faculty members—perhaps two or three percent of the total American professoriate. The vast majority of faculty members—even if the number of experimental cluster colleges should triple or quadruple during the next decade (an utterly remote possibility) —will still be teaching within the conventional program structures ten years from now.

In any analysis of trends, clues given by countertrends are as important as those provided by currently dominant trends, and this fact is especially true when we paint a picture of American postsecondary education during the next decade. A dominant trend often leads to counterforces which mitigate, or in some cases may even reverse, the primary trend. As we have already seen, for example, the current trend toward "open door" admissions policies has been accompanied by an obvious countertrend, increasingly selective admissions policies at many institutions, both public and private. Elitism in higher education is by no means dead—in many ways, it is increasing. A second example of this Hegelian kind of movement is discernible in the "centralization versus autonomy" controversy. While there is clearly a dominant trend toward the centralization of higher education in the United States, there are also strong forces pushing toward decentralization, toward autonomy and independence. During the coming decade, tension is certain to increase between this dominant trend and its counterforce. Almost every institution will be caught in the conflict, and many will probably not succeed in preserving their identity and integrity; and there is no doubt that when this happens, individual faculty members will also feel the impact.

Among the forces pushing toward greater centralization, the most significant has been the growing influence of government agencies. In the private sector of higher education, as we have pointed out, this influence is on the verge of great expansion. In public education, the influence will probably be most obvious in the increasing growth of control over allocations and expenditures, particularly where coordinating boards for higher education have been established in individual states. The increase in federal influence, combined with the growth of state coordinating activities, makes it clear that decision-making mechanisms affecting the future of higher education in the United States are primarily political in nature.

For the classroom teacher, however, there remains one consolation: By and large, within the standard undergraduate model—except for topics the establishment considers taboo in the realms of political ideology, sexual morality, and the like—a faculty member's own classroom will remain a private domain that belongs to him and to his students. And the options for structuring the class session—that is, for choosing from among the possible shapes for the fourth dimension—will continue to be open enough to allow faculty members significant alternatives if they are serious about becoming artists at teaching.

Beyond the Half-Open Door

Every faculty member who teaches undergraduate courses is concerned—probably even anxious—about the progress of the ethnic-minority students in his classes. These students often pose special problems, particularly for humanities professors responsible for literacy and other basic skills typically taught in lower-division liberal-arts courses.

While the immediate symptoms of the problem for the classroom teacher are of a pedagogic nature, every professor knows it is basically not a problem that begins within the teaching-learning cycle, but one that is created by the socioeconomic forces within our society. The problem has a racial dimension as well, which is largely the result of the correlation between family income and educational opportunity. At the present, young people whose families are in the upper half of the income range have three times as good a chance of attending college as those whose families are in the lower half. Accordingly, the most pressing goal American higher education has set for itself during the next decade is to provide adequate educational opportunity and access to college study for all young people who can benefit from it.

In the past, the mere *availability* of free or low-tuition education has not been sufficient to attract and hold the children of lower-class families. In order to increase student enrollments from the socioeconomic lower half, special programs of motivation, recruitment, and intensive orientation for college studies have had to be introduced. Such programs will surely occupy, in the decade ahead, a greater share of the resources and staff devoted to entering freshman students, at least in the community colleges. It is questionable whether the four-year colleges and the universities—where the elitist philosophy of education will probably continue to prevail—will be willing to earmark resources for special programs or, indeed, whether they now have, or intend to hire, faculty members qualified to teach in such programs. But in some of the community colleges, college readiness and educational opportunity programs attempt to prepare academically deprived students to enter college on an equal basis with students from middle-class homes. College preparation programs of this sort usually include more than simple class work; attention is given, as well, to nonacademic factors such as medical and dental care, mental health, and social problems.

There is general agreement with the principle that public funds should be supplied to erase the inequality that has been characteristic of higher education in this country. President Nixon, in his very first message on higher education to Congress, in the spring of 1970, emphasized the goal of access to postsecondary education. "No qualified student who wants to go to college," the President said, "should be barred by lack of money. That has long been a great American goal; I propose that we achieve it now."[5] A key term in the President's statement is *qualified*. The implementation of this goal depends on the definition of this one word.

The open admissions policy has been designed to supply slots—

[5] Quoted in *The Chronicle of Higher Education,* May 2, 1970, p. 1.

chiefly in the community colleges, but in some four-year colleges as well—to be filled by students who can benefit from college study but who, in past years, would not have been encouraged to continue their education beyond high school. In systems where this policy is implemented, the "opportunity" for a college education thus exists, but there remain restrictions as to where one may enroll. There is a distinction between access to a system and access to a particular institution. The term *open admissions* does not include all that the name might imply: it does not mean open admission for any student to any institution, any curriculum, or any course. In every case, there is a limitation; and in many cases, the situation will not bear close scrutiny. Members of an urban black community, for example, have questioned the practice of shunting all "high-risk" students from their community into the nearby large, urban community college; they ask whether the principle of *equality* of opportunity is in fact being violated. One of the most sensitive issues of American higher education during the decade to come will thus revolve around the impact of open admissions policies.

No matter how the phrase "open to any student who can benefit from a college education" is interpreted, the open admissions policy will bring to the colleges an increased number of lower-half enrollees, many of whom will be culturally disadvantaged and "high risk" students. Will the nation's colleges and universities be able to hold these recruits beyond the first college semester? It is almost certain that the majority of faculty members now responsible for freshman programs on almost all of the nation's campuses—and especially those responsible for courses within the humanities area—will not be able to reform those programs sufficiently during the next decade to meet the individual needs of disadvantaged students.

The implementation of an open admissions policy has two components: in addition to the new criteria for admission, there must also be developed appropriate programs for those who are admitted. The successful solution to the problem of access to college thus depends on the flexibility of the curriculum and on instructional practice—on the framework supplied by the structural dimensions of the degree system and the originality of the implemental dimensions of the degree system. If the "high risk" student is routinely placed in a terminal vocational-technical program upon entrance to college, then the philosophy behind the open admissions policy will have been betrayed. For the policy, if it is to be successful in the decade ahead, demands that every lower-half student who has the potential for moving up the educational ladder receive individual encouragement to climb that ladder.

In the implementation of the policy, a professor in one of the various humanistic studies may be able to play a special role. But if he is in a four-year college or at a university, his campus will do little on a collegewide or universitywide basis, and his department will do even less. It will be up to him as an individual teacher to make a contribution. For him, and for the community college teacher, it will not be easy to make that contribution within the setting of conventional courses. It will require him to develop his capabilities as a teacher beyond the mastery of technique, beyond a masterful control of his craft. It will require him to move to the level of art. He must become an artist at teaching: there is no other way.

Epilogue

Daedalus in the Year 2000

The most common form of university instruction is still the lecture. University lecturing has a long and rich tradition, and it is an art of the highest order. But it is a different art from the art of teaching. Unlike the teacher-artist, the lecturer-artist does not actually know his students as individuals and his instructional style does not require him to interact personally with them. He has the same relationship to them as a television speaker does to his faceless audience.

Even among professors who do interact personally with students—and who are, therefore, by our definition, university teachers—we distinguish sharply between teacher-artists and teacher-craftsmen. Our portraits of teacher-artists in the preceding chapters have shown them practicing *evocative* modes of teaching. But teacher-craftsmen practice *didactic* modes: they give cues for drill-like exercises and correct the responses of students, they pose questions for short-answer recitations and evaluate student answers, and they invent academic problems to give students practice in problem-solving. A large number of university teachers do these things with great sophistication. Many are able to achieve a high level of excellence in the craft of teaching.

To be an artist at teaching, however, requires a professor to have relationships with students that are of a different sort from those that students enter into with the professor who is a lecturer-artist or a teacher-

229

craftsman. It has been the object of this book to explicate those differences.

The differences between the teacher-artist and the teacher-lecturer, and between the teacher-artist and the teacher-craftsman, are crucial for the university professor in the seventies—especially for the humanities professor who seeks to escape from the labyrinth in which the educational Establishment has imprisoned him. And those differences will prove to be increasingly crucial for all university professors between now and the year 2000. For by the time we enter the twenty-first century, the lecturer-artist and the teacher-craftsman will have become obsolete. Only the teacher-artist will survive.

Glossary

ADMISSIONS SYSTEM   A major system within the university supersystem. The process through which certain prospective students, considered desirable as degree candidates according to one criterion or another (as determined by a process set by the governance system), are recruited for academic programs and then admitted into them.

ADVISING SYSTEM   A major system within the university supersystem. The process through which candidates for degrees, diplomas, or titles are given information about the way in which the degree system works. This information invariably stresses alternative ways of fulfilling degree requirements, and often also includes facts and opinions relative to career choices. The objective of the academic advising system is to help the student understand each set of alternatives and make the choice that best fits his present needs and hopes for the future.

ART OF TEACHING   As defined in this book, the *art of teaching* contrasts with two other major classroom activities practiced by many university professors, the *art of lecturing* and the *craft of teaching*. For definitions, see TEACHING, LECTURING.

BLUEPRINT MODEL   A technical term (used, in this book, as a contrast to *theoretical model*) referring to a description of structures and/or processes which is formulated at a relatively concrete level. This model has two purposes: (a) to help the practitioner build a new structure or create a new process—for example, a new kind of educational program for culturally disadvantaged students; or (b) if the practitioner faces conditions that do not permit him to start from scratch (or if he prefers to build on existing structures), to help him reform an already existing but dysfunctioning system. The adequacy of a blueprint model is judged by checking against the appropriate theoretical model; only in this way can it be ascertained whether every dimension described in the theoretical model has been translated at a concrete level into mechanisms or structures that carry out the functions pertaining to that particular dimension.

COGNITIVE KNOWLEDGE   A technical term used by educational psychologists to contrast with *affective knowledge*. See KNOWLEDGE for brief definitions of both terms.

COLLEGE   An ambiguous term both inside and outside of the academic world. It often refers to a class of institutions that emphasize undergraduate teaching and do not carry the word *university* in their titles; but very often, and especially as an adjective (for example, in phrases such as "college teaching," "college student," "college newspapers") the word refers to all postsecondary institutions. In this book, *university* is always used, unless explicitly stated otherwise, to mean "college and university." See also UNIVERSITY.

CONVENTIONAL DEGREE PATTERN   An exact synonym, as used in this book, for *standard degree-system model*. See STANDARD DEGREE-SYSTEM MODEL.

CRAFT OF TEACHING   A technical term which contrasts, in this book, with *art of teaching*. See DIDACTIC TEACHING MODES for its definition.

CURRICULAR-INSTRUCTIONAL MODEL   A term only occasionally used in this book. It is an exact synonym for *degree-system model*. See DEGREE SYSTEM and STANDARD DEGREE-SYSTEM MODEL.

CURRICULUM   What is often called a *curriculum* is covered by the three *structural dimensions* of the degree system. In its most common usages, in the academic world, *curriculum* has three quite different meanings: (a) all credit-yielding courses offered in a given subject matter, as in the sentence, "The curriculum in English on this campus consists of over 200 courses"; (b) the courses required of (or taken by) a student who is pursuing a degree, as in the sentence, "Our curriculum for the B.A. in English has a 40-unit minimum"; (c) every learning experience a student undergoes that is organized and supervised by faculty members, whether it actually carries credit or not. See STRUCTURAL DIMENSIONS.

DAEDALUS   Mythological hero and symbol of the artist, after whom James Joyce named Stephen Dedalus, the main character of *A Portrait of the Artist As a Young Man.* Where Apollodorus and Ovid differ in their retelling of the action of the Greek myth, we have in this book followed Apollodorus.

DEGREE PROGRAM   A course of study at the close of which an academic degree or other academic title is conferred upon the student. The term, as it is used in this book, also includes programs, such as those at community colleges, which lead to diplomas or other academic titles. Synonym: *degree curriculum.*

DEGREE SYSTEM   One of a dozen major systems that make up the university supersystem and, seen from the perspective of a university teacher, the central one of those systems. It consists of the processes, and the structures needed to carry them out, through which students in *degree programs* acquire certain kinds of knowledge (as defined by university officials) in order to qualify for an academic degree or other title. In American higher education, it is traditional for the faculty body to have control over the operation of the degree system. See also STANDARD DEGREE-SYSTEM MODEL.

DEPARTMENTAL SYSTEM   A major system within the university supersystem. The process through which everyone employed by the university— professors as well as non-teaching academicians and non-academic employees—are grouped into working units. Generally, these units are sharply divided into two categories, academic and non-academic. Each academic unit is identified as a department or institute or center, or simply "office" —and these are often grouped into larger units called schools or colleges.

DIDACTIC TEACHING MODES   A term used in this book to denote certain classroom styles (which contrast with the *evocative teaching modes*), typical of teacher-craftsmen but not of teacher-artists. The didactic modes stress either cognitive knowledge acquired primarily by memorization, or skills acquired primarily by repetition and practice. Inquiry on the part of the student is not required or encouraged for the successful completion of the learning tasks set by the teacher. See also EVOCATIVE TEACHING MODES.

DIMENSION   In this book, the word dimension always refers to a component aspect of the degree system. There are six:
FIRST DIMENSION   The progression of ideas and skills taught to students in any given program. In standard programs, the basic entity on the first dimension is the *course;* courses are almost always organized in some sequential arrangement. In some experimental programs, however,

courses as such do not exist and the shape of program content is governed by some other principle of organization.

SECOND DIMENSION The scheduling of spaces, times and people. It encompasses all the arrangements by which groups of learners gather in certain specified locations and at specified times—usually together with one or more university officers—to take part in the teaching-learning process. In the standard pattern, the basic entities in the second dimension are the *class* and the *conference*.

THIRD DIMENSION The process of grading and crediting students. In the standard degree-system model, the basic entities that lie in this dimension are grades, grade points, and credit units.

FOURTH DIMENSION Professor and student roles in teaching-learning sessions. The fourth dimension exists only at the times when the teaching-learning group—or any subgroup in it—is in session. (Learning activities or relationships entered into by members of the group at other times comprise the *fifth dimension*.)

FIFTH DIMENSION The pattern of student out-of-class learning; those activities that students must pursue outside of actual class meetings and related group sessions if they are to make satisfactory progress in the program. (It does not include relationships that exist outside the degree system, such as extracurricular activities or residence hall life, unless the student is expected, or otherwise encouraged, to include such activities in his preparation for class or conference sessions.)

SIXTH DIMENSION The power syndrome in the teaching-learning process. In this dimension lies the network of freedoms and controls that are exercised *by* the learners (over themselves and over their teachers) and *over* the learners (by other learners and by teachers) as they move forward toward the degree. In the standard degree model, power over all decisions affecting the course of classroom life, as well as the student's out-of-class preparation for that life, lies entirely in the hands of the professor, who may if he wishes delegate a portion of that authority to his students.

EVOCATIVE TEACHING MODES Classroom styles used by teacher-artists. Their major characteristic is that inquiry and discovery, on the part of the student, are required if he is to complete successfully the tasks set by the teacher. These modes fall into four categories or *prototypes:* the Principles-and-facts Prototype, the Instructor-centered Prototype, and two Student-centered Prototypes. (More information is given under those headings.)

EXPERIMENTAL   See INNOVATIVE.

EXTRACURRICULAR SYSTEM   A major system within the university super-system. The process through which activities and experiences of various kinds (many of them obviously educational) are planned for students by students and faculty. In programs following the standard degree system model, these activities exist outside the degree system altogether; they are not taken into consideration when credits are counted toward the student's degree or when a faculty member's workload is calculated.

FACULTY REWARD SYSTEM   A major system within the university super-system. The process through which faculty members are hired, retained, promoted, given tenure, asked to leave the campus, and in other ways rewarded or penalized by their peers and superiors. It often strongly influences the roles played by professors in the degree system.

GOVERNANCE SYSTEM   One of the most important of the systems that constitute the university supersystem. The process through which any or all of the university's other systems are modified. This process includes the principles that determine *how* the other systems are controlled and changed, *who* decides what changes are made, and *who* is responsible for implementing those changes.

HOUSING AND HEALTH SYSTEM   A major system, within the university supersystem, concerned with the physical needs of the members of the campus community, providing (for certain segments of that community) food services, housing, transportation, and medical attention. There is much variation, from one campus to another, in the way this system affects faculty members.

IMPLEMENTAL DIMENSIONS   The fourth, fifth, and sixth dimensions of the degree system. These are the dimensions we ordinarily associate with the term *instruction*. They differ qualitatively from the other three dimensions (the *structural dimensions*) with which we ordinarily associate the term *curriculum*.

INNOVATIVE   An adjective used in this book to describe two different kinds of degree system change: (a) a planned change that is mild enough to be accommodated entirely within the standard degree-system pattern; (b) a planned change so fundamental as to necessitate a radical departure from the standard system in at least one of the six dimensions—triggering off changes in most (or all) of the other dimensions as well. The term *experimental* is used in this book to refer only to the second of these kinds of change. (It is thus synonymous with the phrase *radically innova-*

tive). The blueprint models presented in Chapter Eleven exemplify each category: Old College is a *mildly innovative* institution while Meiklejohn College is *experimental*.

INSTRUCTION Although commonly used elsewhere as a synonym for *teaching*, in this book the word *instruction* has a broader meaning than teaching. *Teaching* includes some, but by no means all, activities that professors practice in the classroom or lecture hall. *Instruction*, on the other hand, covers all such activities; it is roughly equivalent to everything that occurs in the implemental dimensions (the fourth, fifth, and sixth) of the degree system. See also TEACHING.

INSTRUCTOR A synonym for *professor* or *faculty member*. See PROFESSOR.

INSTRUCTOR-CENTERED PROTOTYPE The mental image of the teacher-at-his-best held by professors who organize their classes around the desire to help the student learn to approach problems as they themselves approach them. They concentrate on transmitting segments of cognitive knowledge, but unlike their colleagues who follow the Principle-and-facts Prototype, they use the force of their own personalities and their own unique points of view to give shape to that knowledge. See also TEACHING PROTOTYPE.

KNOWLEDGE Not only the products of problem-solving processes but the processes themselves and not only the thought processes characteristic of Western thought but all possible ways of organizing experience. Thus, art as well as science, astrology as well as typing ability or linguistic analysis, tolerance of ambiguity as well as the batting averages of major league baseball players are all included in this definition of knowledge. It is common among educators to distinguish between *cognitive* and *affective* knowledge. The first consists of principles, facts, theories, concepts, analytic tools, and the like—the kind of knowledge that can be found in an encyclopedia. The second deals with the attitudinal and emotional development of the student. Objectives like open-mindedness, independence of thought, and respect for fellow human beings are affective goals. A third domain of knowledge includes the motor-kinetic skills.

LECTURING A variety of university instruction which combines the art of composition and the art of oral delivery, and which, in this book, is sharply differentiated from *teaching*, even though the teacher-artist may also lecture from time to time. Teaching is an improvisational art while lecturing—as the term is used in this book—is not. The difference between an artist at teaching and an artist at lecturing lies in the kind of relationship each establishes with his students. See also TEACHING.

LEGAL SYSTEM   A major system within the university supersystem. The process by which the university creates, interprets, and administers its own regulations. It includes all aspects of justice on campus: law enforcement, trials and other legal proceedings, correctional measures, and grievance procedures.

MODEL   See SYSTEMS APPROACH, THEORETICAL MODEL, BLUEPRINT MODEL.

PLANT, EQUIPMENT, AND SUPPLIES SYSTEM   A major system within the university supersystem. The process by which the university acquires and maintains buildings, furniture, books, supplies, and the tools that are needed for instruction, research, and the other functions of the university. This system daily provides many of the university teacher's professional needs, supplying him in particular with the physical tools needed to practice his profession.

PRINCIPLES-AND-FACTS PROTOTYPE   The mental image of the teacher-at-his-best held by professors who organize their classes around their desire to help students master principles, concepts, analytic tools, theories, applications, and relevant facts. It is characterized by two main features: an emphasis on cognitive knowledge, and the systematic coverage of a segment of that knowledge in each of their courses.

PROFESSOR   Synonyms (as the terms are used in this book): *faculty member, instructor*. A member of that segment of the campus population called *faculty body* (or, more rarely, the *professoriate*) which has absolute or virtually absolute control over the operations of the degree system. The term is also used to refer to faculty members in the highest faculty rank—others being associate professors, assistant professors, and instructors—but the word does not occur in this book in that particular meaning. In this book, *teacher* and *professor* (or *teacher* and *instructor*) are not used synonymously but follow the distinction made between *teaching* and *instruction*.

PROTOTYPE   See TEACHING PROTOTYPE.

PUBLIC RELATIONS SYSTEM   A major system in the university supersystem. The process through which images of the university are created for dissemination to various segments of the public. Its purpose is to foster relationships in the outside world which will be favorable to the physical, spiritual, and financial well-being of the university.

SECURITY SYSTEM   A major system in the university supersystem. The process through which members of the campus community and their property, as well as the total holdings of the university itself, are protected against damage, injury, and loss—that is, actual harm—or the threat of harm.

STANDARD DEGREE-SYSTEM MODEL   The pattern of the curricular-instructional system at over 90 percent of American colleges and universities. Its major characteristics: the program consists of *courses* that the student must complete in order to earn his degree or diploma or title, with a certain number of courses required in a single field (typically called a major). Each course, when actually offered, becomes a *class,* for which, generally, a single faculty member is entirely responsible. The work of each student in every class is evaluated by the professor who teaches the class, and by him alone, typically by means of a grade that symbolizes quality of achievement; and for each satisfactory grade, the student receives a specified number of units of *credit* toward the title or degree. The teacher and the student have distinctively different roles in the classroom, and there are strong pressures for them to limit themselves to these roles. Student activity done in preparation for the class is expected to be of *academic caliber;* that is, it is expected to be conceptual, rational, analytic activity of a certain level, usually oriented almost exclusively to books and other printed materials. Finally, the faculty member is in absolute or virtually absolute *control,* and he may (or may not) delegate some of this power. Synonyms: *Conventional degree system; standard degree pattern.* A fuller description is given in Chapter Nine and a summary of that description may be found in the introduction to Part Four.

STRUCTURAL DIMENSIONS   The term describing the first, second, and third dimensions of the degree system—the three dimensions that we ordinarily associate with the *curriculum.* The structural dimensions differ qualitatively from the fourth, fifth, and sixth dimensions of the degree system, which are labeled the *implemental dimensions.* We ordinarily associate the latter with *instruction.* A detailed explanation is given in Chapter Nine.

STUDENT   This word is subject to a variety of definitions, depending on purpose and perspective. From the perspective of the degree system, *student* is synonymous with *degree-seeker* or *degree candidate.* (The term *degree* also includes diplomas and other academic titles.) *Student* thus refers to that segment of the campus population for whom the degree system exists in the first place. *Learner,* in this book, is a synonym for *student;* but their opposites, *teacher* and *instructor* (*teacher* is to *learner* as *instructor* is to *student*), are not used as synonyms in this book. See also PROFESSOR, TEACHING, INSTRUCTION.

STUDENT-CENTERED An ambiguous term that has acquired three layers of meaning during the last half-century. In its first meaning, which derives from the progressive education movement, *student* stands in opposition to *subject-matter*. In its second meaning, which derives from client-centered therapy, *student* stands in opposition to *instructor*. Its third meaning derives from the field of group dynamics and emphasizes the use of the group, in a student-centered class, as an entity that has a life of its own, motivating its members to behave in certain ways.

STUDENT-CENTERED PROTOTYPES The general label used, in this book, for two different teaching prototypes—the *Student-as-mind Prototype* and the *Student-as-person Prototype*. Professors who follow the first prototype emphasize the personal development of the student but limit the scope of their endeavor to the development of the student's mind. Professors who follow the second emphasize the personal development of the whole student—his total personality and not just his mind. Class sessions of the professor who follows the Student-as-mind prototype are organized around his desire to help his students acquire a set of skills and abilities that are intellectual in nature; students are taught to adopt reason and language as their major tools and to use problem-solving as a major means of investigating subject matter. The professor who follows the Student-as-person prototype organizes his classes around his desire to help students develop as individuals, including growth in affective knowledge as well as cognitive knowledge. See also TEACHING PROTOTYPE.

SYSTEMS APPROACH A theoretical framework, which some scholars in higher education have adopted, in which more than a dozen major systems are seen to function within the university, and in which the university itself is seen as a component in even more complex super-systems, such as government agencies, the communications industry, and discipline organizations. In a systems model, each system has a dynamic relationship to all other systems; a change in one will affect all systems in some way. This book distinguishes the systems model from the architectonic model, which envisions the university as a kind of complex edifice constructed out of movable building blocks that stand in a static relationship one to the other. In this conception, a change in the curriculum or admissions policy or a change in a professor's teaching style is seen as the substitution of a new building block for an old one. The analyses presented in this book are built on the systems approach and follow its methodological requirements.

TEACHER   A professor who carries out the activities defined in this book as *teaching*. There are two categories of such professors: *teacher-craftsmen* and *teacher-artists*. See TEACHING, DIDACTIC TEACHING MODES, LECTURING, INSTRUCTION.

TEACHING   One of the kinds of activity professors may carry on in a university classroom. A distinction is made between the art of university teaching and other arts appropriate to other classroom activities, such as the art of university lecturing. Teaching may be practiced at the level of art or at the level of craft. The teacher-artist follows one of four *evocative teaching prototypes* which are identified and described in Chapters One and Two, while the teacher-craftsman follows one of several possible *didactic teaching* modes which are described in Chapter One. Teaching is characterized, in this book, as an improvisational art.

TEACHING PROTOTYPE   A vision every teacher holds in his mind of the teaching style he believes most effective; an image of the teacher-at-his-best. The professor's actual teaching style is the outer reality and the prototype is the inner vision. When an observer watches a teacher in action, it is often not possible for him to understand why the teacher is doing what he does, or how well he is doing it, unless the observer has some idea of the prototype that serves as the teacher's model.

THEORETICAL MODEL   A general model formulated at the highest level of abstraction, intended to describe how objects in a given set (tables, or universities) "work" or how processes in a given set (learning, or doing research) function. In contrast to the *blueprint model*, the function of the theoretical model is to explain; and we judge its success by observing how well it explains the world it purports to analyze. See also BLUEPRINT MODEL.

UNIVERSITY   The word is used in this book to include all postsecondary educational institutions that grant degrees, diplomas, or other academic titles. It includes, then, the institutions in all nine categories of postsecondary education described in Chapter Twelve. Sometimes used in contrast to *university* and sometimes as a synonym, the word *college* is ambiguous in meaning both inside and outside the academic world; it is commonly used as the generic term for all postsecondary institutions offering the Bachelor's degree, even where these are part of larger institutions carrying the word *university* in their title. Many colleges offer graduate work but prefer to think of themselves as, and call themselves, *colleges;* but if their program emphasis is on the preparation of professionals in such fields as business, social work, nursing, or law, and if they offer graduate degree programs, then they probably prefer to carry the word *university* in their title. Courses taught by professors in the humanistic disciplines may vary from one campus to another but these differences are in no significant way correlated to the occurrence of *college* or *university* in the title of the institution at which the program is given.

Index